Classical Music

FOR DUMMIES®

A Wiley Brand

Second Edition

by David Pogue and Scott Speck

Classical Music **For Dummies®, Second Edition**

Published by: **John Wiley & Sons, Inc.,** 111 River Street, Hoboken, NJ 07030-5774, www.wiley.com

Copyright © 2015 by John Wiley & Sons, Inc., Hoboken, New Jersey

Published simultaneously in Canada

For general information on our other products and services, please contact our Customer Care Department within the U.S. at 877-762-2974, outside the U.S. at 317-572-3993, or fax 317-572-4002. For technical support, please visit www.wiley.com/techsupport.

Wiley publishes in a variety of print and electronic formats and by print-on-demand. Some material included with standard print versions of this book may not be included in e-books or in print-on-demand. If this book refers to media such as a CD or DVD that is not included in the version you purchased, you may download this material at http://booksupport.wiley.com. For more information about Wiley products, visit www.wiley.com.

Library of Congress Control Number: 2015940310

ISBN 978-1-119-04975-3 (pbk); ISBN 978-1-119-04974-6 (ebk); ISBN 978-1-119-04972-2 (ebk)

Manufactured in the United States of America

10 9 8 7 6

Contents at a Glance

Table of Contents

Introduction

By opening this book, you've taken a flying leap into the frightening, mysterious, larger-than-life universe of classical music, where 100 people dressed like 18th-century waiters fill the stage, doing some very strange things to hunks of metal and wood, filling the air with strange and exotic sounds.

We can sense the hair beginning to rise on the back of your neck already. But don't be afraid; whether you know it or not, you've experienced classical music all your life — in movies and video games, on TV, on the radio, and in elevators everywhere. We're willing to wager that you already know more than you need to get started.

About This Book

We know that you're a highly intelligent person. After all, you managed to select this book from among a whole shelf (or website) of highly qualified music books.

But in this vast, complex, information-overload society, you're expected to be fully conversant with 1,006,932,408.7 different subjects. (The .7 is for square dancing, which doesn't quite qualify as a complete subject.) So it's only natural that even the greatest genius doesn't know *everything*. It happens that you, O Reader, are still in the incipient stages of Classical Music Geniusdom.

That's why we use the words "For Dummies" with a twinkle in our eye. Truth be told, this book is for intelligent people who want to discover more about a new subject. And for us, it's a chance to share with you what we love.

If you've never touched an instrument or sung a song, *Classical Music For Dummies, Second Edition* can give you the basic understanding you need. If you want an easy-to-read reference when you hear a recording or attend a concert, this book provides it. If you want to get a thorough grounding in the subject, the book allows for that too. Even if you're already very well versed in classical music (and a surprising number of our readers are), you can discover something in each chapter to enhance your delight even further. This book is meant to meet you wherever you are and bring you to a new level. We've even been thrilled to discover that many *teachers* have used our book as a text in classes about music history, theory, composition, orchestration, or appreciation. Well, sure, that works too!

Foolish Assumptions

We, your trusty authors, have made some mighty foolish assumptions about you.

- You have a healthy and active pulse.
- This pulse sometimes races when you hear a surging phrase of classical music, whether on a recording, in a movie or show, in a video, or in a TV commercial.
- You have a sneaking suspicion that a little more understanding of the music that makes your pulse race might add immeasurable joy and fulfillment to your life.
- You'd love to enhance that understanding with one lighthearted, breezy, easy-to-read resource.

If we're right about any of these things (and we're hardly every wrong), then this book is for you. It will deepen your understanding of music, make you comfortable discussing it, and help you understand its form. And although this book isn't a suitable alternative to a graduate degree in music, it's much more fun and costs about $90,000 less.

Believe it or not, you have a great *advantage* over many of the world's classical music fanatics. You enter this amazing artistic realm unencumbered by preconditioning or music prejudice. You enter the concert hall with an open mind, a clean slate, and an empty canvas upon which the great composers can paint their emotional landscapes.

This situation is what many music aficionados often forget: In classical music, the intellect should take a back seat to emotion. More than many other arts, classical music is meant to appeal directly to the senses. In this book, we show you how to activate those senses — and unlock your capacity to experience one of life's greatest highs.

Icons Used in This Book

Throughout the book, icons clue you in about certain topics. They indicate material in which you may be especially interested, or material you may be eager to skip. Let them be your guide.

This icon clues you in on a handy shortcut, technique, or suggestion that can help you get more out of your classical music life.

This icon alerts you to what we think are important pieces of information that you should stow away in your mind.

So that we don't fry your brain by surprise attack, we'll place this icon next to advanced topics and special terminology.

This icon marks an opportunity for you to get up, march over to a keyboard or a sound system, and run a little experiment in real life.

If you go online to www.dummies.com/go/classicalmusic, you can find nine excerpts from the greatest music in the world. Whenever we discuss one of them, this icon lets you know.

Music has been around longer than most countries. This icon alerts you to the beginnings of trends and rituals that are still around today. This information isn't essential to understanding classical music, but it sure is downright interesting.

Beyond the Book

In addition to the very book you're holding in your eager little hands, we provide some delicious online goodies for your enjoyment. For example, take a look at the Cheat Sheet at www.dummies.com/cheatsheet/classicalmusic. There you can find a quick description of the instruments and their locations in a typical symphony orchestra, as well as a timeline of classical music, for easy reference next time you attend a concert.

You also can discover more interesting bits and pieces of information online about how today's concert experience is changing, what it takes to send an orchestra on tour, great music of the 21st century, and more. Head to www.dummies.com/extras/classicalmusic.

Best of all, we provide many, many musical examples, in the form of links to recordings online at www.dummies.com/go/classicalmusic. These recordings are your key to entering the world of classical music — a painless introduction to all different styles and time periods. As we describe some of the great masterpieces, you can actually listen to them right away. These recordings set *Classical Music For Dummies* apart from all the other books on the shelf.

Where to Go from Here

We design this book so that you can start reading anywhere. But to help you figure out what might excite you the most, we give you six different areas to choose from:

- ✔ Part I introduces you to the world of classical music, including a brief history and descriptions of the common packages — such as *symphonies, string quartets,* and so on — that classical music comes in.

- ✔ Part II takes you into the concert hall to experience some real music-making, and then takes you on a backstage tour of the professional classical music world.

- ✔ Part III is a field guide to all the instruments that make up an orchestra.

- ✔ Part IV puts classical music under the microscope, explaining the creative little molecules that make it up.

- ✔ Parts V and VI take you even deeper into classical music and help you get more out of it.

You don't need to finish one part, or even one chapter, before starting another. Use the table of contents or the index as a starting point, if you want. Or, if you're in a romantic mood, turn on some sensual classics, cuddle up with a loved one, and start at the very front of the book. (You may want to skip the copyright page, however, because it can deflate that romantic mood rather quickly.)

Part I
Getting Started with Classical Music

For Dummies can help you with lots of subjects. Check out this book's Cheat Sheet at www.dummies.com/cheatsheet/classicalmusic to discover more interesting information to make your classical music experience more worthwhile.

In this part . . .

- ✔ Discover that you've been listening to classical music all your life — on elevators, in movies, in TV commercials, in video games, and just about everywhere else you want to be.

- ✔ Find out what separates mediocre music from mankind's greatest musical masterpieces.

- ✔ Explore the different packages that classical music comes in, from symphonies to sonatas.

- ✔ Meet all the lovable (and not-so-lovable) characters who collectively created the history of classical music.

Chapter 1

Prying Open the Classical Music Oyster

In This Chapter

▶ Understanding what's so great about classical music

▶ Identifying the seven habits of highly effective composers

▶ Access the audio tracks at www.dummies.com/go/classicalmusic

The world of classical music is a place where idealism reigns, where good conquers evil and love conquers all, where you always get a second chance, where everything comes out right in the end, and where you can have your cake and eat it, too.

Classical music is one of the few living arts. It continues to exist by being constantly re-created, live, before an audience. Unlike the visual arts, classical music envelops you in real time and comes to life before you; unlike literature or theater, it can be understood equally by speakers of any language — or no language; and unlike dance, you don't need to look good in a leotard to perform it.

Classical music is a place to come to for pure enjoyment, for solace, for upliftment, for spiritual transcendence, and — if you follow our suggestions — for less than 25 bucks.

Discovering What Classical Music Really Is

For the purposes of this book, *classical music* is the music composed in the Western Hemisphere during the past few hundred years (not including recent pop and folk music). It's the music generally composed for an orchestra or combination of orchestral instruments, keyboards, guitar, or voice.

Until very recently (at least in geological terms), people didn't make such big distinctions between "popular" and "classical" music. In the 1700s and 1800s, it was all just *music,* and people loved it. People would go to the latest performance of a symphony, concerto, song cycle, or opera just as you might go to a concert in an arena, stadium, club, coffeehouse, or bar today — to have fun! They were enticed by the prospect of seeing their favorite stars, schmoozing with their friends, and hearing their favorite tunes. They came in casual clothes; they brought along food and drink; they even cheered during the show if the spirit moved them. Classical music *was* pop music.

The fact is that classical music is just as entertaining as it ever was. But these days, it's become much less *familiar.* That's all. After you become familiar with this art form, it becomes amazingly entertaining.

Figuring Out Whether You Like It

Not every piece of classical music will turn you on right away. And that's perfectly okay.

First of all, some pieces are, as we euphemistically say in the classical music biz, more "accessible" than others. That is, some have beautiful melodies that you can hum instantly, whereas others, on first listening, sound more like geese getting sucked through an airplane engine.

See what you like best at this very moment. There are no right or wrong answers; classical music is supposed to be fun to listen to. The trick is to find out what's most fun for you.

Play the first minute or so of each audio track at www.dummies.com/go/classicalmusic. Each is a musical masterpiece, each in a different musical style. The track list includes pieces from the Baroque style (roughly mid-1600s to mid-1700s), the Classical style (mid-1700s to early 1800s), early Romantic style (first half of the 1800s), late Romantic style (second half of the 1800s), and more modern, often deceptively chaotic-sounding style (20th century to the present).

Does one piece appeal to you more than all the others? If so, begin your exploration of classical music by delving into other works in that style or by that composer.

Or, if you love them all, fantastic! Our job just got a lot easier.

The Seven Habits of Highly Effective Composers

Despite the incredible variety of styles within the world of classical music, certain consistent qualities make great music great. These sections examine seven of those qualities.

Their music is from the heart

Effective composers don't try to razzle-dazzle you with fake flourishes. They mean what they compose. Look at Peter Tchaikovsky: This guy spent half his life in emotional torment, and — wow! — does his music sound like it. (Listen to Track 7 at www.dummies.com/go/classicalmusic and you'll see what we mean.)

Wolfgang Amadeus Mozart was an incredibly facile composer — melodies just bubbled out of his head effortlessly, and his pieces reflect that ease. Igor Stravinsky was a strictly disciplined, calculating, complex character; ditto for much of his music. Although their personalities were incredibly diverse, these composers wrote great music in a way that was true to themselves.

They use a structure that you can feel

Great pieces of music have a structure, a musical architecture. You may not be consciously aware of the structure while you're listening to a great work; but still, you instinctively feel how that work was put together. Maybe the piece follows one of the classic overarching musical patterns (with names like *sonata form* or *rondo form,* which you can read about in Chapter 3). Maybe it just has a musical idea at the beginning that comes back at the end. In any case, we'd be hard-pressed to name a great work of music that doesn't have a coherent structure.

Recent studies at the University of California show that students who listen to Mozart before an exam actually score higher than students who don't. (Of course, we suspect that these students would've scored higher yet if they'd actually *studied* before the exam.) As you listen to a piece by Mozart, your brain apparently creates a logical set of compartments that process this form. These compartments are then useful for processing other kinds of information, as well. Classical music actually *does* make you smarter.

They're creative and original

You hear again and again that some of the greatest composers — even those whose works sound tame and easily accessible to us — were misunderstood in their own day. Not everyone could relate to the compositions of Ludwig van Beethoven, Johannes Brahms, Gustav Mahler, Richard Strauss, Claude Debussy, Stravinsky, or Charles Ives when those works were first composed. (Actually, that's the understatement of the year; the audience at Stravinsky's *The Rite of Spring* actually rioted, trashing the theater and bolting for the exits.)

The reason for this original lack of acceptance is *unfamiliarity*. The musical forms, or ideas expressed within them, were completely new. And yet, this is exactly one of the things that makes them so great. Effective composers have their own ideas.

Have you ever seen the classic play or movie *Amadeus?* The composer Antonio Salieri is the "host" of this movie; he's depicted as one of the most famous non-great composers — he lived at the time of Mozart and was completely overshadowed by him. Now, Salieri was not a bad composer; in fact, he was a very good one. But he wasn't one of the world's *great* composers because his work wasn't *original.* What he wrote sounded just like what everyone else was composing at the time.

They express a relevant human emotion

Great composers have something important to say. They have an emotion that's so urgent, it cries out to be expressed. The greatest pieces of music (*any* music, from rock to rap to today's chart-topping hits) take advantage of the ability of this art to express the inexpressible.

When Beethoven discovered that he was going deaf, he was seized by an incredible, overwhelming, agonizing frustration. His music is about this feeling. He expresses his frustration so clearly — so articulately, in a musical sense — in every note of his compositions. Beethoven's music is *intense.*

Now, this isn't to say that great composers must be intense. Joseph Haydn, for example, exuded cheerful playfulness in almost everything he wrote. Like all effective composers, *he* had something significant to say, too.

They keep your attention with variety and pacing

Effective composers know how to keep you listening. Their music is interesting throughout.

One technique that achieves this effect is variety. If the composer fills his music with a variety of musical ideas, or dynamics (loudness and softness), or melodies, or harmonies, he's much more likely to keep your interest. In this way, a great piece of music is like a great movie. An explosion near the beginning gets your attention, right? But have you ever seen a movie with an explosion every minute for two hours? Have you noticed how each explosion becomes successively less interesting, until finally you don't even notice them anymore? You need variety — something contrasting and different between explosions.

In a movie, one explosion can be thrilling if it's approached correctly, with a suspenseful buildup. Effective composers know how to use dramatic pacing, too. Their music seems to build up suspense as it approaches the climax. Maurice Ravel's *Boléro* (made famous a generation ago by the movie *10*) is a stunning example. The entire piece of music is one long *crescendo* (getting louder and louder) — the suspense builds and builds for 15 minutes, and the climax is shattering. We recommend it.

Their music is easy to remember

In today's pop music world, the word *hook* refers to the catchy, repeated element in a piece of music. Beatles songs are so catchy because nearly every one of them has a hook. Think "Help!" or "A Hard Day's Night" or "She Loves You" ("Yeah, Yeah, Yeah!"). Catchiness is not a scientifically measurable quality; still, you know a hook when you hear it.

In classical music, the same concept applies. A hook helps you remember, and identify with, a particular piece of music. The compositions of Mozart, Tchaikovsky, Frederic Chopin, Sergei Rachmaninoff, Georges Bizet, Antonin Dvořák, George Gershwin, Edvard Grieg, and Franz Schubert have hooks galore — so many hooks, in fact, that several of them have been pilfered for the melodies of today's rock songs. For example, Barry Manilow's old song "Could It Be Magic?" is a Chopin piano prelude with words added — Barry didn't write the original tune. And "Midnight Blue" is sung to the tune of Beethoven's *Pathétique* sonata. The music of the most effective composers is full of elements that stick in your mind.

They move you with their creations

The most important habit of highly effective composers is their ability to change your life. Ever walk out of a movie or play and suddenly experience the world outside the theater differently? You know, when the real world just after the movie seems to have a feeling of danger, or sadness, or happiness, or just plain wonder, that it didn't have before?

A great musical masterpiece may give you a greater appreciation for the potential of humankind, or enhance your spirituality, or just put you in a great mood. Nothing is more triumphant than the end of Mahler's Second Symphony; after you hear it, you emerge reborn, refreshed, and somehow more prepared to face the world.

Chapter 2

The Entire History of Music in 80 Pages

Every great composer was once a living, breathing human being with a unique personality, family history, and personal hygiene regimen. Knowing about the lives of the great composers makes listening to their music a hundred times more meaningful and interesting.

With very little effort and an inexpensive forklift, you can get your hands on a really fine, comprehensive, 800-page history of music. We, however, intend to fit the entire history of music in Western civilization into about 80 pages. Without using a smaller type size, either. Sometimes we amaze even ourselves.

Understanding How Classical Music Got Started

Music has been around since the Dawn of Man — or at least since the Breakfast of Man. Primitive humans expressed themselves vocally, and the sounds that came out were often musical. (These earliest recordings aren't, however, available on iTunes.)

Over the millennia, music became more complex. Man invented musical instruments to produce the sounds he couldn't sing. Pipes and whistles reproduced the sounds of birds and the wind; drums amplified the sound of a heartbeat. Musical scales became standardized. Unions were formed. Classical music was born.

The first songs were probably religious. Humans, awed and scared by their surroundings, sang prayers and made offerings to the elements. When the wind howled, they howled back; when the skies rained on them, they sang in the shower. They also used song to boast of their conquests, give thanks for a good hunt, and remove stubborn stains.

Rhythm appeared early in the history of music to echo the regular beats of walking, running, and pounding one another on the head with rocks. Dances were invented to appease the gods, and music was performed for the dances.

In those early years, music was passed on orally. Indeed, in some Eastern cultures, music still survives in this way. Only in the past thousand years or so have people thought to write music down.

Chanting All Day: The Middle Ages

The period known as the Middle Ages was an era of plague, pestilence, and self-flagellation, but otherwise it was a rollicking good time. Inside the walls of European monasteries, monks were busy developing one of the greatest achievements of music. No, no, not Lady Gaga — *sheet music.* Here's what you need to know about the musical Middle Ages.

Gregorian chant

Many a millennium of music-making madness passed before anyone had the notion to get the music down on paper. But around the year 600 A.D., Pope Gregory I ("The Great") created a system to explain the musical scales that had been in use in church music up to that time. He gets the credit for giving the notes such imaginative letter names as A, B, C, and D — the same ones that we use today!

From Pope Gregory, we get the name for *Gregorian chant:* a simple, meandering melody, sung in unison with Latin words by a bunch of guys in brown robes. Pope Greg would've popped his little pointy pope hat if he'd known that, late in the 20th century, Gregorian chant would become a smash hit worldwide, when a recording called *Chant* — sung by some hitherto unknown brothers from a monastery in Spain — hit the top of the charts.

This comeback was for a reason: Gregorian chant has a true spiritual depth. If you close your eyes and listen to Gregorian chant, all your daily cares seem to float away. Your breaths become longer and deeper. Your metabolism slows down. Eventually, you gain weight and balloon up like a pig.

But we digress.

A monk named Guido

Guido of Arezzo ("a-RET-so") was a genius monk (not to be confused with Thelonious Monk) who devised numerous musical innovations, such as singing, "do, re, mi, fa . . ." for the notes of the scale. (You may remember Julie Andrews paying homage to Guido in *The Sound of Music* when she sang, "Doe, a deer, a female deer; ray, a drop of golden sun . . .") This system of singing standard syllables on certain notes of the scale, a centuries-old skill practiced by opera singers and music majors worldwide, is called *solfège* (pronounced, more or less, "sol-FEDge").

Guido of Arezzo also devised a new music notation system, using a rudimentary version of the musical staff we use today (see Chapter 11).

It's hard to imagine what would have happened to the world of music without the innovations of Guido of Arezzo. Luckily, we don't have to. Guido existed; his musical staff still thrives; and, to this day, scholars everywhere have the pleasure of pronouncing the funniest name in the history of music (with the possible exception of Engelbert Humperdinck).

Mass dismissed!

But monks weren't the only factors influencing the course of musical history. Their system of worship did, too — especially the Catholic mass. Some of the greatest choral and orchestral works ever written have been masses.

The Catholic mass (or *missa* in Latin) got its name from the closing words of all Latin masses in the old days: *"Ite, missa est"* (rough translation: "Scram, you're dismissed!"). Every mass and musical piece based on the Catholic mass has the same set of lyrics. Even if you're not Catholic, you've probably heard some of them before: *Kyrie eleison* ("Lord have mercy" — another ancient piece that was reincarnated as a disco hit single); *Gloria in excelsis Deo* ("Glory to God in the highest" — familiar from many a Christmas carol); *Credo* ("I believe"); *Sanctus, Sanctus, Sanctus* ("Holy, Holy, Holy" — another Christmastime fave); and *Agnus Dei* ("Lamb of God"). If you listen to a musical mass of practically any time period from the Renaissance to the present, you hear these words.

Born Again: The Renaissance

About 400 years after the death of Guido and his monkly cohorts, society entered the phase now known as the *Renaissance* (French for "rebirth"). The arts flourished during the Renaissance, funded by art-loving rich folks and royalty with no taxes.

One of the most famous Italian composers of the Renaissance was Giovanni da Palestrina (1525–1594), who's pictured in Figure 2-1. A great favorite of the pope — a veritable pope's pet — Palestrina was known for his songs written for voices alone, without instrumental accompaniment. Unlike Gregorian chant, the music of Palestrina wasn't just a melody sung *in unison* (everyone singing the same notes at once). Instead, he explored amazing harmonies that resulted from singing several simultaneous independent melodies. And thus it was that Palestrina helped build the on-ramp for the long road to Gladys Knight and the Pips.

Palestrina was a great composer of masses and other religious music. But around the same time, composers looked beyond the church for words they could set to music. Long passages from great Roman poets, non-religious writing — even Dante's *Inferno* — were turned into tunes. Here are some of the ways they turned words into music.

Figure 2-1:
Giovanni da Palestrina, one of the greatest composers of the Renaissance.

Source: Creative Commons

The madrigal takes off

The most popular musical form for these songs was the *madrigal* ("MAD-drig-gull"). A madrigal is a piece for at least three voices, usually without accompaniment. During the Renaissance, families or groups of friends would get together and sing these madrigals, each person taking a different vocal line and elbowing one another when they hit wrong notes.

Madrigals were fun to sing because they often involved a clever technique known as *word-painting*. Whenever the lyrics included a particularly descriptive word, the composer wrote music that depicted the word literally. On the word *sigh,* for example, the composer had the vocal line start up high in a singer's range and then fall wearily to a lower note. On the word *run* or *fly* or even *happy,* the composer wrote a flurry of fast notes. Fortunately for the word-painters, such lyrics as "I'm your boogie man" and "I am the walrus" were still centuries away.

Opera hits prime time

Composer Claudio Monteverdi (1567–1643) lived during the height of the Italian Renaissance. Monteverdi added more hummable melodies and instrumental accompaniment to the already popular madrigal form.

Monteverdi was also one of the inventors of music-dramas, otherwise known as *opera.* Like so many aspects of the Renaissance, opera was an attempt to re-create the glories of ancient Greece. In this case, the model was the Greek play, which was performed in outdoor amphitheaters with an accompaniment of woodwind and string instruments. Monteverdi and his friends strove to re-create this form in their own time — and music has never been the same. Unfortunately, Monteverdi never got a dime in royalties.

Getting Emotional: The Baroque Era

Monteverdi and his followers paved the way for a new period in the history of music, known these days as the Baroque era ("ba-ROKE," as in, "If it ain't Baroque, don't fix it").

The following sections examine some aspects of the Baroque era (the mid-1600s to the mid-1700s), which was a time of flowery, emotional art — and flowery, emotional music. The creative types of the Baroque period filled their works with fancy little swirls and curlicues, as you can see in Figure 2-2.

Figure 2-2:
The florid
Baroque
style.

Source: Creative Commons

Renegade notes on wheels

When you listen to Baroque music, you may be surprised to discover that it was considered highly emotional. Today, it sounds relatively well-behaved. But at the time, all those florid melodies, noodling up and down all over the place, were considered music gone wild. Composers experimented with all different kinds of musical structure, breaking the rules of how music was supposed to move from one section to another.

The *word-painting* that had been so popular in Renaissance madrigals found its way into Baroque music, too — and expanded. Previously, a singer may have sung some wearily falling notes to illustrate the word *sigh*. But now a composer could use those same weary notes in an instrumental composition that didn't *have* any singing. The audience knew that the falling note pattern stood for a sigh, even if nobody said so in the music. Word-painting without words became one of the most basic emotional elements in Baroque music.

Kings, churches, and other high rollers

If you were a young musician in Europe 300 years ago, a career counselor of the time would have advised you to look for work in one of three areas: a noble court, a rich man's house, or the Christian church.

All the great composers of old, whose names you probably know today, had jobs such as these. Some were luckier than others; many famous-name composers in wealthy households wound up spending most of their time doing housework. After all, how often do you need a new composition written for your family, and how often do you need your socks washed? 'Nuff said.

Here's an example: Giuseppe Sammartini (circa 1700–1775) was a great Italian oboist, composer of some of the world's first symphonies, and a great influencer of the up-and-coming Wolfgang Amadeus Mozart. Want to know what kind of job he had? He worked for the Prince of Wales as *head of the household staff.* Can't you see it?

> **Prince of Wales:** That was a wonderful lasagna, Giuseppe.
>
> **Giuseppe Sammartini:** I offer great thanks to Your Highness for lavishing such undeserved praise upon my humble work. And what does Your Highness desire that I prepare for next Sunday?
>
> **Prince:** I think I'd like one of your exquisite oboe concertos. I love your ornamentation, your florid melodies, and your noodling up and down!
>
> **Sammartini:** I blush with pride, Your Most Excellent Excellency.
>
> **Prince:** Oh, and Giuseppe, could you please not put so much starch in my shorts?
>
> **Sammartini:** Okay.

Antonio Vivaldi

Antonio Vivaldi (1678–1741), Italian celebrity of the Baroque period, worked for the Catholic Church. Talk about prolific: This guy wrote more music in his lifetime than just about anyone else on the planet. Aside from his 50 operas, more than 40 pieces for choir and orchestra, and 100 works for orchestra alone, he wrote nearly 500 concertos for various solo instruments with orchestra. Vivaldi's caffeine consumption must have been prodigious.

Now, some of Vivaldi's jealous critics — and they're still around today — snipe that Vivaldi actually wrote the same piece of music 500 times. To that we say: balderdash! Why would anyone write the same piece 500 times? What a waste of effort. Personally, we would never write the same piece more than 200 times, and even then, we'd do it only to meet a publishing deadline.

Vivaldi's music does have a very consistent style, however — hence the accusation that it all sounds alike.

The little priest that couldn't

Vivaldi grew up in Venice; after he came of age, he decided to enter the priesthood. This decision, plus his blazing red hair, gave him the nickname "The Red Priest."

But Vivaldi didn't last very long as a priest; stories of his misadventures abound. One day during Mass, for example, a great tune popped into his head. Without hesitation or apology, he stepped down from the altar and dashed into the next room to get the tune on paper. The congregation was stunned. (It didn't take much to stun a congregation in those days.)

Vivaldi was brought before a tribunal to determine his punishment. Luckily, the Inquisition was in a good mood. Its verdict: Genius Gone Awry. The punishment: Vivaldi was not allowed to say Mass ever again. We have every reason to believe that this sentence was perfectly okay with him.

And so the Red Priest became simply Red.

The Wayward Girls Philharmonic

Vivaldi's next job lasted 35 years, until the end of his career. He became a violin teacher at the *Ospedale della Pietà* (literally, "Mercy Hospital"). This was a unique hybrid institution: It was a conservatory of music/school for illegitimate girls. No institution in America today — not even the Juilliard School — can make this claim.

Over the years, Vivaldi gradually took on more and more duties at the *Ospedale,* until he was practically running the place. He organized weekly concerts that became renowned throughout Europe. Whenever he wanted to show off the musical talents of one girl or another, he would simply write a *concerto* ("con-CHAIR-toe") for her. (For more — much more — on the subject of concertos, see Chapter 3.)

Vivaldi's concertos have three movements, and they all follow a set format, which became the model for many other Baroque composers. Here's the formula:

Fast — Slow — Fast

Listening to Vivaldi's music

We promise that you've heard the music of Vivaldi, especially his most famous piece ever: *The Four Seasons.* It's a set of four concertos for a violin with orchestra, in which each concerto evokes the feeling of a different season.

Spring is full of bird songs, a quick thunderstorm with lightning, a sleeping goat-herd complete with barking dog, dancing shepherds, and nymphs. (*Especially* nymphs.) In *Summer,* you feel the heat of the burning sun; you hear the cuckoo; you get a few mosquito bites; and you experience the full force of a fluke hail-storm. *Autumn* begins with a drunken harvest bacchanal and ends with a wild hunt, complete with simulated hunting horns. And in *Winter,* you freeze; you shiver; you stamp your feet; you sit by the fireside for warmth; and then you go outside again, only to slip and fall through the ice. Kind of sadistic, actually. All this feeling comes through wonderfully in the music.

We love *The Four Seasons;* so do the countless commercials, movies, and TV shows that have incorporated this music. It's a great piece to own; go get it.

And if you're hungry for more, we suggest these tasty tidbits:

- Concerto for Guitar in D major, RV 93
- Concerto for Two Trumpets in C major, RV 537
- Sonata for Two Violins, RV 60
- Gloria (oratorio for three solo singers, chorus, and orchestra), RV 589
- Concerto for Two Cellos in G minor, RV 531
- Double Orchestra Concerto, RV 585

(Notice that, in the preceding list, the title of each work is followed by an RV catalog number, which helps you locate the piece in a record store. This number refers to the number of times that you could fit that piece, end to end, into a standard recreational vehicle.)

George Frideric Handel

While Vivaldi was composing away in Venice, another composer was turning heads in Germany and England: George Frideric Handel (1685–1759; see Figure 2-3). He too had a great influence on the direction that music took during and after his lifetime. The following sections help you get a handle on Handel.

Figure 2-3: George Frideric Handel, composer of *Messiah* and other great oratorios.

Source: Creative Commons

The most Italian of German Brits

Handel (it's actually pronounced "HEN-dle," but many people say "HAN-dle") was born in Germany and trained in Italy. Which explains, of course, why he's considered to be one of the greatest of the *English* composers. Try not to think too hard about this one.

Actually, there's logic here. Handel was the son of a German barber-surgeon (not the kind of guy you'd want to do your tummy tuck). With dad spending his days removing one vital body part after another, it's no surprise that the young George Frideric took up the organ. At 18, he left home for the big city — Hamburg, where he found work as a composer and performer.

Handel knew that Italian opera was going to be the next big thing in Europe. And so, at age 22, he went off to Italy to learn how to write in the Italian style. He got to meet the superstar composers of the day — including Antonio "Xerox machine" Vivaldi, whose concertos he emulated. After a stint back in Germany, Handel ditched his homeland and moved to London.

Handel wrote 36 operas in England, many of which were masterpieces of their kind. But public taste was changing. The trend of the day was musical entertainment based on the Bible. Handel obliged; he started writing *oratorios* — pieces for solo singers, chorus, and orchestra, usually with words taken from the Bible.

The most famous of his oratorios was *Messiah,* first performed in 1742. Talk about a mega-hit: *Messiah* became so popular that gentlemen were encouraged to attend performances without their swords, and ladies without their hoops, so as to make more room.

"Get a Handel on yourself!"

Handel, for all his musical talent, was famous for his explosive temper. News of Handel's irritability got around in musical circles, and he became a prime target for practical jokes. It was well known, for example, that Handel couldn't bear to hear the sound of instruments tuning up. So whenever he was to conduct a concert, he ordered that all the instruments be tuned before he even showed up at the theater.

One evening, a prankster snuck into the theater and untuned all the instruments before the concert began. As Handel started conducting, what the audience heard was the screeching, dismal, harsh cacophony that only 50 out-of-tune instruments can produce. Handel went ballistic. In a rage, he grabbed an enormous double bass and tipped it over; then he picked up a kettledrum and, with all his might, lobbed it at the first violinist. (Not easy to do! *We* can never even get it past the violas.) In the frenzy, his wig came flying off, and the audience burst into uncontrollable laughter as Handel stormed off the stage.

A royal disaster

In 1749, Handel composed the *Music for the Royal Fireworks* to commemorate the signing of a treaty with Austria. The first performance was one of the greatest disasters in all of music history.

For this special occasion, the king hired an architect to build a huge backdrop for the concert, which was to culminate with a spectacular fireworks display. The architect obliged with a building 400 feet long and 100 feet high, crowned with an enormous sun on a 200-foot pole. The whole thing looked like the set for an Andrew Lloyd Webber musical.

When the day came, Handel himself began conducting the piece. Everything went great for the first half of the piece. And then the fireworks began.

Handel was probably annoyed enough that the fireworks were shooting off during his lovely music. But to make matters worse, some of the fireworks landed on the brand new building, which responded the only way it knew how: by catching fire. The crowd panicked, running for their lives as Handel doggedly continued conducting.

Handel was livid. He had a notoriously explosive temper, so we're guessing that he provided the king with a display of private fireworks the next morning.

Listening to Handel's music

Handel's compositions are some of the best examples of the Baroque style. They're fresh, spirited, often dancelike, and often emotionally charged. Amazing, considering Handel's speed; he composed his famous *Messiah* oratorio — which lasts more than two hours and is sung in major cities worldwide every Christmas and Easter — in about three weeks.

Handel was prolific, and his recordings are easy to find. In particular, we recommend the following titles:

- ✔ *Messiah,* an oratorio for solo singers, chorus, and orchestra
- ✔ Concerto Grosso, opus 3, no. 1-6
- ✔ Concerto Grosso, opus 6, no. 1-12
- ✔ *Water Music,* Suites 1, 2, and 3 (You can hear one movement of this delightful music — written to be performed on a barge as King George floated up and down the Thames River — if you go online to www.dummies.com/go/classicalmusic, and listen to Track 1.)
- ✔ Royal Fireworks Music

Johann Sebastian Bach

Most musicians count Johann Sebastian Bach (1685–1750; see Figure 2-4) among the handful of greatest musicians who ever lived. And some — we're among them — would nominate him as The Greatest of Them All. Not just because every one of his compositions is a knockout, but also because every subsequent composer owes a great debt to him. These sections highlight a few important aspects of Bach.

Figure 2-4: Johann Sebastian Bach, master of the organ.

Source: Creative Commons

A few minor posts

Bach (pronounced "BAHkhh") got his first big job at age 23: court musician in the city of Weimar, Germany. There he wrote some terrific organ pieces, many of which are still played today.

The fact that these works survive at all is remarkable for two reasons: First, compositions in those days weren't made to last. A composer would write a piece for a specific occasion, never expecting to hear it a second time. Some of Bach's immortal sonatas were rescued for posterity only moments before being used to wrap fish or butter. (We shudder to think how many of his compositions actually *did* get used to lock in freshness, never to be heard again.)

Second, in the tradition of public unappreciation that persists to this day, most composers and artists remained relatively obscure while still alive. Bach was well-known — even venerated — in the century following his death, but as an *organist,* not as a composer.

The organmeister

Bach was one of the most highly skilled organists who ever lived. Not only did he have fast, fleet fingers, but he was a mean pedaler, too. (See Chapter 6 for a description of the organ pedals that play the lowest notes.) People came from miles around to see Johann S. Bach, the guy with the flying feet.

Bach was also a master improviser. He could take almost any tune and make up new music based on it, on the spot, just as jazz musicians do today. That's the kicker: Because nobody ever wrote down improvisations, we'll never know what Bach's on-the-spot flights of fancy sounded like.

Prolific in more ways than one

Bach was another of the most prolific composers. One person would need several decades just to *write down* all the music that Bach wrote.

But Bach was prolific in more ways than one. With the help of his two wives, Bach had 20 children — that he knew of. Several of those children became composers themselves: Wilhelm Friedemann Bach, Carl Philipp Emanuel Bach, and Johann Christian Bach, to name the most famous ones. They assisted their dad at least in copying out his musical compositions.

At 38, Bach got the last job of his life: cantor at the church of St. Thomas in Leipzig, Germany. In this job, too, Bach was incredibly prolific. He wrote one big choral piece — a *cantata* — for each Sunday and holiday of the Christian calendar, and then he did that *three more times!* In all, he wrote at least 215 cantatas.

Bach's music is full of *counterpoint:* two, three, four, or more melodic lines played at the same time, creating interesting harmonies. He perfected the art of the *fugue* — an astoundingly complex composition usually written for four musical lines, or voices. Each melody is similar, but one doesn't begin until another has already started. (Think "Row, Row, Row Your Boat," with each person starting at a different time, and you get the basic idea.) Bach's fugues involved incredibly complex melodies that, even though they started at different times, wound up sounding good together. That's the way Bach's mind worked; he was so good that he could take a musical idea — just about any idea you could think of — and turn it into a fugue on the spot.

Listening to Bach's music

You can hear one of Bach's masterful keyboard works by going to www.dummies.com/go/classicalmusic and listening to Track 2. If you want to hear more, check out these pieces:

- Brandenburg Concertos, no. 1-6, BWV 1046-1051

- *Magnificat,* a sacred oratorio for solo singers, chorus, and orchestra, BWV 243

> ✔ *The Passion According to St. Matthew,* a sacred oratorio for soloists, chorus, and orchestra, BWV 244
>
> ✔ Concerto for Violin, Oboe, and Orchestra in C minor, BWV 1060
>
> ✔ Orchestral Suite no. 3 in D major, BWV 1068
>
> ✔ Concerto for Harpsichord (or piano) in D minor, BWV 1052

Note: The letters *BWV* refer to a catalog number, which can help you find the right piece on YouTube, on iTunes, or in a music store.

Tightening the Corset: The Classical Style

Johann Sebastian Bach's music was the height of the Baroque style in music, and the Baroque period pretty much ended with him. The musical style that followed is known today as the *Classical* style.

We hasten to point out the difference between the Classical style, or period, and *classical music.* We use the term *classical music* for all the music discussed in this book. But the Classical *period* (the middle of the 1700s through the early 1800s) is only one of the musical eras that make up classical music. And music from that period is in the Classical *style.*

The Classical style was, in some ways, a reaction to the excesses of the Baroque. Whereas Baroque music had been florid, extravagant, and emotional, music in the Classical style was sparer, more reserved, and more controlled. It was music with a corset on.

During the Classical period, three particular forms of music got a lot of airplay: *sonatas, symphonies,* and *string quartets.* For an in-depth look at each of these forms, see Chapter 3.

The three best composers of the Classical period were the three masters of these forms: Haydn, Mozart, and Beethoven. These three geniuses all knew one another — they all spent a considerable amount of time in Vienna, Austria, which was the music capital of the Western world.

Joseph Haydn

Joseph Haydn (1732–1809), pictured in Figure 2-5, was the most pleasant, cheerful guy you could ever hope to meet. He was constantly playing little jokes on people, making fun of things, and making fun of himself. And his music shows it.

Figure 2-5:
Joseph Haydn, a merry old soul.

Haydn ("HY-dn") grew up in a part of rural Austria that bordered on Croatia, Slovakia, and Hungary. As a boy, he heard lots of peasant folk music-making, and he came firmly to the conclusion that music was to be enjoyed. He had a beautiful singing voice, and at age eight he was selected to go to Vienna and join the choir of St. Stephen's Cathedral.

In Vienna, Haydn, which the following sections discuss, became acquainted with all the musical masterpieces of the day, decided to become a composer, and nearly got castrated (see the sidebar, "Haydn the soprano").

Like so many composers before him, Haydn's primary income was serving as a royal court musician. His longest job was working at the castle of Prince Esterházy (pronounced "*ESS*-ter-HAH-zee") — the ultimate plum job.

Life at Esterházy's Castle

Servant was Haydn's official job description, but he was treated like a king. He had his own maid and his own footman, plus a great salary. He spent his days writing new music and performing it for (and sometimes with) the prince, who was no slouch of a musician himself.

This job afforded Haydn the perfect opportunity to experiment with various musical forms. (See Chapter 3.) During the 30 years that he spent at Esterházy's castle, Haydn practically single-handedly standardized the structures of the symphony and the string quartet. That's why he's known as the father of the symphony, and that's why Beethoven (and others) called him "Papa." To this day, music writers refer to the composer as "Papa Haydn."

Alas, Haydn's cushy palace job came to an end after Prince Esterházy, in a rare display of thoughtlessness, died. Haydn moved back to Vienna and was based there for the rest of his life.

Haydn the soprano

As a young boy, Joseph Haydn was a prized boy soprano at St. Stephen's Cathedral in Vienna. As he grew older, his teacher told him that he would be able to retain his beautiful high voice forever if he were to have a "very simple little operation." Having been spared the specifics, young Haydn was eager for this miracle. He was all ready to go in for the operation when — just hours before the surgery — his father found out and prevented it.

Imagine what would have happened if Haydn had had the operation! Sure, he would have kept his beautiful high voice. But he may never have been hired as a composer by Prince Esterházy. He may never have had the opportunity to use the court orchestra as a crucible for his musical experiments. He may never have developed the string quartet and the symphony as we know them. And nobody — not even Beethoven — would ever have called him "Papa."

Going into Haydn

The *Surprise* symphony (no. 94) is a must-listen: It's one of Haydn's best pieces, and it's a perfect example of Haydn's style. There's a great story behind it, too: Haydn, working in London, had noticed that his after-dinner audiences tended to fall asleep when the music was slow or quiet. For revenge, he wrote a movement that was slow *and* quiet and grew more so as the piece went on. Sure enough, many in his audience nodded off — just in time for the deafening, full-orchestra crash. Exactly as he had mischievously hoped, the huge chord woke (and entertained) everyone in the room.

As Haydn got older, he also incorporated more and more of the peasant folk melodies he'd heard in his youth. A perfect example of this is the final move-ment of his final symphony, no. 104 (the *London* symphony).

If this kind of music turns you on, here are some excellent orchestral works by Joseph Haydn to listen to:

- Trumpet Concerto in E-flat major, Hob. VIIe:1
- Violin Concerto in G major, Hob. VIIa:4
- Cello Concerto in C major, Hob. VIIb:5
- *Lord Nelson Mass,* for soloists, chorus, and orchestra, Hob. XXII:11
- Symphony no. 48 in C major (*Maria Theresia*)
- Symphony no. 94 in G major (*Surprise*)
- Symphony no. 104 in D major (*London*)

By the way, "Hob." refers to the Hoboken catalog numbers, which can help you find the recording you're looking for.

Wolfgang Amadeus Mozart

We said earlier that we consider Bach to be the Greatest Composer Who Ever Lived. But many people like to bestow that title on Mozart (1756–1791 — see Figure 2-6). From the very beginning of his life, Mozart ("MOAT-sart") mastered music with a natural ease almost unparalleled in the history of music. He was the Michael Jordan of composers.

Figure 2-6. At left, Wolfgang Amadeus Mozart, boy wonder. At right, Mozart in his later years.

Source: Creative Commons

Wolfgang's own father, Leopold, was a respected composer and music theorist himself, but he sacrificed his own blossoming career to foster his prodigy son's talent. He taught young Wolfgang piano, violin, and music theory as the boy grew up in Salzburg, Austria.

With his dad's nurturing, young Wolfgang was composing piano concertos by age 4. Shortly thereafter, he wrote his first symphony. And he wrote the opera *Bastien and Bastienne* when he was 11.

Mozart joins the circus

Leopold knew genius when he saw it; he packed up young Wolfgang and his older sister Nannerl and toted them all across Europe. Everywhere they went, Leopold touted his son as a scientific phenomenon. One of his posters in England said: "To all lovers of sciences: The greatest prodigy that Europe or that even Human Nature has to boast of is, without contradiction, the little German boy Wolfgang Mozart." (And we thought *our* dads had high expectations.)

The young Mozart displayed such stunts as improvising at the keyboard, performing at first sight difficult pieces he'd never seen before, and playing with his hands hidden under a cloth so that he couldn't see the keys. Nannerl helped out, too, wowing the public with her harpsichord playing.

Together, they were a traveling circus act.

Mozart gets a kick in the pants

By age 13, Wolfgang found a job in the court of the archbishop of Salzburg, where he worked for 12 years. But his constant traveling and angling for better jobs irked the archbishop. Finally, with absolutely no clue how politically incorrect he'd look to future generations, the archbishop fired Mozart. The archbishop's secretary — in one of the least subtle gestures in music history — gave Wolfgang Amadeus Mozart a kick in the pants.

Mozart moved to Vienna to seek his fortune. He knew that Vienna was a major center of European musical activity, and he had been successful on tour there as a child prodigy. But Mozart wasn't a child prodigy anymore — well, at least he wasn't a child. He had a hard time finding work. The musical establishment at court had deteriorated, and not as many royal commissions were available as before. But Mozart found something else: Joseph Haydn.

Papa Haydn took an immediate liking to his younger colleague, and they struck up a lifelong friendship. After Mozart dedicated a set of string quartets to the older master, Haydn remarked to Mozart's father, Leopold: "I tell you before God, and as an honest man, that your son is the greatest composer that ever lived."

Papa Leopold, we're sure, forgave Papa Haydn for the understatement.

Mozart makes a living

Without a steady job, Mozart sustained himself around Vienna by writing operas, which were as popular with the public as movies are today. (See *Opera For Dummies,* by David Pogue and Scott Speck [John Wiley & Sons, Inc.], for more on Mozart's operatic career.)

As you can see in the classic play and movie *Amadeus,* Mozart drove his rivals nuts because composing was so easy for him. Musical ideas sprang into his head, fully formed, as if he were taking dictation — all he really needed to do was to write them down!

During this time, Mozart fell in love with a lovely young woman named Aloysia Weber, whom he'd met five years earlier during his travels. After she turned him down (evidently unaware that he'd one day be a movie and a Broadway show), Mozart turned his affections to Aloysia's sister, Constanze, who married him. In honor of the wedding, Mozart wrote his great C-minor Mass.

Aloysia wasn't the only one who failed to appreciate Mozart. The Viennese public itself, a tough and fickle crowd, saw him as just another in the parade of young composers writing fun little entertainments for Saturday night.

Things went better when Mozart visited Prague, now part of the Czech Republic. The city went nuts over his opera *The Marriage of Figaro*. One year after that great success, in 1787, Prague commissioned him to write an opera to celebrate the marriage of the emperor's niece. And what solemn story did he choose to musicalize for this sacred union? The tale of Don Juan, the sleaziest sex maniac of them all.

The opera was called *Don Giovanni*. It was a smash hit.

The Minuteman

Tales of Mozart's speed in writing music became legendary. When a beggar approached him on the street, for example, he found himself without his wallet — so he whipped out a sheet of paper, drew staff lines on it, and wrote a minuet and trio in a couple of minutes. He gave the new composition to the beggar and sent him to a music publisher, who purchased it on the spot. (We suspect that Mozart would have less luck with this technique in today's New York City.)

This kind of composition speed went along with Mozart's hyper personality. In the middle of a conversation, he'd suddenly burst out laughing, jump up and down, turn somersaults, and leap tall tables and chairs in a single bound.

We've had coffee like that, too.

Farewell to Papa Haydn

Meanwhile, Mozart continued to stay in touch with his friend and mentor, Joseph Haydn. In 1790, when Haydn was an "old man" of 58 and Mozart just 34, the two spent a long day together. After dinner, when the time came to part, Mozart said to Haydn, "This is probably the last time we will say goodbye in this life."

He was right. Within a year, *Mozart* was dead.

For years after his death at age 35, the rumor (perpetuated by *Amadeus*) circulated that Mozart had been poisoned by Antonio Salieri, a jealous fellow composer. But, most likely, he simply died from exhaustion.

Mozart's final composition was his *Requiem,* commissioned by an unnamed stranger. You may remember the scene in *Amadeus* where Salieri dons a monstrous disguise, impersonates the stranger, and terrorizes Mozart into delirium and eventual demise. That scene was a complete fabrication; in fact, the stranger was probably just a minor nobleman who intended to pass off the commissioned masterpiece as his own.

But from the beginning, Mozart was convinced that he was writing this *Requiem* for his own death. He raced feverishly to complete the piece, only intensifying his illness. In the end, he completed only a few movements and a sketchy outline of the rest. Mozart's pupil Franz Süssmayr completed it after his death; that's the version you hear in most performances.

Since Mozart's death, the music world has never seen anyone with his combination of musical genius, compositional facility, and divine inspiration. His music is the essence of the Classical style: elegant, graceful, refined, high-spirited, and unsentimental, but with a deep vein of emotion.

Listening to Wolfgang

No music written by Mozart is bad. You could go to a music store *blindfolded* and pick out a Mozart masterpiece every time (although you may have trouble coming up with correct change).

Selecting a short list of compositions to recommend, therefore, is difficult for us. But we know how much you trust us, and our solemn duty is to give it a shot, so check out the following masterpieces:

- Clarinet Concerto in A major, K. 622
- Piano Concerto no. 22 in E-flat major, K. 482 (You can hear the final movement of *this* concerto on Track 3 at www.dummies.com/go/classicalmusic.)
- Piano Concerto no. 24 in C minor, K. 491
- Violin Concerto no. 5 in A major (*Turkish*), K. 219
- Sinfonia Concertante (concerto for violin and viola) in E-flat major, K. 364
- Symphony no. 38 in D major (*Prague*), K. 504
- *Requiem* (completed by Franz Süssmayr), K. 626

If Wolfgang blows you away, listen to these pieces for piano:

- Piano Sonata in G major, K. 283
- Piano Sonata in F major, K. 332

And check out these lovely serenades for small groups:

- Serenade in G major for Strings (*Eine kleine Nachtmusik* — or *A Little Night Music*), K. 525
- Serenade no. 6 in D major (*Serenata notturna* — or *Nocturnal Serenade*), K. 239

Note: In all these titles, the letter *K* refers to a catalog number that can help you find the recording you want.

Ludwig van Beethoven: The man who changed everything

Even Mozart didn't influence the course of classical music as much as Ludwig van Beethoven (1770–1827 — see Figure 2-7). Born in Bonn, Germany, Beethoven ("BAY-toe-ven") was the son of a court musician named Johann. Like Mozart's dad, Johann tried to turn his son into a famous child prodigy. Unlike Mozart's dad, Johann did it the hard way, by beating his son when prodigyhood was too slow in coming. Despite this harsh treatment, Ludwig became an excellent pianist.

Figure 2-7: Ludwig van Beethoven changed everything.

Source: Creative Commons

At age 22, Beethoven moved to — where else? — Vienna, where the musical action was. There he wrote music for various individuals, special occasions, and public concerts of his own compositions, in the process making a better living than Mozart ever did.

Both Beethoven and his music were fiery, impulsive, and impetuous; people loved to watch and listen as he played his passionate piano compositions. Offstage, however, his fiery personality got him into fights with his landlords and girlfriends. Beethoven wasn't a long-term kinda guy, in either apartments or relationships.

We all know characters like that: geniuses who, despite their incredible abilities and talents, are so much easier to deal with when they're dead. Keep reading for more about Beethoven.

Papa Haydn teaches Ludwig a thing or two

But Beethoven's main reason for moving to Vienna was to study composition with Joseph Haydn. (After Prince Esterházy's death, Haydn moved back to his permanent home in Vienna.) This teacher-student relationship, alas, was no less stormy than any of Beethoven's other relationships; still, Haydn tolerated his new pupil out of respect for his prodigious talents.

Just as Mozart had, Beethoven learned how to write a symphony and a string quartet — Haydn's two greatest specialties. In fact, in Beethoven's first two symphonies, Haydn's influence is everywhere. In form, structure, and length, they're nearly identical to Haydn's symphonies of the day.

But then something happened that changed Beethoven forever. At 31, he began to realize that he was gradually losing his hearing. This is the worst thing that can happen to a musician — let alone the hottest-tempered one of all. The approaching deafness had a deeply disturbing effect on Beethoven.

One day, Beethoven walked through a forest with his friend and pupil Ferdinand Ries, who remarked on the beautiful piping of a shepherd's flute nearby. Beethoven heard nothing — and became overwhelmingly depressed. He later wrote of his torment in a document that's both pathetic and courageous, now known to musicians as the *Heiligenstadt Testament:*

> Oh, you men, who think or say that I am evil or misanthropic, how immensely you wrong me. You do not know the secret reason. . . . For six years now, I have been horribly afflicted. . . . Ah, how could I possibly admit a weakness in the one sense which ought to be more perfect in me than in others, a sense which I once possessed in the greatest perfection? Oh, I cannot do it; so forgive me when you see me retreat when I would have gladly spoken with you. . . . I must live alone, as if banished.

Beethoven's compositions of this period bear the mark of a man desperate to be the master of his own fate. If you're aware of his condition of the time, his music makes much more sense. In expressing his pain, Beethoven single-handedly took music from the Classical style into the Romantic period, where the most important element in music was the expression of *feelings*.

Put another way: Without Ludwig van Beethoven, we'd have no Barry Manilow.

The Heroic Symphony

If one single piece of music revolutionized music history, it was Beethoven's Symphony no. 3, known as the *Eroica* (meaning "heroic") Symphony. With this piece, Beethoven ceased to be merely the successor to Haydn and Mozart and found his own unique voice.

The pendulum of classical music

You may have noticed a funny thing about musical tastes throughout history: They're a pendulum. Each period of music represents an overreaction to the style of the music before it.

The Baroque style, with its florid ornaments and improvisations, was an attempt to be freer emotionally than the cool spiritualism of medieval and Renaissance music. After the Baroque, the Classical period put a bridle on emotion once more. And the Romantic period burst violently out of that bridle.

Beethoven was the one who did the bursting.

From the start, Beethoven conceived this symphony on a grand scale, intending to evoke the life and death of a great hero. Originally, the hero was to have been Napoleon Bonaparte, but that changed in 1804, as Beethoven's friend Ferdinand Ries wrote:

> Beethoven greatly admired Bonaparte at the time. I saw a copy of the score lying on his table, with the word "Bonaparte" at the very top of the title page, and at the very bottom "Luigi van Beethoven," but not another word. . . .
>
> I was the first to break the news to him that Bonaparte had proclaimed himself emperor. He flew into a rage and cried out: "Is he then, too, just an ordinary human being? Now he, too, will trample on all the rights of man and satisfy only his ambition. He will become a tyrant!" Beethoven seized the title page, ripped it in two, and threw it to the floor. The first page was later rewritten, and only then did the symphony receive the title *Sinfonia eroica* (*Heroic Symphony*).

The piece is almost twice as long as any symphony that came before it, and the proportions were changed dramatically. Especially unusual is the second, slow movement — it's a somber funeral march with moments of great mourning and passionate outbursts of grief.

In all, Beethoven wrote nine symphonies; they challenged and expanded all the symphonic forms that existed up to that point. With each work, he tried to make his music do more, say more, and boldly go where no music had gone before.

Taking the Fifth

Of course, Beethoven's most famous symphony is his Fifth. It's the one that begins in the austere key of C minor, with the famous four-note snippet that everybody knows: "Da-da-da-DAAAAAAAAAAAAAAAAAH!"

After four movements of Herculean toil, the symphony comes to a close — but instead of ending in C minor (the serious key that began the piece), Beethoven finishes in the cheerful, triumphant, exuberant key of C major.

Now, in musical terms, the difference between a minor chord and major chord is just one note. (See Chapter 11.) But in emotional terms, the difference is *enormous.* If you go from minor to major, you feel as if the storm has passed, the clouds have lifted, the sun has come shining through, and you've found a free parking space *right* in front of the restaurant.

Listen to the first movement on Track 4 at www.dummies.com/go/ classicalmusic — and follow along by reading Chapter 5. But to fully appreciate the tormented musical journey of Beethoven's Fifth Symphony, you've got to listen to the whole thing.

From sketch to final symphony

Unlike Mozart, Beethoven wasn't a facile composer; in fact, he'd wrestle with his work in his sketchbook for weeks and months and *still* he wasn't satisfied.

One of the simplest melodies ever to enter Beethoven's sketchbooks eventually became one of the most profound themes in history: the "Ode to Joy" theme from his Ninth (and last) Symphony. You may recognize this melody as the tune to "Joyful, joyful, we adore thee."

"Ode to Joy" was a long, beautiful poem by Friedrich Schiller. From the age of 23, Beethoven had wanted to set it to music. He finally found the right place to put it — right at the end of the Ninth Symphony — 20 years later.

Up until that moment, every symphony ever written had been designed to be played by an orchestra alone. But in his Ninth Symphony, for the first time ever, Beethoven added four solo singers and a huge chorus to sing the words of Schiller's poem. For music critics of the time, adding the singers was an act of treason. Debate raged in musical circles for decades.

Fortunately, the public didn't care much about musical circles; the first performance was a great success. After it was over, the audience rose to its feet, cheering Beethoven in a thundering ovation. But by this time, Beethoven was totally deaf; he sat onstage facing the orchestra, unaware of the audience's reaction. In a famous act of kindness, one of the singers gently grasped Beethoven's shoulders and turned him around to see the adoring audience.

By the time Beethoven died, he was a hero; 30,000 mourners attended his funeral. One of the coffin bearers was Franz Schubert — the next musical guy you can read about in this chapter.

Hearing Beethoven

If you'd like to hear more music by Beethoven (and you *really* should), check out these orchestral masterpieces:

- The symphonies — all nine of them are amazing
- Piano Concerto no. 4 in G major, opus 58
- Piano Concerto no. 5 in E-flat major, opus 73
- Violin Concerto in D major, opus 61

While we're on the subject, we may as well tell you about Beethoven's piano sonatas, too. Here are his three most famous — you may even find all three recorded together:

- Piano Sonata no. 14 in C-sharp minor, opus 27, no. 2 (*Moonlight*)
- Piano Sonata no. 8 in C minor, opus 13 (*Pathétique*)
- Piano Sonata no. 23 in F minor, opus 57 (*Appassionata*)

Then there are his chamber works (that is, pieces for small groups of musicians). Some of our favorites are:

- Sonata for Violin and Piano no. 9 in A major, opus 47 (*Kreutzer*)
- Trio in B-flat major for Clarinet (or Violin), Cello, and Piano, opus 11
- String Quartets opus 59, no. 1-3 (the *Razumovsky* Quartets)

Schubert and his Lieder

Beethoven was 20 when his future pallbearer Franz Schubert ("SHOE-bert") was born. Shrewdly observing that every great composer of the Classical period eventually moved to Vienna, Schubert chose to save the plane fare and just be born there.

As with Mozart, melodies poured from Schubert (pictured in Figure 2-8) like honey from the bottle; after one piece was finished, he simply began another. And his melodies are extremely hummable — even in his symphonies. These sections point out interesting aspects about Schubert.

Schubert evenings

Schubert was a decent pianist, but not a virtuoso like Mozart or Beethoven; he didn't make much money by playing. But his piano came in handy for lots of fun evenings with musical friends, which came to be known as

Source: Creative Commons

Figure 2-8:
Franz
Schubert
(1797–1828),
one of the
most prolific
songwriters
in history.

Schubertiads. They'd gather together, play charades, and dance to music that Schubert composed on the spot.

His fun-loving nature — and his fun-filled parties — made Schubert immensely popular among his friends, despite the fact that he wasn't a handsome man. Not at all. In fact, his friends called him "Mushroom." (With friends like that, who needs enemies?)

Furthermore, his circle of friends became even closer after, broke and jobless, Schubert had to move in with them for long stretches. Vienna was still swooning over Haydn, and Beethoven was making his mark, so Schubert had trouble competing in the symphony department. And a young composer named Gioachino Rossini was packing them in with his great operas (such as *The Barber of Seville*), so Schubert wasn't scoring with his operas, either.

Unfinished!

Nonetheless, Schubert's symphonies are exquisite. His most famous symphony, no. 8, is known as the *Unfinished* Symphony. He didn't leave it unfinished because of any great life interruption, such as death; actually, nobody knows exactly why he wrote only two movements instead of the usual four. But we'll venture three guesses:

- **Theory 1:** The two movements stand just fine by themselves.
- **Theory 2:** Schubert couldn't come up with any more movements of that quality to match.
- **Theory 3:** He did — but they were lost. (A sketch for the beginning of a third movement does exist.)

In fact, some people have tried to reconstruct a third and fourth movement for the symphony, but to our ears, they don't sound right with the first two.

After the *Unfinished* Symphony, Schubert wrote Symphony no. 9. Its nickname is *Die Grosse — The Great —* for good reason: It's by far the longest of his symphonies. (Which isn't necessarily saying much, considering the length of Schubert's *preceding* symphony.)

The Songmeister

But as good as Schubert's symphonies are, Schubert was best at writing *small* musical pieces — for example, short piano pieces called *Impromptu* (which means "impromptu") or *Moment Musical* (which means "musical moment").

Most of all, however, he was great at composing songs. In all, he wrote more than 600 of them. He called them *Lieder* ("LEE-der"), because he didn't speak English.

Schubert wrote his Lieder to be sung by one voice, accompanied by piano. In fact, maybe the word *accompanied* is inappropriate, because in these songs, the piano has an equal role to the voice. When the voice sings of Gretchen at her spinning wheel, the piano plays a spinning figure over and over, suggesting both the turning of the wheel and the agitation of a young girl's romantic thoughts. When the voice sings of a man and his child riding a galloping horse, the accompaniment graphically depicts the horse's galloping. When the voice sings of a trout swimming down the river, the piano is the river — and the trout. The more you listen to the songs of Schubert, the more musical detail you can hear in them.

Piano for two

Always the socialite, Schubert also wrote scads of piano *duets* — pieces for two players. (To be technically accurate, Schubert wrote these pieces "For four hands." He didn't mind if one player had three hands and the other had only one.)

Duets are fun because they require a social get-together just to hear how they sound — a fact not lost on Schubert. Often, while composing a piano duet, he'd deliberately write the notes so that the players' hands crossed each other. Then he'd invite some good-looking local female pianist over to play his new composition with him. The resulting minutes of light hand brushing, we're guessing, were often as close as old Mushroom could get to the real thing.

One year after being a pallbearer at Beethoven's funeral, Schubert himself died, of typhoid fever. He died as he lived, very poor and very young — he was 31.

Schubert in the record store

If you want to be a Schubertian, we'd better get you ready. First, listen to the following orchestral works:

- Symphonies no. 4, 5, 8, and 9
- Mass (for solo singers, chorus, and orchestra) no. 5 in A-flat major, D. 678

(In these works, the letter D refers to a catalog number that can help you locate the piece you want in a record store.)

Then check out these pieces for smaller forces:

- Quintet, opus 114 (*The Trout*)
- *The Shepherd on the Rock,* song cycle for soprano, clarinet, and piano
- Die schöne Müllerin (*The Miller's Beautiful Daughter*), song cycle for voice and piano

Felix Mendelssohn

Meanwhile, back in Germany, yet another genius was growing up, writing great stuff, and dying young: Felix Mendelssohn (1809–1847 — see Figure 2-9).

Felix was a child of privilege. His father was a banker; his grandfather (Moses Mendelssohn) was a philosopher. After his parents discovered Felix's immense natural abilities, they helped Felix begin developing his

Figure 2-9: Felix Mendelssohn, the man who rediscovered Bach.

Source: Creative Commons

great potential. Like Mozart, he started composing early, but Mendelssohn's childhood music is even more mature-sounding — especially the Octet for Strings (written at age 16) and the Overture to Shakespeare's play *A Midsummer Night's Dream* (written at age 17).

About 17 years later, Mendelssohn composed some background music for the same Shakespeare play. Among those new snippets is the single most famous piece Mendelssohn ever wrote: the wedding march that gets played right after "You may now kiss the bride." That little piece has become so familiar, so much a part of popular culture, that it often surprises people to hear that it was actually *composed* by somebody!

Like Mozart, Mendelssohn simply wrote down music from his head, fully formed, without any need for a first draft. Fellow musicians would carry on long, pleasant conversations with Felix, marveling as he notated music on paper in mid-conversation.

The piano that wouldn't die

Mendelssohn was one of those rare composers who achieved fame and fortune without having to die first. His Piano Concerto no. 1 in G minor, for example, was such a hit that, for a while, it was the most-performed piano concerto ever written. In fact, the composer Hector Berlioz (who appears a bit later in this chapter) went around telling the story of a piano at the Paris Conservatory. This particular piano, the story goes, was so used to playing that Mendelssohn concerto that it continued playing the music even if nobody was touching its keys! The local piano-maker tried everything to make the piano shut up: sprinkling holy water on it, throwing the piano out the window, chopping up the keys with an ax; still the piano wouldn't stop. Finally, he got serious: He threw the remaining pieces of the piano on a roaring fire — and the concerto was silent at last.

We know how the poor guy felt; we lived through the disco era.

Mendelssohn rediscovers Bach

Though of Jewish descent, Mendelssohn was baptized as a Lutheran, and he composed many pieces on religious subjects.

As an adult, Mendelssohn conducted the orchestra in Leipzig, Germany, where Bach had written his sublime masterpieces a century earlier. In fact, Mendelssohn played a major role in popularizing Bach's music. As you may remember, Bach was famous as an organist, not as a composer; many of his compositions languished in storage (or were thrown away) after his death.

Felix Mendelssohn unearthed and performed Bach's monumental *St. Matthew Passion* for the first time since Bach's death. From that point on, Bach became revered, admired, and beloved the world over.

He's just that good

When the time came to conduct the first performance of St. Matthew Passion, Felix Mendelssohn walked up to the conductor's podium and opened the huge book of sheet music on the music stand. Only one little problem: As the audience members were settling into their seats, Felix discovered that he had the wrong music score! The book looked the same as the actual Bach piece — same thickness, same leather binding — but it was a completely different piece by a different composer.

No matter. Mendelssohn lifted his baton and began to conduct Bach's piece, turning the pages of his impostor score every so often so as not to alarm the musicians. He managed to conduct Bach's entire Passion (which is more than two hours long) from memory, with no noticeable mistakes.

He must have listened to it a lot on his MP3 player.

Mendelssohn sought to continue the tradition of Bach and Handel in his own oratorios, such as *Elijah* and *Hymn of Praise.* But Mendelssohn's symphonies are even more famous than his oratorios; the Fourth Symphony, called the *Italian,* is especially great. In it, Mendelssohn captures the breezy, festive atmosphere that he experienced on vacation in the Italian countryside. You can almost taste those little frozen fruit-ice things that the vendors sell.

The sounds of Mendelssohn

Listen to these wonderful works of Felix Mendelssohn:

- Piano Concerto no. 1 in G minor, opus 25
- Violin Concerto in E minor, opus 64
- Overture and Incidental Music to *A Midsummer Night's Dream*
- *Fingal's Cave* Overture
- *Elijah,* an oratorio for solo singers, chorus, and orchestra
- Symphony no. 4 in A major (*Italian*), opus 90

And here's that neat octet he wrote when he was just 16: Octet for Strings in E-flat major, opus 24.

Falling in Love: Hopeless Romantics

By the time Mendelssohn died, a new age in music was well underway. The Classical years, filled with intellectual, rational-sounding music, had slowly given way to the Romantic era, where what counted was feeling, emotion, and nursing one's inner child. Romantic composers, which we discuss in these sections, often took as their inspiration forces of nature, such as sunrises, thunderstorms, and crop circles.

Carl Maria von Weber

Like any self-respecting Romantic composer, Carl Maria von Weber ("VAY-ber" — see Figure 2-10) composed lots of very Romantic-sounding music. But these days, he's also remembered for his contributions to music as a *lifestyle*.

Figure 2-10: Carl Maria von Weber, one of the earliest Romantic composers and a great innovator in virtually every aspect of his medium.

Source: Creative Commons

Weber (1786–1826) was the first conductor to draw up a standard seating arrangement for orchestra players — a system of sectional clumps that's still used today; the first to hold separate rehearsals ("sectionals") for each section of the orchestra; the first to conduct every concert by using a baton and standing on a podium (instead of conducting from the keyboard or pounding a staff on the ground); and the first to demand complete artistic control of all aspects of the productions he conducted. And as if *that* weren't enough, he was one of the best pianists in the world. Not bad for a guy whose middle name was Maria.

Weber also became known as the father of German Romantic opera, but that's neither here nor there. (Well, okay, it *is* there — in *Opera For Dummies*.) And to seal his place as One of the Guys Who Really Defined the Romantic Era, Carl even managed to die in a very Romantic way — of tuberculosis, the leading cause of death among sick Romantics.

Many of Weber's important works are operas, but he wrote several purely instrumental works as well, including wonderful concertos for piano, clarinet, horn, and bassoon. He also wrote two rarely heard symphonies.

Weber was a master of moods. He created many atmospheric effects, including a shivering, shuddering, devilish, supernatural feel during a climactic scene in *Der Freischütz*. It was a lot like Gothic horror. In fact, it *was* Gothic horror. This was the same period during which Mary Shelley wrote *Frankenstein*.

Weber lent a new style and identity to Romantic music. And in doing so, he influenced all the composers who came after him.

For a taste of the many sides of Weber, we recommend

- Overture to *Der Freischütz*
- Overture to *Euryanthe*
- Clarinet Concerto no. 2 in E-flat major, opus 74

Hector Berlioz

Most of the great names in music history are well known because they changed the rules. Hector Berlioz (1803–1869), pictured in Figure 2-11, became famous by *ignoring* the rules.

Figure 2-11: Hector Berlioz: Romantic, visionary, compositional genius, loony tune.

Source: Creative Commons

Berlioz (pronounced "BARE-lee-O's") was, in some ways, even more of an innovator than Beethoven. Listen, for example, to a Beethoven symphony and then to Berlioz's *Symphonie fantastique* — written just three years after Beethoven died. From the sound of it, you'd think that Berlioz came from a different planet. The following sections explain a bit about Berlioz.

Berlioz nearly dies at a dissection

Berlioz was born in France, near Grenoble. His dad, a physician, encouraged his son to follow in his footsteps. But once in Paris to study medicine, Berlioz became the most famous in a long line of doctors-to-be who ditched the medical world in favor of music. What changed his mind? Maybe it was the ineffable lure of music. Or maybe it was having to dissect a corpse. He wrote:

> When I walked into that horrifying house of human remains, littered with pieces of limbs, and saw the terrible faces and heads cut off at the neck, the bloody cesspool where we were standing, with its horrible stench, the flock of sparrows fighting each other for scraps, and the rats in the corners gnawing on bleeding vertebrae, such a feeling of terror seized me that I jumped out of the window and sprinted home as if Death and all his evil entourage were behind me.

Well, Hector, when you put it *that* way . . .

Creating a new kind of music

Berlioz went to the Paris Conservatory to study with Luigi Cherubini, a notoriously strict Italian composer. Unfortunately, Berlioz hated everything Cherubini stood for — including his slavish obedience of the rules of music at the expense of interesting thoughts. Rebel Berlioz wanted to create a new kind of music — and he couldn't stand the nearsightedness of those who didn't understand him.

During his career, every aspect of music went under his microscope — the rules of harmony, the structure of a symphony, the way to write a melody, the number of players in an orchestra, and so on. If he felt that these conventions helped him express what he wanted to express, he kept them. If not, he broke them.

Berlioz puts on a dress

At age 27, Berlioz won the coveted *Prix de Rome,* a composers' scholarship that gives the recipient four years, all expenses paid, in Rome. Actually, he didn't get much composition done there — he was too wrapped up in exploring the city itself — but he did get a lot of inspiration for his later works, including the *Roman Carnival* Overture, one of his most popular works today.

Perhaps another reason why Hector didn't make much headway was his infatuation with a young woman back in Paris named Camille. When, after four months in Rome, he heard that she had a new boyfriend, he went into a jealous tizzy. Intending to murder the new boyfriend (and hoping to land himself on the daytime talk-show circuit), he bought a gun, dressed up as a woman, and took a train headed for Paris. But by the time the train reached Genoa, Italy, Hector decided that killing the guy was too melodramatic. Instead, he decided to kill *himself* by leaping into the Mediterranean.

His suicide attempt was unsuccessful, however — he got fished out so that he might live to write his most famous symphony, the *Symphonie fantastique,* one of his few successful attempts to get women via his composition.

A fantastique story

One night, Berlioz was watching a performance of *Romeo and Juliet* in English. From the moment the actress playing Juliet walked onto the stage, Berlioz (who, as you've probably noticed, wasn't terribly subtle about his crushes) fell madly in love with her.

The Irish actress, Harriet Smithson, didn't speak a word of French. Naturally, the language barrier only fanned the flames of his obsession. He sent her letters, gifts, and love notes; he traveled to where she was in hopes of "bumping into" her. Eventually, he succeeded — in terrifying her completely.

His obsession with Harriet led Berlioz to write a strange, five-movement symphony called the *Symphonie fantastique*. It's based on a story he made up about a young artist who's insane with love for an unresponsive woman (surprise, surprise!). Berlioz wrote a musical theme to represent this obsession, and he called it an *idée fixe* ("fixed idea"). This particular melody keeps coming back in each movement of the symphony.

The *Symphonie fantastique* was so different from anything that had come before it that Berlioz had to write notes to the conductor, such as: "This is not a clerical error. It's *really* supposed to sound like this. Please don't 'correct' the notes."

For Berlioz, however, the *Symphonie fantastique* was successful for a completely different reason: It actually *worked*. Harriet Smithson showed up at the premiere performance and was blown away. After the concert, she met Hector; they dated; and — cue the violins! — they actually got married.

We'd love to end the story there, but journalistic integrity beckons. Even after years of marriage, Harriet *still* didn't speak any French. And Hector never did learn English. And as many a divorcée can tell you, a communication-free marriage isn't exactly fulfilling. Eventually, driven mad by the sheer boredom of silence, Hector and Harriet split up. *C'est la vie,* Hector.

Berlioz on your MP3 player

You're gonna go nuts over the wild music of Berlioz, especially the following pieces:

- *Symphonie fantastique*
- *Roman Carnival* Overture
- *The Corsair* Overture
- *Requiem* (an enormous, amazing piece for chorus and orchestra, with four brass bands to boot!)

Frédéric Chopin

While Hector Berlioz was living and working in Paris, another great composer was rising into the headlines: Frédéric Chopin (1810–1849), a thin, frail virtuoso pianist from Poland (see Figure 2-12). Chopin ("sho-PAN," except that you don't really pronounce the final N; instead, you send it flying through your nose) single-handedly revolutionized the world of piano music. He changed everybody's idea of what was possible on the piano (intimate, brilliant, singing, diverse tone colors) and what was not (apparently nothing). Keep reading for more information about Chopin.

Figure 2-12: Frédéric Chopin revolutionized the sound of the piano.

Source: Creative Commons

A Polish boyhood

Like so many of the composers in this chapter, Frédéric Chopin was a boy wonder. At age seven, he published his first composition in Poland; only a year later, he made his debut as a concert pianist. His childhood was rich with the sounds of Poland's national dances, such as the *polonaise* and the *mazurka* — musical influences that filled his head and his music forever after.

Frédéric composed all his pieces at the piano, and he loved to improvise as he performed them. In fact, he hated to write them down, because that meant freezing them in one form. Unfortunately, all of Chopin's on-the-spot genius is lost to history; in those days, video recording was still in the testing labs.

After Chopin came to Paris at age 21, his virtuosity caused a sensation; nobody had heard music like his before. Unfortunately, because he was so fragile and sickly, he couldn't play many concerts. Still, he managed to support himself by selling his compositions and giving piano lessons. He limited his live performances primarily to small, less stressful "salon" concerts — concerts in somebody's home. In these, he was wildly successful.

Tiny digits, big heart

We once got to see (and actually touch) a bronze replica of one of Chopin's hands. From this experience, we can conclude the following: His fingers were tiny, delicate, shiny, and metallic.

Yet even with such small hands, young Frédéric sure could get around the keyboard. His music is a flurry of notes, like a whirlwind, flying from bottom to top and back again. His music is warm, romantic, and tender; in a typical Chopin recording, you don't often hear the sounds of agony and pain (except possibly from the pianist).

Fred, George. George, Fred.

In Paris, Frédéric Chopin had a famous love affair with an author named George. George was female, by the way. She used the pen name George Sand only to boost sales of her books (and to save time; her real name was Amandine-Aurore-Lucile Dupin).

Actually, George was somewhat masculine in more than name alone; she loved to dress like a man, drink and smoke cigars, and dominate her relationship with Frédéric. Once, as her little dog was merrily chasing its little tail, George said to Fred, "If I were as talented as you, I'd compose a piece of music based on the dog."

Chopin walked directly to the piano and obediently composed his Waltz in D-flat major, known, of course, as the Little Dog Waltz (otherwise known by its familiar title, the Minute Waltz).

If you think that you've never heard Chopin, you're wrong. The famous funeral march music, so somber and lugubrious, so often borrowed in Road Runner and Bugs Bunny cartoons, is by him; it was originally part of a piano sonata. And then recall that old Barry Manilow hit "Could It Be Magic"; take away Barry's voice, and the piano part that remains is unmistakably Chopin's Prelude opus 28, no. 20 in C minor.

Shoppin' for Chopin

If you'd like a taste of Chopin, you can find much to chew on in your local record store. We especially recommend these works for solo piano:

- 24 Preludes, opus 28
- Ballade no. 4 in F minor, opus 52

And look for these works for piano and orchestra:

- Piano Concerto no. 1 in E minor, opus 11
- Piano Concerto no. 2 in F minor, opus 21

Robert Schumann

Robert Schumann (1810–1856; see Figure 2-13) was one of the foremost German Romantic composers, although not everybody knew it at the time. His life story, punctuated as it was by periods of great emotional trauma, would have been number one on the self-help bestseller list. Here's all you need to know about this certifiable eccentric.

Figure 2-13: Robert Schumann, one of the foremost German Romantic composers.

Source: Creative Commons

Another prodigy

Schumann ("SHOE-mahn") showed an incredible talent for the keyboard as a child. Unfortunately, Mrs. Schumann, like mothers of many musician wannabes even today, hoped for a more "upstanding" career for her son — such as law. Reluctantly, Robert shuffled off to law school at the University of Leipzig. Unfortunately for Mrs. S., her son met Felix Mendelssohn, also in Leipzig, and they became pals. Soon enough, like Berlioz, Schumann bagged school to be a musician.

Robert began studying piano full-time with a fabulous teacher named Friedrich Wieck — and, hormones raging, promptly fell in love with his teacher's teenage daughter, Clara.

Desperately seeking Clara

Clara was a musical prodigy herself. At age 9, she'd toured Germany as a piano virtuoso; now, at 16, she had a good career going. As you can imagine, her father was less than ecstatic about the 25-year-old Schumann's interest in her; "Cradle robber," he undoubtedly muttered in German.

Clearly, Papa Wieck had missed out on one basic precept of child-rearing: If you forbid your teenager to do something, she'll *definitely* do it. Sure enough, Clara married Schumann. It took five years and a lawsuit, but they finally tied the knot.

Personally, the following years were the happiest of Schumann's life. Professionally, however, he blew it big-time. In an attempt to strengthen the ring finger on his left hand — which has less range of movement than any other finger (try it!) — Schumann devised an invention. He attached a string to that finger and tied the other end to the ceiling while he slept. In theory, this contraption would gradually stretch the tendon in his hand and give him more flexibility. In practice, he completely paralyzed his finger.

With his piano career trashed, Schumann turned his attention full-time to composition. He wrote mostly piano pieces, plus four fine symphonies and a terrific piano concerto.

A true Romantic

In the true Romantic tradition, expressing emotion in music was more important to Schumann than form, reason, or logic. And Schumann wasn't lacking emotions to express; his personality swung wildly between two poles — one extroverted and hard-working, the other languid and self-absorbed. He felt as though he were two different people — in fact, he even gave names to his two characters: Florestan for the outgoing one and Eusebius for the introverted one. (Frankly, we're more interested in his *third* personality — the one who dreamed up the names Florestan and Eusebius.)

These days, we know the clinical term for Schumann's problem: He was bipolar. (Beethoven may have been, too.) Unfortunately, his manic depression was accompanied by hallucinations later in his life. At 44, in the throes of midlife crisis, Schumann tried to kill himself by throwing himself into the Rhine River. Not having read Berlioz's biography, however, he didn't realize how ineffectual self-hurling can be; like Berlioz, Schumann was fished out of the water, bedraggled but alive. Alas, his final two years of life were spent in an asylum.

Listening to Schumann

Schumann's best works are his *cycles* (groups) of pieces for solo piano. Listen especially to these pieces:

- *Carnaval*
- *Fantasiestücke* (Fantasy Pieces)
- *Kreisleriana*
- *Kinderszenen* (Scenes from Childhood)

And check out these works calling for full orchestral forces:

- Symphony no. 2 in C major, opus 61
- Symphony no. 3 in E-flat major (*Rhenish*), opus 97
- Piano Concerto in A minor, opus 54

Johannes Brahms

Like Mozart and Beethoven before him, German-born Johannes Brahms (1833–1897 — see Figure 2-14) was a musical child prodigy. Luckily for him and for us, his father (a bass player) recognized and nurtured his talent during the formative years.

But unlike his musical predecessors, who acquired musical posts in such exalted surroundings as cathedrals and castles, Brahms, who we discuss more in these sections, got jobs playing piano in Hamburg's taverns and brothels. (For more on brothel experiences, we gently refer you to another *For Dummies* book — the one written by Dr. Ruth Westheimer.) Still, a job was a job, and Brahms became familiar with a huge amount of music — especially dance music, which he performed every night during his teenage years.

Figure 2-14:
Johannes
Brahms,
one of the
greatest
of all
composers
of classical
music.

Source: Creative Commons

A lucky break

Brahms was 20 when he got to meet the famous Robert Schumann. Upon experiencing Brahms' music, Schumann knew he was in the presence of a genius.

But Robert wasn't the only Schumann who took an interest in young Brahms; so did Robert's pretty wife, Clara. History doesn't record exactly *how* close she and Brahms became — except to note that after Robert Schumann's death, Brahms and Clara spent more and more time together.

Eventually, Brahms became one of the leading composers of the day; his fame spread throughout his native Germany and beyond.

The big leagues

The celebrity German pianist/conductor Hans von Bülow coined the phrase "the three B's: Bach, Beethoven, and Brahms." This honor must have been incredibly flattering to Brahms, but it also saddled him with a great feeling of responsibility to carry on the great German-Austrian tradition in music. He even settled in Vienna, where all the greatest masters had lived.

Brahms carried out his responsibility well, adding a warm, rich, Romantic expressiveness to the forms and structures of Baroque and Classical music. But he was one of the most self-critical composers in history. He threw out dozens or even hundreds of compositions before anyone had a chance to hear them. In fact, he didn't publish his first symphony until he was 43. By way of contrast, by the time *Mozart* was that age, he'd published 41 symphonies, died, and been buried for eight years.

What's amazing to us now is that Brahms' music, so lush in harmony and charming in style, was considered academic, plodding, harsh, and sometimes even dissonant by the public of his time. (Listen to Track 5 at www.dummies.com/go/classicalmusic and judge for yourself.) As recently as 1930, a concertgoer at a major American concert hall added some graffiti to an exit sign to make it read: "Exit in Case of Brahms."

The reason for these complaints, we think, is that melody was not Brahms' strongest suit. Like Beethoven, he often worked with little musical ideas called *motives* — just two- or three-note licks, for example — and worked them out in ingenious ways, exploring all the possibilities and permutations. The result was stunning, but not always what you'd call hummable. Brahms certainly *wished* that he'd been blessed with a gift for catchy tunes, however. "I would give up everything I have ever composed," he once said, "to have written the *Blue Danube Waltz!*"

Boning up on Brahms

Because there's perfection aplenty in most of Brahms' works, you can start almost anywhere and get an awesome sampling. But here are some of our favorites.

For orchestral forces, try the following:

- ✔ All four of his symphonies — but listen to no. 2 first!
- ✔ Variations on a Theme by Joseph Haydn
- ✔ Piano Concerto no. 2 in B-flat major, opus 83
- ✔ Violin Concerto in D major, opus 77
- ✔ *Ein Deutsches Requiem* (also known as *A German Requiem*) for solo singers, chorus, and orchestra

And for smaller forces, check out these pieces:

- ✔ Sonata for Violin and Piano no. 1 in G major, opus 78
- ✔ Intermezzi for Piano, opus 118

The superstars: Paganini and Liszt

Rock stars didn't originate with Elvis. Two of the greatest rock stars the world has ever seen lived in the 1800s (see Figure 2-15), dazzling the crowds and making the young girls scream and faint.

Figure 2-15:
Niccolò
Paganini
(left) and
Franz Liszt,
classical
music's first
superstars.

In his day, Niccolò Paganini (1782–1840) was the most astoundingly talented violinist who'd ever lived. He had a perfect technique, flying fingers, a bow that made sparks fly, and a fervent, emotional style of playing that drove audiences wild.

Paganini ("pah-gah-NEE-nee") completely changed the nature of violin playing. True, he could toss off pieces that were considered unplayably difficult; but he was also one of classical music's biggest self-promoters, presenting himself to his public as a phenomenon. Before a concert, for example, he'd prepare his violin by sawing most of the way through three of his four strings. During the performance, these strings were bound to break, forcing him to finish the music all on one string.

Women (and some men, too) actually fainted at Paganini's concerts. Sometimes he asked for the lights to be dimmed while he improvised a particularly scary-sounding showpiece. After the candles were lit again, the audience looked like a battleground, bodies sprawled everywhere.

But becoming a media sensation isn't all screaming fans and glory. The gossip-mongers of the 1800s delighted in spreading rumors that Paganini had cut off his wife's head; that he had learned to play the violin while spending eight years in a dungeon for having stabbed one of his rivals; and even that he had sold his soul to the devil. (Paganini's long, thin, sallow face; taciturn, almost sinister expression; long, bony fingers; and customary long, black cloak didn't do much to quell those devil rumors.)

To show off his astonishing feats of virtuosity, he wrote six violin concertos. As music, they're pretty good, but mainly they're dazzling showpieces that feature one special effect after another. We recommend no. 1 and no. 2, which are the ones most widely performed today.

Liszt follows Paganini's lead

If Paganini was a master showman on the violin, Vienna-trained Franz Liszt ("LIST") was his equivalent on the piano, touring all across Europe to sold-out concert halls. Like Paganini, Liszt (1811–1886) turned his own performances into rockin' road shows: removing a trademark pair of white gloves with a flourish just before playing, insisting on a backup piano onstage in case he broke strings with his violent crashes on the keyboard, and showing off his memorization skills by dramatically tossing the sheet music over his shoulder before beginning to play.

Paganini made the ladies swoon with his playing, but Liszt went one better — he'd swoon *himself* at the end of a particularly emotional, wrenching piece. Of course, his fans went wild. So many people wrote to him asking for a lock of his hair that he had to get a dog — he cut off little pieces of fur whenever necessary. *Lisztomania* — as it was called even then (we're not making this up!) — was out of control.

To showcase his talents, Liszt composed an enormous number of solo piano pieces — some of the most difficult music ever written. Some of his more virtuosic compositions are the Hungarian Rhapsodies for piano and the Piano Sonata in B minor.

At age 37, Liszt shocked the world by ending his piano-playing career. He settled down at the court of Weimar, Germany, as music director. There he conducted opera and symphonic performances and composed a series of tone poems, two symphonies, and two piano concertos. We recommend his Piano Concerto no. 1 — it's his finest orchestral masterpiece.

Seventeen years later, Liszt shocked the world yet again when he moved to Rome to become a clergyman, paving the way for future stars, from Cat Stevens to Little Richard, to abandon their adoring fans and immerse themselves in religion.

Richard Wagner

Liszt liked to call his daring style of music, filled with unusual harmonies and structures, "Music of the Future." (Perhaps it's just as well that he never heard gangsta rap.) But the prime proponent of "Music of the Future" was Richard Wagner (1813–1883), pictured in Figure 2-16. Wagner (pronounced "VAHG-ner") became Liszt's friend and brother in arms — or, more precisely, son-in-law in arms: Wagner married Liszt's daughter Cosima (after courting her away from her first husband). If you want to know a bit more about Wagner, read on.

Figure 2-16:
Richard
Wagner,
the height
of German
Romantic
music.

Source: Creative Commons

An opera guy

Wagner was an opera guy. He tried to create a new art form, a music drama that married famous German folk tales with great spectacle and great tunes. You can find out an incredible amount about Wagner in our own modest attempt titled *Opera For Dummies* (John Wiley & Sons, Inc.). You'll soon see why more biographies were written about this man than anyone in history except Jesus. You'll also see what an arrogant, dishonest, jealous, hypocritical, racist, sexist scumbag Wagner was.

We include Wagner in *this* particular opus, however, for three reasons:

- ✔ Wagner spawned a Music of the Future *movement* whose members included all kinds of different composers, operatic and otherwise. For a time, composers aligned themselves with one of two philosophical camps: those who looked to the future (such as Wagner, Liszt, and Berlioz) and those who looked to the past for inspiration (for example, Brahms, who was, as you may recall, conservative in his composing).

  Brahms and Wagner, in fact, were the centerpieces of a raging, divisive controversy, perpetuated largely by their fans. In private, Brahms was actually a fan of Wagner; in public, he played along with the media hype. When someone brought Brahms the news that a member of Wagner's orchestra had died, he quipped: "The first corpse."

- ✔ Wagner developed in his operas the practice of assigning a musical theme to each main character. Each little melody, called a *Leitmotif* (pronounced "LIGHT-mo-teef"), comes and goes with its character. This technique, influenced by Berlioz's "fixed idea" invention, was the direct ancestor of some of the melodies by future composers such as Richard Strauss (we'll introduce him next) — not to mention the ancestor of the Darth Vader theme, the Luke Skywalker theme, the Princess Leia theme, and the Obi-Wan Kenobi theme.

- Wagner's operas have great overtures — sometimes known as *preludes* — that can stand very well on their own as orchestral pieces, and often do in concerts.

Listening to Wagner

Here are the best of Wagner's overtures, in our humble opinion:

- *Tannhäuser* Overture
- *Rienzi* Overture
- *Die Meistersinger* Overture
- *Tristan und Isolde:* Prelude and Love-Death (also known as *Liebestod*)

And then you should hear *Die Walküre: Ride of the Valkyries*, just to be able to say that you've heard it (if you haven't already, blasting out of the helicopters in the classic war movie *Apocalypse Now*).

Strauss and Mahler

If you think of Richard Wagner as a brick dropped in a pond, his ripples touched most everyone who came later — especially his two most ardent disciples, Richard Strauss (1864–1949) and Gustav Mahler (1860–1911), pictured in Figure 2-17. The next sections look more closely at these two men.

Richard Strauss: the tone painter

Born in Germany, Richard Strauss (you have to say it German: "REEEKKHH-art SHHHHTRAUSS") received plenty of early training in music from his father, a French horn player. No wonder his compositions are so horn-heavy; his two horn concertos are staples of the horn-player's repertoire, and some astoundingly difficult and heroic horn solos in his *orchestra* pieces have made Richard Strauss a favorite composer of horn players everywhere.

Strauss firmly believed that, after the age of Wagner, making music in the old, established forms was no longer possible. "From now on," he wrote, "there will be no aimless phrase-making . . . and no more symphonies."

For Strauss, the future was in music with a *program* — music that tells a story, that's *about* something. He called such pieces *tone poems*. You can read about tone poems in Chapter 3; Strauss was the tone poem's greatest proponent. His best ones are *Don Juan, Don Quixote, Ein Heldenleben (A Hero's Life), Also sprach Zarathustra (Thus Spoke Zarathustra),* and *Tod und Verklärung (Death and Transfiguration).*

Figure 2-17: Richard Strauss (left) and Gustav Mahler, two of the most ardent disciples of Richard Wagner.

We've never met you, but we *know* that you've heard Richard Strauss's music. It's been used in movies aplenty — especially in the beginning of *2001: A Space Odyssey*. Have you seen the beginning of that movie, when the apes are looking at the Giant Black Rectangle from Outer Space? You hear three long notes for trumpet, followed by a huge crash ("DA-Daaaaah") for the entire orchestra and the pulse of kettledrums. That's Strauss's *Also sprach Zarathustra* (*Thus Spoke Zarathustra*).

True to his philosophy, Strauss's tone poems all follow a story. In *Don Juan,* you can hear the world's greatest lover making conquest after conquest. In *Tod und Verklärung,* you can hear the old man's weak and arrhythmic heart falter as he is about to die. In *Don Quixote,* you can hear the distracted Don attacking an "army" of bleating sheep, rampaging against the windmills, or falling off his horse. Richard Strauss once boasted to a friend at dinner, "I can translate *anything* into sound. With my music, I can describe what it sounds like to pick up your spoon and fork from one side of your plate and lay them down on the other side." (We're betting *that* tone poem never went platinum.)

Richard Strauss's music borrows several tricks from Wagner's book. He associates a particular melody (a *Leitmotif*), for example, with a particular opera character. He also uses a lot of *deceptive cadences,* which are stretches of harmonies that seem just about to settle happily on the ending chord — and then don't.

Strauss was also a prominent conductor, which may explain why he was one of the rare composers to get rich and famous while still alive. Though he was a musical genius, you'd never know it from his conducting: He conducted sitting down, sober, expressionless, his baton moving unemphatically through the air. He once proclaimed that a conductor's left thumb never needs to leave the pocket of his waistcoat. (Generations of future conductors, not knowing what a *waistcoat* is, have searched in vain for a place to stick their left thumbs ever since.)

Chronologically, Strauss was a 20th-century composer for half his life, but musically, he belonged to the Romantic era. Though he continued experimenting with new ideas, he never completely gave up *tonality* in his music (basing it mostly on traditional harmony); in fact, his writing became more traditional-sounding as he neared his death in 1949. As a young man, he wrote *Death and Transfiguration;* 60 years later, as he was dying, the master of musical paintings said, "Death is just as I wrote it."

Strauss on recording

Of Richard Strauss's eight tone poems, listen to these first:

- *Till Eulenspiegel's Merry Pranks* (also known as *Till Eulenspiegels lustige Streiche*)
- *Don Juan*
- *Death and Transfiguration* (also known as *Tod und Verklärung*)

And for a taste of the simpler, more conservative Strauss, make sure that you listen to these pieces:

- Suite for Wind Instruments in B-flat major, opus 4
- Suite from *Le Bourgeois Gentilhomme* (music written to accompany the comedy by Molière)
- Horn Concerto no. 2 in E-flat major

Finally, we want to recommend one of our all-time favorites: *Four Last Songs* (for solo soprano and orchestra) belongs in the category of Most Ravishing Music Ever Composed.

Gustav Mahler, neurotic

As a contrast to the sober, emotionally well-balanced Strauss, Wagner's second most loyal devotee was a neurotic, tortured genius: Gustav Mahler (1860–1911).

Born in Bohemia (now part of the Czech Republic), the son of a Jewish liquor distiller, Mahler got started early on a life of anguish. "And what do you want to be when you grow up, little boy?" asked a kindly passerby (in Czech). "A martyr," he replied.

He got his wish; his life was dominated by tragedy. Mahler's daughter died of scarlet fever (for which the superstitious Mahler felt guilty; he had just composed a set of songs called *Songs on the Death of Children*). And Mahler himself had a very weak heart, making him obsessed with death. From the beginning, Mahler also felt alienated from his surroundings: "I am three times homeless: as a Bohemian native in Austria, as an Austrian among Germans, and as a Jew all over the world."

His upbringing was full of disturbing moments. His father, a cruel man, regularly abused the family, especially his mother. After one particularly painful episode of abuse, the young Mahler ran from the house, unable to take it anymore. Just as he got to the street, a hurdy-gurdy was playing a popular Viennese drinking song. Later, in a psychotherapy session with Sigmund Freud, Mahler realized that this episode had caused him to associate happy, trivial music with great tragedy.

Actually, most of Mahler's music is full of such contrasts: quick alternations of loud and soft or high and low; instruments screaming at the extremes of their range; moments of ethereal beauty, rage and torment, desolation, or triumph. (Some of his symphonies end in hair-raising blazes of glory, including Symphony no. 2 [*The Resurrection Symphony*] and Symphony no. 8 [*Symphony of a Thousand*], which featured 1,379 musicians performing at the premiere — orchestra, soloists, and an immense chorus. The program booklet probably didn't have enough room to call it the *Symphony of One Thousand, Three Hundred Seventy-Nine.*)

Meanwhile, Mahler became a shockingly busy (and demanding) opera conductor, at one point conducting both the Vienna State Opera and New York's Metropolitan Opera. He didn't just conduct the music; he attacked it, lunged at it, and absolutely became it.

His devotion to the highest standards of music-making drove him to exhaustion and collapse, but they won him universal admiration and success as a conductor. His compositions, on the other hand, didn't do so well at first: It took later conductors like Leonard Bernstein, one of Mahler's greatest champions, to bring his work to international prominence.

Mahler's music follows Wagner's lead in taking tonality closer and closer to the breaking point. Nearly every piece of music before Wagner's time was very clearly in a particular key; Mahler's music, on the other hand, has long stretches that don't seem to be in a key at all.

The Mahler experience

Mahler wrote nine symphonies and a series of dark German song cycles. For a good introduction to Mahler's music, you can't go wrong with these recommendations. Start with the first ones on the list; they're the easiest to listen to.

- Symphony no. 4 in G major
- Symphony no. 1 in D major (*The Titan*)
- Symphony no. 2 in C minor (*Resurrection*)
- Symphony no. 5 in C-sharp minor
- *Rückert Lieder* (songs based on texts by the poet Rückert)
- Symphony no. 8 in E-flat major (*Symphony of a Thousand*)

Saluting the Flag (s): Nationalism in Classical Music

Through the 1850s, the bigshots in Germany and Austria monopolized the direction of classical music. Composers from all across Europe went to such places as Vienna, Leipzig, and Weimar to learn from the great masters. No matter what country a composer was from, he was a nobody until he'd mastered the German-Austrian style.

But the last part of the 19th century was one of the most interesting periods in music history. That was when the composers of each country threw off the bonds of convention and asserted the flavors of their own native countries.

Each country had always had its own folk music, which until this time had been kept separate from the music of its "serious" classical composers. But now, that very same folk music was suddenly embraced as the very *basis* of classical compositions. (Think that the highbrow elite getting turned on to the music of the peasants and the uneducated is peculiar? Well, just remember how that jerky, hand-held, amateurish camerawork has become a trendy style for music-video directors — and certain movies — for the past 30 years.)

Anyway, music became the symbol of national pride, and these new native influences that we discuss in these sections spilled over national borders to the rest of the world.

Bedřich Smetana

One of the first nationalistic composers was Bedřich Smetana ("BED-r-zhikhh *SMEH*-ta-nah" — hey, nobody said classical music was going to be easy). While such composers as Brahms were still exploring the possibilities of old Germanic forms, composer/conductor/pianist Smetana (1824–1884) was creating a completely different kind of music — music that represented his native Bohemia.

In Smetana's time, the Austro-Hungarian Empire ruled Bohemia (roughly the area now called the Czech Republic). Smetana, upset at having to grow up under a foreign power, joined a group of rebellious buddies who tried to create an independent Bohemian state. After their coup failed, he jogged over to Sweden for a while and then boomeranged back to Prague. You could call him a bounced Czech.

A river runs through it

One of Smetana's most appealing compositions is a set of six tone poems (freeform orchestral works meant to *depict* something) called *Má Vlast* (*My Fatherland*). The second tone poem in the set is the most famous: *The Moldau* (or *Vltava* in Czech), the name of the mighty river that runs through much of the country.

Smetana set this river stunningly to music, beginning with two solo flutes representing the two mountain streams that form the source of the river. As *The Moldau* grows, so does the orchestral sound, with one instrument entering after another, until a mighty river of sound flows. This river flows through woods, where hunting horns are heard; through fields, where a wedding celebration is taking place; through a nighttime scene of water and wood nymphs; over great rapids; through the great city of Prague; and finally off into the distance, all the while picking up remarkably little in the way of industrial runoff.

Smetana remains immensely popular in his country. On a recent trip to the Czech Republic for the purpose of researching this book (at least that's what we told the IRS), we flew Czech Air. From the moment we boarded the plane in New York, the strains of *The Moldau* poured from the plane's speakers. In the tiny town of Litomišl, we visited Smetana's birth house; there the elderly woman tour guide (a not-too-distant relative of Smetana himself) turned on the stereo as soon as we arrived — yup, the old vinyl record that happened to be on the turntable was *The Moldau,* which she played over and over until we left. Then, on the flight home, we were treated once again to *The Moldau.* We never want to hear *The Moldau* again.

Keeping an ear out for Smetana

Well, of course you must hear *The Moldau* (also known as *Vltava*), as well as the other five tone poems that make up *Má Vlast* (*My Fatherland*). And then you should hear the overture from his most famous opera, *The Bartered Bride,* which is set — naturally enough — in a Bohemian village.

Antonín Dvořák

Antonín Dvořák (or "Tony," as he would have been called in Brooklyn) was also a Bohemian. His childhood was filled with country folk music, rustic dances, and merry peasant tunes. His father was the last in a long line of Dvořák butchers, but he played zither on the side for weddings. Young Antonín (1841–1904 — see Figure 2-18) got a lot of his early musical training by playing fiddle next to his father.

Figure 2-18:
Antonín
Dvořák.

Source: Creative Commons

At the age of 16, Dvořák moved to Prague, where he first heard some of Bedřich Smetana's stuff. Antonín got all fired up about writing original music based on the folksy Bohemian musical language. With this simple but highly marketable idea, Dvořák eventually became a professor of composition at the Prague Conservatory. These sections give a few facts about him.

Cheerful success

By classical music standards, Dvořák (pronounced "d(a)-VOR-zhak") was something of a freak: He wasn't especially disturbed, tormented, or nuts, as were his more famous brethren (such as Beethoven, Berlioz, and Schumann). He actually had a sunny personality, despite the fact that he looked more like a full-bred bulldog than any other composer in history. That cheery disposition found its way into his music without the aid of antidepressants.

Dvořák was also a simple, mild-mannered man, with simple tastes and six children. He loved raising pigeons, watching locomotives, and drinking himself silly. As a cosmic reward for his simple likability, Dvořák became a freak in another way: He was successful without having to die first. His music was immediately popular — he had a great gift for melody, and his Bohemian folk-sounding stuff was instantly familiar to his audiences.

The most important audience member of all was Brahms (remember? the guy who wished he could write more-hummable tunes?), who became a great proponent of Dvořák's music. He introduced the younger composer to his publisher, who accepted Dvořák's music for publication, too. Their kinship was more than social: You can actually hear a lot of Brahms's musical influence in some of Dvořák's symphonies, especially no. 7. In fact, you may even hear the musical styles in these pieces bounce crazily back and forth: Germanic, Bohemian, Germanic, Bohemian.

An invitation to America

At age 51, in 1892, Dvořák was invited to America to take over the newly founded National Conservatory of Music, in New York. He was deeply reluctant, citing his national pride, his rich Bohemian heritage, his family, and his fans. Then he found out that the salary was 25 times what he was earning at the Prague Conservatory. He was on the next boat.

Dvořák stayed in the United States for three years. But he was deeply homesick and wound up spending a good deal of his time in a Bohemian colony in Iowa. During his US stint, having been turned on to American Indian and African-American music, Dvořák composed his most well-known piece, his Symphony no. 9 (*From the New World*). The slow, melancholy English horn solo in this symphony's second movement is reminiscent of an African-American spiritual, and the third movement scherzo describes (according to the composer) a great Indian dance feast in the forest.

If you listen to the *New World* symphony, you'd swear that it's *American* music. But play it for a Czech, and she'll assure you that it sounds *Bohemian*. That's quite a stunt for a composer — to enable two different groups to lay claim to the same ideas. Too bad Dvořák never ran for Congress.

Listening to Dvořák

These are the pieces you should hear first. After you've heard them all, you can find many, many more to enjoy.

First, the orchestra pieces:

- Cello Concerto in B minor, opus 104
- Symphonies no. 7, 8, and 9
- Romance for Violin and Orchestra in F minor, opus 11

Then try these lovely serenades:

- ✔ Serenade for Strings in E major, opus 22 (You can hear a movement of this lovely serenade on Track 6 at `www.dummies.com/go/classicalmusic`.)
- ✔ Serenade for Winds in D minor, opus 44

And check out this splendid work of chamber music: String Quartet no. 6 in F major (*American*).

Edvard Grieg

What Dvořák and Smetana were to Bohemia, Edvard Grieg ("ED-vahrd GREEG") was to Norway. (That's not a typo, by the way; they use V instead of W in Norway, because it's such a small country.)

Like any self-respecting great-composer wannabe, Grieg (1843–1907 — see Figure 2-19) dutifully trooped off to Leipzig, Germany, to study the techniques of the great masters. Unfortunately, he worked himself so hard that he developed a lung disease that dogged him the rest of his life.

Boosting Norwegian morale

When he came back to Norway, Grieg became wrapped up in his homeland's struggle for independence. Norway had been ruled by Sweden since 1814,

Figure 2-19: The Norwegian Edvard Grieg (left) was one of the most well-known nationalist composers. Jean Sibelius (right) became a Finnish national hero.

Source: Creative Commons

and Norwegians were starving for freedom. Politically oriented artists such as playwright Henrik Ibsen encouraged Grieg to join them, and he did so with all his heart. He swore off the German influence and began writing music based on the rhythms and melodies of Norwegian folk music.

The Norwegian audiences loved his stuff in a big way. As thanks, when Grieg was only 29, the Norwegian government granted him a government pension for life. Two years before his death, Grieg's zealous nationalism paid off — Norway became free of Sweden's rule. On the day of his funeral in Bergen, Norway, more than 40,000 people crowded the streets. (Most were there for his funeral.)

Many of Grieg's compositions have a sunny, happy character. His delicious tunes have a simple clarity to them. When you hear them, you think, "How come nobody thought of that before?"

Recordings of Grieg

Here are the most popular works of Edvard Grieg, which are well worth getting to know:

- ✔ Piano Concerto in A minor, opus 16
- ✔ *Peer Gynt* Suites no. 1 and no. 2 (incidental music to a play by Henrik Ibsen; they include many familiar melodies)
- ✔ *Holberg Suite* for strings, opus 40

Jean Sibelius

Jean Sibelius (pronounced "YAHN si-*BAY*-lee-us"), also pictured in Figure 2-19, became a famous composer partly because he was in the right place at the right time. Just as Sweden had dominated Norway for many years, so Finland was under Russia's rule at the end of the 19th century. These sections examine Sibelius a bit.

A saga of Sibelius

Like so many composers before him, Jean (yes, "Jean" was a boy) started out pursuing a "respectable" career to please his mom — in his case, law. But you can't keep a great composer down; Jean dropped out of law school after a year and began studying music at the Helsinki Conservatory. Eventually, he received a grant to study music in — surprise! — Berlin and Vienna.

But after he returned from Austria, he found that his beloved Finland had fallen under Russia's domination. He joined a rebel group called the Young

Finns and, like Edvard Grieg before him, cast off the Germanic influence from his compositions. Sure enough, in Sibelius's pieces you can feel the cold weather; the long nights and short days; the bleak, snowy, windswept landscapes; the fiery soul of the Finnish people; and some extremely fine vodka.

This feeling comes across most brilliantly in his tone poem *Finlandia*. From its austere beginning, through its passionate, lyrical theme, to its moving, triumphant conclusion, this piece embodied the Finnish soul and came to be the anthem for Finnish independence. As you can imagine, the Russians weren't crazy about the piece; in fact, they banned it. Even neighboring countries were a little nervous about how it got the Finns whipped up; when it was performed in Germany or France, for example, it was called simply *Fatherland*.

After Finland finally broke free from the yoke of Russia in 1918, Sibelius became a national hero; he truly crossed the Finnish line. To this day, the Finnish people consider Sibelius as important to them as Americans consider Abraham Lincoln or Justin Bieber. All across the country, statues, monuments, museums, and schools stand in honor of Sibelius.

P. S. On top of being a great composer, Sibelius sometimes appeared to be psychic. They say that he could always tell if one of his pieces was being broadcast on the air. "He sits quietly reading a book or a newspaper," wrote his wife. "All of a sudden he gets restless, gets up and goes to the radio, turns it on, and then one of his symphonies comes blasting out!"

Either that, or their "radio" was actually a CD player.

Hearing Sibelius

Sibelius's pieces are generally profound and stirring. For a good start, you should listen to these:

- *Finlandia,* opus 26
- Symphony no. 1 in E minor, opus 39
- Symphony no. 2 in D major, opus 43
- *The Swan of Tuonela* (from Legends), opus 22, no. 2

Carl Nielsen

Grieg and Sibelius became superstars far beyond their homelands during their lifetimes. The Danish nationalist composer Carl Nielsen (1865–1931), on the other hand, didn't. To this day, many classical music buffs still don't know Nielsen's music — and that's a shame, because his compositions are brilliant, strikingly original, expressive, and written with a great economy of notes. Plus, you don't need any funny symbols to spell his name. The following sections introduce this great composer a bit more.

Island life

Nielsen (along with Hans Christian Andersen) was born on the Isle of Fyn off the coast of Denmark. This island, with its harsh changes of season and simple, traditional living, had a great effect on Carl's music. By age 17, he was composing; by 18, he was off to a Copenhagen music conservatory.

But, fed up with his instructors' old-fashioned musical ideas, Carl went off to (can you guess?) Germany to find out what was going on in the centers of music-making. Like the other nationalist composers in this chapter, Carl studied German/Austrian music, deeply absorbed its lessons, and then went home and ignored it completely. "Those who make the hardest fist will be remembered the longest," he wrote at that time. "Beethoven, Michelangelo, Bach, Berlioz, Rembrandt, Shakespeare, Goethe, Henrik Ibsen, and people like them have all given their time a black eye."

Nielsen made a fist, too, especially with his six symphonies. Each explores new musical territory and has some amazing moments — such as the spot in the Fifth (first performed in 1922) where Nielsen instructs the snare drum player to "destroy the music." (In our experience, snare drum players often need no such prompting.)

Despite his music's new sound, often filled with "wrong"-sounding dissonances and unusual harmonies, Nielsen was eventually admired throughout the music world. These days, Nielsen's music is finally beginning to receive the worldwide acclaim that it deserves.

Nielsen for the record . . .

You're best off approaching Nielsen by beginning with his most *accessible* (meaning "not too way-out sounding") pieces. We recommend that you first listen to the following works:

- Little Suite, opus 1
- *Maskarade* Overture

Next, move on to these more substantial masterpieces:

- Symphony no. 3, opus 27 (*Sinfonia Espansiva*)
- Symphony no. 4, opus 29 (*The Inextinguishable*)
- Concerto for Flute and Orchestra
- Concerto for Clarinet and Orchestra, opus 33

Glinka and the Mighty Fistful

Russia may have had a tyrannical, greedy government bent on clutching in its cold talons such helpless countries as Finland, in the process stirring up rebellious young hellions such as Jean "I'm actually a boy" Sibelius. That's not to say, however, that Russia didn't have a few nationalist composers of its own. As you've probably figured out from this chapter, the old adage "Where you find peasant folk music, you also find nationalist classical music" holds true just about anywhere — and Russia had plenty of both.

Mikhail Glinka (1804–1857) was the composer who first brought the folk music sound into Russian classical music. You may have heard his most famous piece, the Overture to *Ruslan and Ludmila;* it's a staple of orchestra concerts because of its contrast of light, bubbly sections and loud outbursts; because of the great melody it offers the violas and cellos; and because it's not very hard to play.

Glinka was a master of long, complete melodies (unlike the Germans, who instead wove together many short fragments in their compositions), and these melodies had a distinctly Russian flavor. He was hailed as a hero by the Russian composers of the Romantic era. In emulation of Glinka, a group of five composers called the Mighty Five, or the Mighty Fistful, decided to banish Western European influences from their music, embracing Russianness to the max. The individual fingers of the Mighty Fistful were Mily Balakirev (1837–1910), who first got the group together; Cesar Cui (1835–1918); Alexander Borodin (1833–1887); Modest Mussorgsky (1839–1881); and Nikolai Rimsky-Korsakov (1844–1908). The following sections examine them a bit more.

All of them were decent musicians, but only one (Balakirev) had originally entered music as a profession. Cui was a professor of military engineering; Borodin was a chemist; Mussorgsky was a civil servant; and Rimsky-Korsakov was a naval officer. They were the original Village People.

Best of five

When we were kids, we thought Rimsky-Korsakov was a songwriting team, like Rodgers and Hammerstein or Lerner and Loewe.

As a child, Rimsky-Korsakov was an excellent pianist, but his passion was the ocean. At age 12, he was studying at the Naval Academy in St. Petersburg. After graduation, he spent 22 years in the Navy — 11 as a sailor and 11 more in charge of the Navy bands.

While a naval officer, Rimsky-Korsakov met the aforementioned Mily Bala-kirev, a Russian composer. In Balakirev's opinion, composers of the day relied too heavily on the musical themes of the famous French and German composers; instead (as he told Rimsky-Korsakov one day on the poop deck), they should look to their own Russian heritage for inspiration. Balakirev was eager to recruit R-K and other young talents to join his cause. Thus was born the "Mighty Five" (which Balakirev thought sounded much more convincing than the "Mighty *One*").

After he finished his Navy stint, R-K got a job as professor of composition at the St. Petersburg Conservatory. Imagining just how he secured this position is difficult, considering that his résumé listed 22 years of sailing and 0 years of professional composition. But Rimsky-Korsakov was a very good teacher, even to himself; after landing the job, he taught himself just enough harmony, form, analysis, and counterpoint to stay a step ahead of his pupils.

Eventually, some of Nikolai's protégés became great composers in their own right — Sergei Prokofiev and Igor Stravinsky, among others. Rimsky-Korsakov taught them the obligatory music subjects, but he excelled in one particular technique — *orchestration* (converting a piece of piano music into a piece that's arranged for a complete orchestra). Rimsky-Korsakov even wrote a classic book on the subject that composers still use today. He would have called it *Orchestration For Dummies* if he hadn't worried about being sent off to Siberia.

Rimsky-Korsakov's most famous piece is called *Scheherazade.* In the story, a spectacularly creepy sultan, king of the Male Chauvinist Pigs, has decided to kill off each of his wives after the wedding night. But one particular wife, named Scheherazade, is able to save her life by telling him incredible stories. Each ends with a cliffhanger, thus keeping the sultan interested in the outcome (and, therefore, postponing her execution) for more than 1,001 nights. By the end of those 2.74 years, the sultan at last gives up his bloody plan. (Scheherazade, we assume, writes up her tale as a screenplay and moves to Hollywood.)

One of R-K's other famous marks on history was helping out his friend Modest Mussorgsky, best known for his *Pictures at an Exhibition.* Although he was the most imaginative, forward-looking musician of the Five, Modest had trouble finishing his pieces, partially because he lacked compositional technique and partly because he was a roaring drunk. Rimsky revised several of his friend's compositions, including the famous *Night on Bald Mountain,* without asking for a penny in royalties.

A fistful of mighty pieces

Here are some pieces by some of the Mighty Five that you should hear:

- **Rimsky-Korsakov:** *Scheherazade,* opus 35
- **Rimsky-Korsakov:** *Russian Easter Overture,* opus 36

- **Mussorgsky:** *Night on Bald Mountain* (orchestrated by Rimsky-Korsakov)
- **Mussorgsky:** *Pictures at an Exhibition* (either the version for piano or the symphonic version orchestrated by Maurice Ravel)
- **Borodin:** Prince Igor: Polovtsian Dances
- **Borodin:** Symphony no. 2 in B minor
- And from the man who started it all . . . **Glinka:** Overture to *Ruslan and Ludmila*

Peter Tchaikovsky

The best Russian composer of them all wasn't a member of the Mighty Fistful. He was, however, a self-absorbed, neurotic, vulnerable, intense guy whose entire life consisted of suffering. So that's gotta count for something. His name was Peter Ilyich Tchaikovsky ("chai KOFF skee"; 1840–1893). (See Figure 2-20.)

Figure 2-20: Peter Ilyich Tchaikovsky, the best of the Russian Romantic composers.

Source: Creative Commons

Tchaikovsky's well-to-do parents noticed his innate talent but were smart enough to realize that nobody makes money being a musician — and they packed him off to law school in St. Petersburg. In the tradition of many musical lawyers-not-to-be before him, however, Peter quit law to concentrate on music at the St. Petersburg Conservatory.

Eventually, Tchaikovsky, the subject of the following sections, was good enough to teach music at a new conservatory being formed in Moscow. He was, however, stone broke.

In one of the few lucky breaks this poor guy would ever get, the wealthy recent widow of a railroad entrepreneur, Nadezhda von Meck, fell in love with his music. She probably had the hots for *him,* too, which was something of a no-no among wealthy recent widows of 19th-century railroad entrepreneurs. She sent him money again and again but insisted that they never meet. Needless to say, he was extremely grateful for her funding, and he even dedicated his Fourth Symphony to her: "To my best friend."

We got trouble

Nadezhda's cash eased Tchaikovsky's financial troubles, but his other problems were just beginning — primarily because he was gay. Homosexuality was a crime in Russia, punishable by exile to Siberia. Tchaikovsky spent most of his life concealing his nature in resolute misery. At one point, thinking that he could "cure" his torment, he even married a female admirer — but the marriage was disastrous, leaving him miserable, divorced, and worse off than before.

Pain and music

Despite his private anguish, Tchaikovsky's music — symphonies, ballets, operas, and overtures — became immensely popular, and his fame spread around the world. He even conducted at the gala opening concert of New York's Carnegie Hall in 1891.

Tchaikovsky's greatest gift was melody. In the tradition started by Glinka, Tchaikovsky wrote *entire* melodies into his pieces, rather than little snippets. And you've definitely heard his melodies. The theme from his *Romeo and Juliet,* for example, is the soaring, lush music you hear in practically every TV show and commercial when two characters fall in love. And everybody knows *The Nutcracker,* which has become the most popular ballet in the world.

Given the torment in most of his life, Tchaikovsky's ability to write such cheerful music as *The Nutcracker* is amazing. But his best music is far from cheerful. His Symphony no. 6, known as the *Pathétique,* is the most personal and deeply felt piece of music ever to pour from the pen of this tormented artist.

Tchaikovsky's inward struggle is the motivation behind the *Pathétique* symphony. Many musicians believe that its soaring, longing melodies reflect the agony of having to live a secret life. Most devastating is the final movement, in which Tchaikovsky gives up his will to live. You can find this movement in its entirety on Track 7 at www.dummies.com/go/classicalmusic, along with a detailed description in Chapter 5.

This most autobiographical of all Tchaikovsky's music was perhaps his greatest achievement. It was also prophetic: Just a week after the first performance, Tchaikovsky died.

Listening to Tchaikovsky

We can't possibly oversell the music of Tchaikovsky: It blows you away. Listen to these, for starters:

- *Romeo and Juliet* Overture-Fantasy
- Suite from the ballet *Swan Lake,* opus 20
- Piano Concerto no. 1 in B-flat minor, opus 23
- Violin Concerto in D major, opus 35
- Symphonies no. 4, 5, and (especially) 6

Sergei Rachmaninoff

Although he lived until 1943, Sergei Rachmaninoff ("rock-MAHN-i-noff"; 1873–1943), pictured in Figure 2-21, was a true Russian Romantic. He grew up in St. Petersburg and studied at the conservatory there, absorbing everything that the great Russian masters such as Tchaikovsky and the Mighty Fistful had to offer. (At his graduation, Tchaikovsky gave him the highest mark anyone had ever seen: the equivalent of "A++++." On the other hand, Tchaikovsky never was one for moderation.)

When Rachmaninoff moved to the United States around the time of the Russian Revolution, he brought the spirit of his country with him. Beneath his cold, forbidding appearance lurked one of the warmer hearts in the business. (Don't be put off by the fact that his works are almost all in a minor key or that they have such titles as *Isle of the Dead.*) Keep reading for more facts about Rachmaninoff.

Sergei gets hypnotized

Early in his career, Rachmaninoff went through a long period of "composer's block." After the disastrous premiere of his Symphony no. 1, Rachmaninoff suffered a serious nervous breakdown, lost his inspiration, and couldn't compose another note. Only after he visited a *hypnotist* could he get past his block. ("You are getting sleeeepy. . . . You are writing a C minor chord. . . . You will dedicate your next piece to meeeee. . . .")

After his recovery, Rachmaninoff's next creation was the Second Piano Concerto — by far his most popular piece. He dedicated the piece to his hypnotist.

Figure 2-21:
Sergei
Rachmanin-
off, the
Russian
piano
master.

Source: Creative Commons

Sergei was a phenomenal pianist, and he wrote many of his famous compositions (such as that piano concerto) for himself to play for a particular occasion. Today, he's best known for those piano pieces — and for his nicknames. Musicians refer to him as "Rocky"; his Second Piano Concerto is called "Rocky 2"; and his demonically difficult Piano Concerto no. 3 — the one that gave pianist David Helfgott a nervous breakdown, as dramatized in the 1996 movie *Shine* — is known as "the Rach 3," or just "Rocky 3."

Rocky on recording

Here are the pieces of Rachmaninoff that we think you should hear first. For orchestral forces, try these:

- Piano Concerto no. 2 in C minor, opus 18
- Piano Concerto no. 3 in D minor, opus 30
- Rhapsody on a Theme of Paganini, opus 43
- Symphony no. 2 in E minor, opus 27

And for piano solos, give these a listen:

- ✔ Prelude in C-sharp minor, opus 3, no. 2
- ✔ Prelude in D major, opus 23, no. 4
- ✔ Piano Sonata no. 2 in B-flat minor, opus 36

Listening to Music of the 20th Century and Beyond

After attending a few concerts of modern music, you too may develop a nervous eye tic on merely hearing the *words* "20th-century music." Much of the music composed in the past century was written by composers who aimed to break the traditional rules. Unfortunately, some of the rules they broke included "Music should sound good," "Music should have melody and rhythm," and "Music should not send the audience bolting for the parking lot."

First, you may actually *like* some modern classical music — even the more strange-sounding stuff. Second, some of the composers of this century had brilliant musical ideas, resulting in fresh, interesting music that, after you're used to it, can actually get you fired up. Finally, just because it's modern doesn't necessarily mean that it's dissonant; many recent composers have as much a gift for melody and beauty as their predecessors. These sections take a closer look at modern composers.

Debussy and Ravel

If one composer started 20th-century music, it was probably the French composer Claude Debussy (1862–1918 — see Figure 2-22). Then again, he had a head start: He began writing 20th-century music in 1894.

Debussy (pronounced "de-bu-SEE," or "WC" if you say it really fast) was one of a group of composers known as *Impressionists*. He tried to portray in music the *impressions* created by sights, sounds, fragrances, and tastes, much the way that such painters as Claude Monet and Pierre-Auguste Renoir depicted blurry fields of dappled light, Paris in the rain, and so on.

To create such impressionistic sounds, Debussy needed a new musical language. The tried-and-true harmonies and chord structures weren't enough anymore. He needed different chords — and different progressions of chords — to produce his special effects.

Figure 2-22:
Claude
Debussy
was one of
the brightest
lights on the
Impression-
ism scene.

Source: Creative Commons

Debussy flunked composition at the Paris Conservatory, where unortho-
dox harmonic progressions were frowned upon. In fact, several years later,
another conservatory student was expelled just for having a Debussy score
in his possession!

As you can imagine, the audiences in Paris took a long time to get used to
these new sounds in music. Today's audiences find Debussy's music lush and
sensual, but what his audiences heard was utter chaos.

One of Debussy's most interesting innovations was his use of the *whole-tone
scale.* In Chapter 11, you can find out how to play a normal scale on the
piano: You move up the keyboard, playing *adjacent* keys or every *other* key
in a specific sequence. But in a whole-tone scale, you play every other key
from start to finish. The result is a magical, dreamy, harplike sound that's not
in any one key. (*Any* time a TV or movie character goes into a trance, starts
having a daydream, or thinks back to an earlier time — or parodies such
a flashback — the harp plays a whole-tone scale up and down to create a
dreamy Debussy ripoff.)

Debussy's first important piece was *Prelude to the Afternoon of a Faun,* based
on a poem by Stéphane Mallarmé. The music fits the mood of the poem,

which concerns the afternoon adventures of a faun (half man, half goat). It's dreamy, sensuous, and vague; the story is your basic Goat-Meets-Nymph, Goat-Chases-Nymph, Goat-Loses-Nymph, Goat-Eats-Grapes.

The musical examples available at www.dummies.com/go/classicalmusic include the third movement of Debussy's greatest orchestral composition, *La Mer* (*The Sea*). In this piece, the water rises and falls, little waves play with one another, and the wind whips the ocean into a frenzy of excitement. If you don't get the feeling of the endless, heaving sea while listening to this piece, your earbuds need adjustment.

Debussy on your MP3 player

If you're going to listen to Debussy, you must hear *Prelude to the Afternoon of a Faun* (also known as *Prélude à l'après-midi d'un faune*) and *La Mer*.

Then listen to the evocative, highly sensual pieces *Nocturnes* and *Images,* and the popular little piano piece *Clair de lune*.

Unraveling Ravel

Claude Debussy was a hero to Maurice Ravel (1875–1937), another Frenchman. Ravel ("rah-VELL") was also a Paris Conservatory-trained Impressionist composer, but his style isn't as hazy and gauzy sounding as Debussy's. Ravel's music was also influenced by American jazz, which he experienced during a brief visit to the United States in 1928.

Ravel might not have become very well known if not for one particular composition: *Boléro.* This piece, based on one particular Spanish rhythm (a *bolero,* of course), consists of a simple melody repeated over and over, louder and louder, played by successively more and more instruments, for 15 minutes, until it reaches a shattering climax that just wipes you out. Depending on how you look at it, this long, slow music buildup is either totally maddening or astoundingly exciting. Because its building intensity is so overtly sexual, Hollywood loves this piece; you hear it in critical lovemaking scenes in movies, such as *Bolero* and *10.*

Another of Ravel's best compositions does for the waltz what *Boléro* does for the bolero. It's called — what else? — *La Valse* (*The Waltz*), and it was written shortly after the end of World War I. At the very beginning, the orchestra, heard through an ominous mist, plays a simple, lovely waltz tune, which represents the elegant, graceful society of the past (before the war). But as the piece progresses, the waltz becomes stranger and more distorted, depicting European society's decline. Again, Ravel builds the music to a shattering finish, in an extremely violent crash of the full orchestra.

Our favorite Ravel piece, however, is the ballet *Daphnis and Chloé.* He wrote it for the Ballets Russes (the same dance group for which Igor Stravinsky wrote his three famous ballets). Like Debussy's *Afternoon of a Faun,* it's about nymphs, but don't prejudge — hey, some of our best friends are nymphs.

Recordings of Ravel

You must, absolutely must, hear *Daphnis and Chloé* Ballet Suite no. 2. Then listen to these other terrific Ravel pieces:

- ✔ *Boléro*
- ✔ *La Valse*
- ✔ *Rhapsodie espagnole* (a lovely and exciting evocation of Spain)

Igor Stravinsky

To many (including us), the Russian Igor Stravinsky (1882–1971; refer to Figure 2-23) was the most important composer of the 20th century. After Stravinsky ("stra-VIN-skee"), nobody could write music without thinking about Stravinsky's ideas and then either accepting or rejecting them.

Figure 2-23: Igor Stravinsky, the most important composer of the 20th century.

Source: Creative Commons

Stravinsky's youth followed the standard Classical Music Composer Formula: he was born into a successful family, got packed off to law school, and felt tugged enough by the lures of music to bag law and become a composer. Keep reading for more about Stravinsky.

The Firebird jump-starts his career

Stravinsky first made his mark by writing ballet music. A famous Russian producer named Sergei Diaghilev, who founded the Ballets Russes in Paris, was looking for a composer to write music for a ballet based on the legend of the Firebird. He originally hired a guy named Anatol Liadov to write it. But as the rehearsal period approached, he asked Liadov how the composition was going. Liadov's response: "Great! I just bought the music paper!" Diaghilev panicked and gave the commission to his second choice: Stravinsky.

Igor's music for *The Firebird* was a milestone. At its premiere in Paris, nobody had ever heard such complex rhythms and strange, shocking dissonances. Still, the audience was impressed by the excitement of the piece and the new sounds that Stravinsky (a student of the great orchestrator Rimsky-Korsakov) had created. The ballet was a hit. Stravinsky became Diaghilev's favorite composer, and his career in Paris was assured.

The Petrushka Chord

Next on the list was *Petrushka,* a ballet based on the antics of — get this — a sex-starved puppet. This ballet has even more dissonance; for example, Stravinsky deliberately wrote two simultaneous harmonies that clashed horribly with each other. If you've got a piano handy, here it is: the now-famous *Petrushka Chord* (which, much as it may resemble the title of an airport bookstore paperback, is actually a perfectly good cocktail party term):

This clash, however, has a purpose: It represents a musical nose-thumbing on the part of the puppet. The audience understood the effect, and this dance, too, was a success.

The most famous premiere in music history

But then, in 1913, the 31-year-old Igor wrote the bombshell: *The Rite of Spring.* The subtitle of this ballet, "Scenes of Pagan Russia," tells all. As Stravinsky wrote: "I saw in my imagination a solemn pagan rite; sage elders, seated in a circle, watched a young girl dance herself to death. They were sacrificing her to propitiate the god of spring." Not exactly a day at the beach (unless you live in certain parts of Southern California).

His music for this scenario offers the sonic impact of a baseball bat in the gut: exceedingly harsh, with short, repetitive melodic fragments; sudden, jarring dissonances; instruments screaming at the edges of their ranges; and hideous, pounding, brutal rhythms. In short, it's *great*. At the opening-night performance — the most famous premiere in music history — the audience responded by trashing the theater.

Not everyone hated the performance; the audience included some of the leading artists in Paris (including Claude Debussy, the famous French composer), who shouted out their energetic approval for the music. Unfortunately, this enthusiasm only fanned the riot's flames, making the music's detractors even more vocal. Fistfights broke out; people scrambled over each other to get out of the theater; at least one person challenged another to a duel. Stravinsky himself ducked out through a window in a dressing room and pretended to join the rioting crowd outside.

Only a year later, the music from the ballet was played in a concert performance, and the audience stood up and cheered. Go figure.

After the Rites

A long excerpt from *The Rite of Spring* is online at www.dummies.com/go/classicalmusic. In Chapter 5, we explain in detail what's going on as you listen. But for now, we should say that the best way to enjoy a lot of Stravinsky's early music is to let it roll over you like thunder. It's a kick.

Stravinsky was still a young man when he composed his three earth-shaking ballets. Shortly thereafter came the Russian Revolution and World War I, and Stravinsky fled Russia, first to Switzerland and then to the United States. (He actually bought a house in Hollywood.)

In his later years, Stravinsky became very cerebral and experimental, composing in a number of styles, including the *Neoclassical* (meaning, simply, "new-Classical") style. (To oversimplify a bit, Neoclassical music was a return to the balance and restraint of Classical music, but with a lot of "wrong notes.") Although he continued to write music into his old age, nothing Stravinsky wrote ever achieved the musical importance of *The Rite of Spring*. He died in New York in 1971.

Stravinsky for the record

You can guess what we're going to suggest in your Stravinsky listening list. Start with his three great ballets, in order of composition:

- *Firebird* (also known as *L'oiseau de feu*)
- *Petrushka*
- *The Rite of Spring* (also known as *Le sacre du printemps*)

Then proceed to the Neoclassical *Pulcinella* Suite. Then, if you're still with us, move on to *Symphony of Psalms*, an incredible composition for orchestra and chorus. If you *still* haven't yanked off your earbuds, a whole world of music lies in store for you. Read on.

Sergei Prokofiev

Speaking of Russians writing in the Neoclassical style, meet Sergei Prokofiev (1891–1953). His music isn't widely known by the general concertgoing public, except for his famous children's story, *Peter and the Wolf*. But his ballet version of *Romeo and Juliet* is a masterpiece, as are several of his symphonies, especially the Fifth.

Prokofiev ("prah-COFFEE-eff"), one of the few composers who didn't drop out of law school (at least in part because he never *went* to law school), managed to mix the balance of the Classical era with the pain and longing of Russian music. Largely because of the "wrong notes" that appear in an otherwise traditional-sounding harmony, much of his music sounds biting, sharp, and even sarcastic.

Listen to these pieces for a dose of Prokofiev:

- *Peter and the Wolf,* opus 67
- Suites from *Romeo and Juliet*
- Symphony no. 1, opus 25 (also known as the *Classical Symphony*)
- Symphony no. 5, opus 100
- *Alexander Nevsky* Cantata (Prokofiev wrote this music for a famous Sergei Eisenstein movie, *Alexander Nevsky.* These days, this music is often performed by an orchestra and chorus, in the dark, while the silent film is projected on-screen.)

And for music written for smaller forces, check out his wild Piano Sonatas no. 3 and 7.

Dmitri Shostakovich

After Russia was replaced by the Soviet Union following the 1917 revolutions, the new, totalitarian society had problems — and music — of its own. Chief among the Soviets was Dmitri Shostakovich ("shos-ta-KOH-vitch"), considered the best composer the Soviet Union ever produced.

Unlike Stravinsky, who escaped before the country became totally totalitarian, Dmitri Shostakovich (1906–1975) lived his entire life as a composer within the Soviet Union. Another prodigy, Shostakovich wrote his first symphony, cryptically titled "First Symphony," at age 18. (It's still considered one of his best.) The symphony sounds buoyant, brash, and defiant, and it's often dissonant in harmony. The officials of the still-new Soviet Union loved it: It seemed to embody the zealous revolutionary drive that they themselves felt.

Dmitri dgets in dtrouble

But as the new government aged, feelings slowly changed. By the mid-1930s, "brash" and "defiant" weren't good things in the USSR's view; the government much preferred music that glorified the status quo.

In 1935, Shostakovich was one of the most celebrated composers in the Soviet Union. His modernistic opera, *Lady Macbeth of Mtsensk,* was enjoying a wildly successful run, both at home and abroad. Shostakovich had every reason to believe that his future as a composer was bright and secure.

Then, one day, an editorial in the Soviet newspaper *Pravda* condemned his work and everything he stood for. The editorial was called "Chaos Instead of Music." "The purpose of good music is to inspire the masses. . . . This is very dangerous music," it said.

Lady Macbeth of Mtsensk was immediately pulled from the stage. Shostakovich was ostracized from professional circles, having been designated an official "enemy of the people." In fact, newspapers announcing his concerts read, "Tonight at 8 p.m.: a concert by Enemy of the People Shostakovich." In the United States, ads like that would double the ticket sales, but in the USSR it was professional death. Shostakovich became extremely depressed.

If this bad news had befallen *Tchaikovsky,* he would have been on the phone to his analyst in a nanosecond. But Dmitri Shostakovich was an artist of a different sort. He set about to rehabilitate himself as a composer in the eyes of the Soviets — and he did so ingeniously. In the tradition of humble-pie-eating celebrities everywhere, Dmitri wrote a symphony (no. 5) subtitled, "A Soviet Artist's Reply to Just Criticism."

The critics were stunned; this piece was just the kind of Soviet music that they had been asking for. Shostakovich was completely rehabilitated in the eyes of the Stalinist regime. He became a star again, and his music was played across the country.

Dmitri's revenge

Shostakovich, however, had the last laugh. Despite the subtitle, the *music* was anything but a tribute to the creeps running the country. If you really listen to the piece, you hear musical metaphors that describe a totalitarian regime battering down the optimism of its people. Years later, in fact, the composer admitted that he had indeed intended a scathing condemnation of Stalin's regime: "I think it is clear to everyone what happens in the Fifth Symphony. You've got to be a complete oaf not to hear it. . . . The rejoicing is forced, created under a threat. It's as if someone were beating you with a stick and saying, 'Your business is rejoicing, your business is rejoicing.' You get up, stunned, saying, 'My business is rejoicing, my business is rejoicing. . . .'"

As you may imagine, Shostakovich had to be careful what he composed thereafter. And, in fact, you can feel this caution in some of his pieces; he had to keep his soul well hidden for a good part of his career.

TECHNICAL STUFF

We can only hope that it was some consolation that his was the first music in history to be performed extraterrestrially. The first cosmonaut, Yuri Gagarin, sang one of his songs over the radio for Mission Control.

Listen to Shostakovich

These pieces are the best introduction to the music of Dmitri Shostakovich:

- Piano Concerto no. 1, opus 35 (piano, solo trumpet, and strings — a brilliant, buoyant work)
- Symphony no. 5 in D minor, opus 47
- Symphony no. 1 in F minor, opus 10
- Cello Concerto no. 1, opus 107

And check out his amazing string quartets, especially no. 3 and no. 8.

The Second Viennese School

Millions of famous composers up until 1900 had lived and worked in Vienna: Haydn, Mozart, Beethoven, Schubert, Brahms, and all their sisters and their cousins and their aunts. These masters had shaped the direction of music-writing for centuries. But as the new century dawned, a new group of composers wanted to change music forever; because they lived in Vienna, too, they adopted the witty moniker "Second Viennese School." Their leader was Arnold Schoenberg (1874–1951).

Schoenberg (pronounced "SHERN-bearg," kind of) began his musical career writing pieces that sounded somewhat melodic and you-can-almost-tell-what-key-you're-in — similar to those of Wagner, Strauss, and Mahler before him. But after years of stretching tonality almost to the breaking point, Schoenberg finally decided to break it once and for all. He started writing a

FOR VIRTUOSOS

Schoenberg explained — somewhat

If you find middle C on a piano and play all the white notes in order up to the next C, you've just played the seven notes in the key of C. About 99 percent of the world's music has been written in the key of something. That's why so many famous pieces of classical music are called such things as Symphony in D major or Sonata in F.

But notice something about the key of C: In traveling up the piano from C to shining C, you skip all the black keys. Arnold Schoenberg's big concept was that these keys shouldn't be second-class citizens just because they're a different color. His new kind of music, 12-tone music, used all 12 of the notes between C and C, white and black — equally.

Not only did Schoenberg decide that all those previously ignored in-between notes deserved more importance, but he actually instituted the world's first affirmative-action quota system for those notes. He decided that if he wrote the note C on his music paper, he wasn't allowed to use a C again until he'd used all 11 of the other notes first!

After he saw how intellectually satisfying such self-imposed rules were, he went even further. He'd make up a specific order of those 12 notes — for example, C, E-flat, G, A-flat, B, C-sharp, B-flat, D, F-sharp, F, A, E — and force himself to use these notes in that order, over and over again, for an entire piece. He'd permit himself to use whatever rhythms he wanted, and he was allowed to combine the notes into "chords" — but he always went in order.

When things were getting really dull, he made up a couple more rules: Playing the series of 12 notes backward *(in retrograde)* was okay, too. He even permitted himself the luxury of flipping a 12-note series upside-down (or *in inversion*) on the music paper. And for years and years, he had all kinds of fun mixing up these rules to make music (such as playing those 12 notes backward and upside-down — known as *retrograde inversion*).

This new kind of music was dubbed serialism, which has almost nothing to do with Schoenberg's passion for whole-grain breakfast flakes.

new kind of music that wasn't in *any* key, ever. This kind of music was non-tonal, or *atonal*. Atonal music is *dissonant* (it sounds as though *all* the notes are "wrong").

Serial music: It isn't just for breakfast anymore

After several years of experimentation, Schoenberg went even further: he started substituting rules of math and intellect for blind inspiration in choosing which notes to write down. Today, we call this kind of music *12-tone music,* or *serialism* (see the accompanying sidebar "Schoenberg explained — somewhat" if you're interested). Composers such as Alban Berg ("BEARG," 1885–1935) and Anton Webern ("VAY-bern," 1883–1945) followed suit.

A box of serial music and assorted goodies

If you'd like to hear some examples of the Second Viennese School's experimentation, we can point you in the right direction. Listen to the following pieces:

- **Schoenberg:** *Pierrot Lunaire,* opus 21 — for a singer with small instrumental ensemble. In this piece, Schoenberg uses a technique called *Sprechstimme* ("speak-voice"), in which the singer doesn't dwell on notes as in traditional music, but just touches upon them, sliding up and down between them — and he wrote it years before Bob Dylan existed!

- **Berg:** *Violin Concerto* — a 12-tone piece that also manages to quote from Bach and Austrian folk music. Even though it's wildly atonal, it has an intensely personal, passionate, Romantic feeling about it.

- **Webern:** Six pieces for orchestra, opus 6 — a series of very short pieces totaling only 12 minutes, exploring fleeting moments of shifting moods and very short — really short.

The Americans

While the Second Viennese School in Europe was creating a complex, involved, dark kind of music, a new kind of uniquely American music was evolving: music that expressed the strong, hopeful, optimistic emotions of the American spirit. These sections point out a few notable American composers.

Aaron Copland

Aaron Copland (1900–1990) is America's most beloved classical music composer. (See Figure 2-24.) A native of Brooklyn, New York, and the son of Russian immigrants, Copland captured the spirit of the American heartland. Listen to one of his pieces, and you're practically wiping flecks of wheat-field chaff from your eye.

The earliest music of Copland ("KOPE-land") echoed some of the musical currents in Europe at the turn of the century. But as he progressed, he tried to create a style that would resonate with American audiences. He added jazz rhythms and harmonies to some of his serious pieces, and he wrote music about legendary American subjects, such as Billy the Kid.

Copland's most popular composition by far is *Appalachian Spring* ("appa-LÄTSCH-en S-PRINNG"), a ballet that tells the story of a newlywed farmer couple moving into a new farmhouse in the Appalachian Mountains. In this piece, you can *feel* the dew falling on the countryside, *sense* the joy of the wife and husband as they begin their new life together, and *touch* the Appalachian road dust that tends to dirty up the otherwise nicely painted windowsills of the couple's new house.

Figure 2-24: Aaron Copland (left) and George Gershwin, two of America's most beloved composers.

Appalachian Spring was a hit from its first performance in 1944. The following year, it won the Pulitzer Prize, and it remains to this day the best-known piece of American classical music.

George Gershwin

The second-best-known piece belongs to George Gershwin (1898–1937), who was also born in Brooklyn. Gershwin died of a brain tumor at age 39, but in his short lifetime he managed to single-handedly bridge the musical gap between Tin Pan Alley and Carnegie Hall. (Check out Figure 2-24.)

The piece that did the trick was *Rhapsody in Blue,* a short concerto originally for piano with jazz band. (In a later version, an orchestra replaces the jazz band.) The piece was featured at a now-legendary concert of the Paul Whiteman Orchestra called "An Experiment in Modern Music."

Gershwin wrote *Rhapsody in Blue* at the last minute, just a few weeks before the concert, having been inspired by the sounds and sights of a train ride from New York to Boston. The piece spectacularly combined a classical piano concerto with American jazz and blues, but Gershwin was much more at home with jazz than classical. The player-piano rolls he recorded testify to his skill as a jazz pianist, and he made a living writing the music for Broadway shows, with his brother Ira as lyricist.

Through it all, George felt insecure that he had little formal training in music theory or composition. (*Classical Music For Dummies* was still 50 years away.) As a result, he constantly asked successful classical composers for their help and advice. He even befriended (and played tennis with) Arnold Schoenberg, grandpa of nontonal, nonmelodic music. Fortunately, the older composer refused to give Gershwin composition lessons. "I would only make you a bad Schoenberg," he said, "and you are such a good Gershwin already!"

Good thinking, Arnie. *Rhapsody in Retrograde* probably wouldn't have done so well.

Samuel Barber

Samuel Barber (1910–1981) wrote the third-best-known piece of American classical music: Adagio for Strings, which rips your emotions to shreds in war movies like *Platoon*.

Barber completed the Adagio when he was just 23 years old, following formal training at the Curtis Institute in Philadelphia. The piece gradually caught on across America; after World War II broke out, it became famous worldwide, an unofficial anthem in remembrance of the young soldiers who died in battle.

In a time when much of the classical music world was experimenting with everything from atonality to jazz, Barber remained unabashedly Romantic; his pieces remained lush and melodic. His music explores a deeper, more personal vein than the music by any other American.

And more . . .

Many more gifted American composers have blessed concert halls with music in the 20th and 21st centuries. Unlike the European composers you've read about, the Americans don't generally dash off to Vienna at 18 for training or hurl themselves suicidally into rivers or drop out of law school (well, okay, a few did that). But some have succeeded nonetheless. Check out the following:

- ✔ **Charles Ives** (1874–1954), an insurance salesman by trade who invented the concept of estate planning, had a secret life as a composer. Most of his works ended up in his attic, but once rediscovered, they were hailed as highly original masterpieces from a unique American voice. We especially enjoy his short piece *The Unanswered Question* and his Symphony no. 2.

- ✔ **Leonard Bernstein** (1918–1990), a legendary conductor of the New York Philharmonic, wrote many serious compositions that explore the juxtaposition of jazz and classical music. He also composed one of the best Broadway musicals ever: *West Side Story*.

- **John Cage** (1912–1992) revolutionized and bewildered the music world by introducing the concept of *chance* — four radios playing at once, for example, all tuned to different stations. He also wrote the piano piece called *4'33"*, in which the pianist opens the lid of the keyboard, sits there for four minutes and 33 seconds without playing a note, and closes the lid again. (We ourselves can play this one *really* well.) Cage introduced an element of fun into an art that had become ultra-serious, but, just between us, his pieces are actually more fun to hear *about* than to hear.

- **John Adams** (born in 1947), together with composers such as **Steve Reich** (born in 1936) and **Philip Glass** (born in 1937), developed a musical style called *minimalism.* In this kind of composition, very repetitive snippets of music, with subtly shifting rhythms and harmonies, are supposed to lull you into a sort of altered state. It's soothing and mostly tonal, and it's beautiful to listen to. Rent the movie *Koyaanisqaatsi* (entirely accompanied by Philip Glass's music) to see what we mean. All three of these composers have subsequently gone beyond minimalism, exploring interesting new paths in their music.

- **John Corigliano** (born in 1938) came to international prominence with his Symphony no. 1, dedicated to those who had died from AIDS. He also composed a sparkling and original opera, *The Ghosts of Versailles,* for the Metropolitan Opera in New York. Corigliano is considered to be one of the most important composers of his generation.

And many more composers continue to strike out in fascinating new directions, many of them quite tonal and melodic. If your appetite for modern music needs more whetting, check out the music of Christopher Rouse, Michael Daugherty, Michael Torke, Kevin Puts, Mason Bates, Jennifer Higdon, and Christopher Theofanidis. And those are just a handful of the American composers active today! Classical music composition is alive and well and thriving.

American music for the record . . .

In your exploration of 20th-century American music, don't miss these pieces:

- **Copland:** *Appalachian Spring* and *Fanfare for the Common Man* (heard on many a sports broadcast, this piece is a compact, distilled version of Copland's musical style, played by brass and percussion)

- **Gershwin:** *Rhapsody in Blue* and Concerto in F for Piano Solo and Orchestra

- **Barber:** Adagio for Strings, Symphony no. 1 in one movement, opus 9; and *Medea's Meditation and Dance of Vengeance*

- **Ives:** *The Unanswered Question*

- **Bernstein:** Symphonic dances from *West Side Story*

- **Cage:** Sonatas and Interludes for Prepared Piano (a *prepared piano* has all kinds of things [paper, nails, you name it] put inside to change the sound)

- **Adams:** *Short Ride in a Fast Machine* (a fun, jaunty, super-rhythmic, wild ride of a fanfare, lasting just a bit more than four minutes; the perfect introduction to this composer) and *Harmonielehre* (a three-movement piece; in our opinion, the best piece of minimalist music to date)

- **Corigliano:** Symphony no. 1 (since its premiere in 1990, this raging, brutal, emotional piece has received hundreds of performances around the world)

People who hate composers (and the composers who love them)

The great English conductor Sir Thomas Beecham was once asked whether he had heard any Stockhausen (a composer of modern electronic music). "No," he replied, "but I believe I have trodden in some."

From the beginning of time, the public has been slow to embrace new ideas in music. Back in the days when all you ever heard on the radio was Gregorian chant, the first sounds of Renaissance music — filled with multiple, simultaneous melodies — must have seemed unbelievably strange.

At the time they first appeared on the scene, even Beethoven and Brahms were considered ugly and dissonant (not to mention their music).

So were Berlioz, Debussy, Mahler, Nielsen, Schoenberg — well, with Schoenberg you've got a point. But you get the idea. Show us a beloved composer who opened exciting new doors in classical music, and we can show you a composer who was reviled in his own time.

Composers write their music in the hope that it will someday be understood — even loved. If our great-great-grandparents hadn't given Brahms a chance, his masterpieces wouldn't be bestsellers today.

So keep an open mind. Don't forget that your best friend was once a complete stranger. Music can work that way, too.

Chapter 3

Knowing How to Spot a Sonata

Although today's concert music often has creative titles, composers weren't so creative with their titles in the heyday of classical music. In the 18th century, for example, you were much more likely to encounter a piece titled "Symphony No. 1" than, say, "Dr. Doom Gets a Root Canal." Most classical works were simply named according to the category of music they represented.

These categories can be confusing (and sometimes even intimidating) to the uninitiated. In your listening and concert-going career, you'll meet these musical formats again and again; this chapter, therefore, introduces you to them one by one.

Symphonies

The word *symphony* has two meanings, and for the sake of your cocktail-party reputation, we'd better help you get them straight. *Symphony* usually refers to a musical work written in a certain form. But the term can also refer to a *symphony orchestra,* meaning a group of musicians who perform that kind of music.

If you hear your friend say, "I went to the symphony last night," that means that she went to hear an orchestra — specifically, an orchestra that habitually plays symphonies. (In fact, the orchestra may not have played a *symphony* at all that night; maybe it played a bunch of overtures or dances

A brief history of the symphony

The symphony as a musical form has existed for more than 200 years. It's a piece of music for a large body of instruments, and it usually consists of four different sections (or *movements*) of music. Composers used to demonstrate their mastery of the elements of music by writing symphonies: Having written one became a status symbol. So, over the years, the symphony became one of the most common musical forms. Nearly every composer we talk about in this book wrote symphonies. Johannes Brahms wrote 4; Ludwig van Beethoven wrote 9; Wolfgang Amadeus Mozart wrote 41. Joseph Haydn wrote 104 (but he didn't get out much).

instead.) But if your friend goes on to say, "And they played a wonderful symphony," she's referring to the piece of music itself.

The parts (or movements) of a symphony are usually free standing, with one movement ending, a pause, and then the next movement beginning. But the sections, conceived as parts of a whole, somehow relate to one another. The German word for movement is *Satz,* which means "sentence." The four movements of a symphony fit together like the four sentences in this paragraph.

With rare exceptions, the four movements of a symphony conform to a standardized pattern. The first movement is brisk and lively; the second is slower and more lyrical; the third is an energetic *minuet* (dance) or a boisterous *scherzo* ("joke"); and the fourth is a rollicking finale.

Actually, composers and music jocks make a big deal over the structure *inside* each of the four movements, which we discuss in the following sections.

First movement: brisk and lively

The first movement of a symphony usually has a structure called *sonata form.* Sonata form is simple, and understanding it will enhance your appreciation of almost all classical music. What follows is simplified further still, but it applies to the first movement of most classical symphonies.

A movement in sonata form has two musical themes (or *melodies*). The first is usually loud and forceful; the second is quiet and lyrical. These themes are often referred to as the *masculine* and the *feminine* melodies. (Yes, this stuff was invented *way* before political correctness.) You may also think of them as iron and silk, or *yang* and *yin,* or jalapeño and Jell-O. Whatever. In any case, the entire movement is based on these two themes.

- At the very beginning of the movement, you hear the strong first theme; then, after a brief bit of interesting activity in the harmony department, the softer second theme comes in. This whole section's purpose in life is to introduce, or *expose*, the two melodies; therefore, musicians call this part of the first movement the *exposition*.

- Then comes a new section. Here the composer develops the two themes, varying them and making interesting musical associations. Logically enough, this section is called the *development* section.

- Finally, the main ideas are reintroduced in the same order as at the beginning: first the strong, powerful theme and then the quieter, more lyrical one. The composer restates these themes in a slightly different form, but they're very recognizable for what they are. This section is called the *recapitulation*.

At the risk of repeating ourselves, here's the structure, simplified still further:

EXPOSITION — DEVELOPMENT — RECAPITULATION

All movements in sonata form have this sequence of events. Nearly all the symphonies, string quartets, and sonatas of Haydn, Mozart, Beethoven, and countless other composers begin with a first movement in sonata form. (See Chapter 2 for more on all these old guys.) In fact, you can hear a perfect example of it at www.dummies.com/go/classicalmusic, on Track 4: the first movement of Beethoven's Symphony no. 5.

Second movement: slow and lyrical

Back to our symphony in progress: After the lively and energetic first movement, it's time to relax. The second movement is usually slow and lyrical, with a lilting, songlike theme (giving the composer a chance to show off his melodic ability). No battle-of-the-sexes melody thing goes on here, and the structure can be looser than in the first movement. Sit back and drink it in.

Third movement: dancy

The third movement of a symphony is dancelike — either a *minuet* (based on the old courtly dance) or a *scherzo* (meaning "joke" — a quick, often lighthearted tune). The third movement is usually written in three-quarter (¾) time; that is, each bar has three beats. (If you count "ONE-two-three, ONE-two-three," you're counting three beats to the bar.) Joseph Haydn (1732–1809), the papa of symphonic form, first made the minuet standard equipment in a symphony. Listen, for example, to the third movement of just about any Haydn symphony, from no. 31 to no. 104.

This third movement usually consists of three sections. First you hear the minuet or scherzo itself. Then comes a contrasting section (often for a smaller group of instruments) called a *trio*. Finally, the minuet or scherzo section comes back again.

So the entire third movement sounds like this:

MINUET — TRIO — MINUET

or

SCHERZO — TRIO — SCHERZO

The next time you listen to a symphony, try to distinguish these sections of the third movement. We bet that you can.

Finale: rollicking

Now on to the rollicking finale. The final movement is usually fast and furious, showing off the virtuosic prowess of the orchestra. This finale is usually quite light in character — that is, it doesn't have a great deal of emotional depth. The finale's much more concerned with having a good time. But wait — there's more! Very often, this final movement is in *rondo form*. Yes, this last movement has a substructure of its own.

In a rondo, you hear one delightful theme over and over again, alternating with something contrasting. Here's an example of a rondo, in written form:

I will not raise taxes.

I have character.

I will not raise taxes.

I will be tough on crime.

I will not raise taxes.

I will make things the way they used to be, which is a heck of a lot better than they are now.

I will not raise taxes.

If you call "I will not raise taxes" theme A, and the other three themes B, C, and D, then you can describe this rondo form as follows:

A-B-A-C-A-D-A

You can find another great example of rondo form at www.dummies.com/go/ classicalmusic. It's Track 3: the finale of Mozart's Piano Concerto no. 22.

Sonatas and Sonatinas

A *sonata* is a symphony composed for a much smaller instrumental force — for one or two instruments. Composers have written hundreds of sonatas for piano alone and countless others for piano plus one other instrument (violin, flute, clarinet, trumpet, horn — you name it).

The word *sonata* simply means "sounded." Such a piece gives an instrument the chance to show off its sound. But it's usually in a strict form, especially in the first movement. The sequence of events in that opening section has become so standardized that it's often called *sonata form.* Hey, you already know that one! As we said, symphonies' first movements are generally also written in sonata form.

Now, what's a *sonatina?* In your musical travels, you're very likely to encounter this term. A *sonatina* is nothing more than a sonata of smaller proportions. (It's good to know that *-ino* or *-ina* at the end of a word means "little." Just as *concertino* means "little concert," just as *Katerina* means "little Katherine," just as *wrestlerina* means "little wrestler," so *sonatina* means "little sonata.") A sonatina is little in many ways. It may have fewer movements than a sonata — only two, perhaps. And each movement is short. The first movement usually has no development section, and we get to the recapitulation quickly.

Sonatinas are generally easier to play than sonatas. Often, they're composed for beginning or intermediate players, like a bicycle with training wheels. If MTV played classical music, this is the kind it would play — sonata lite.

Concertos

Concerto ("con-CHAIR-toe") started life meaning "concert" in Italian. In today's musical lingo, though, a concerto is a piece of music in which one player (the *soloist*), who often comes from New York and is paid astronomical fees, sits or stands at the front of the stage playing the melody while the rest of the orchestra accompanies her. The concerto soloist is the hero or heroine, the lead of the play, the prima donna. She doesn't even have to look at the conductor — the conductor follows *her.*

In most great concertos, the orchestra doesn't just accompany the soloist by playing quiet oompahs under the soloist's melody. In the greatest concertos, the orchestra has an equal part, conversing back and forth with the protagonist, "Dueling Banjos" style. The third track available online at www. dummies.com/go/classicalmusic is a movement from one of the greats: Mozart's Piano Concerto no. 22.

Sometimes (as in the great concertos of the Danish composer Carl Nielsen [1865–1931]), one other member of the orchestra even acts as *antagonist,* seemingly arguing back and forth with what the soloist has to say. (This argument is done musically, of course — although we feel that concert attendance would go up if the antagonist could *really* argue with the soloist. "What?!? You call that a melody? Get off the stage, you amateur!")

Concertos are a lot of fun for the audience. If you haven't heard one, you're in for a treat. Many audience members go to a concert *mainly* for the concerto. They come to hear a great, famous soloist; to witness her flashy pyrotechnics; to be swept away by her outpouring of musical passion; and to check out her outfit.

For this, soloists are paid dearly — sometimes $50,000 to $100,000 for *one* performance. Orchestras pay because they know that they're going to make the money back. Sometimes concertgoers buy a season ticket just to have the chance to hear a single famous soloist.

If you're going to an orchestra concert that includes a concerto, buy a seat a little to the left of center. The soloist almost always stands or sits just to the left of the conductor. If it's a piano soloist, sit even farther to the left (the extreme left is okay, as well). The piano is always situated with the keyboard on the left side, and you'll have more fun if you can see the pianist's hands. (You'll have *no* fun sitting front-row center, however, because the piano *completely* blocks your view.)

Concerto structure

The average concerto lasts about 30 minutes. Concertos almost always have three movements — that is, three contrasting sections separated by pauses. For most classical composers of old, a concerto was expected to have three movements, just as most Hollywood movies are two hours long, just as most Broadway shows have exactly two acts, just as a limerick has exactly five lines, just as most rock songs are three minutes long, just as Lady Gaga's hair color changes every six weeks.

In most cases, the three movements of a concerto fall into this scheme: FAST-SLOW-FAST. This setup, which has been around for centuries in all kinds of music (and, we should also mention, movie plots), works especially well in a concerto, enabling the soloist to show off her amazing technique in the first and last movements and to bring the listener into a more intimate, soulful world in the middle.

Soloists almost always play from memory, unlike the musicians in the orchestra, who read from sheet music, or the conductor, who's probably using a big, bound score. This habit is a holdover from the days of the great virtuoso superstars, such as Franz Liszt (1811–1886), who were the "rock stars" of their generation. The audience expects to see a star, and stars don't mess with sheet music.

Meanwhile, the orchestra is chugging along like a train on its track, unable to deviate from the written music. In other words, the soloist *cannot* slip up. But sometimes she does — with hair-raising results. The conductor and orchestra must react with split-second timing. If the soloist skips three pages of music — which is entirely possible, because the music at the beginning of a piece often repeats at the end — the conductor must figure out where she skipped to and *somehow* signal to the orchestra when to come back in.

If conductor and orchestra can react quickly, the audience may never even notice the mistake. But sometimes orchestra and soloist are out of sync for a minute or more. And in some cases, the conductor must resort to desperate measures to let the orchestra know where the soloist has gone. If you're ever listening to a concerto and the conductor yells, "Skip to Letter F!" you know what happened.

The cadenza

Near the end of every movement of a concerto is usually a moment where everything seems to stop — except the soloist. The soloist takes off on a flight of fancy, all by herself, lasting anywhere from ten seconds to five minutes. *This* is not a mistake. It's called the *cadenza:* a moment devised by the composer for the soloist to show off.

Cadenza is Italian for "cadence" (not to be confused with *credenza,* Italian for "piece of dining room furniture"). A *cadence* is a simple falling progression of harmonies, one chord to another, ending with a natural resting-place chord.

But toward the end of a concerto movement, this falling progression is *interrupted.* Before the final chord or chords of the progression can be heard, suddenly everything stops and the soloist does her thing. (Check it out online at www.dummies.com/go/classicalmusic, Track 3, at 8:50. You'll hear a beautiful little cadenza at this point in Mozart's Piano Concerto no. 22.) If the soloist does it well, she can actually create suspense and anticipation, just like a sneezer who goes, "Ah . . . *ah* . . . AH . . ." and makes you wait for the "*choo!*"

Then, just as the soloist finishes, the orchestra comes in with the final chords. It's great.

In the old days, soloists made up their own cadenzas on the spot. The great composers, who were often wonderful soloists themselves, took special pride in doing this kind of improvisation. But other composers, including Beethoven, wrote down specific notes to be played in their cadenzas. These days, soloists usually play a cadenza that somebody else has composed. In any case, the cadenza is meant to *sound* improvised. If you get the impression that the soloist is making up the whole thing as she goes along, she's playing it well.

Just about every cadenza ends with a *trill*. A trill is the quick alternation of two notes that are next to each other. Try it — it's easy and fun!

1. **Sing any note.**

2. **Now sing the note right above it.**

3. **Repeat steps 1 and 2, faster and faster.**

   This is a trill.

A trill is actually quite a bit easier to play on an instrument. In the old days, a trill was the signal from the improvising soloist that she was just about done with her cadenza. It was the sign to the orchestra and conductor to wake up, put their magazines down, and get ready to come in with the final chords. At the end of the trill, the soloist and conductor watch each other, breathe together, and play those final chords together.

Dances and Suites

As we explain in Chapter 2, the earliest music was composed primarily for singing (for example, in church) or dancing. Very little "easy listening" took place in ancient times.

If you go to a concert and hear a minuet, you're hearing a form that was originally meant strictly for dancing. In the old days, the only people who simply *listened* to minuets were people without dates.

But as concert music began to develop, composers drew upon what they knew. And so it was that certain rhythms, changes in harmonies, and musical structures — originally created strictly for dances — found their way into music that people just listen to. Ironically, these days, virtually nobody in the concert hall gets up and starts dancing when a minuet begins.

Much of the classical music you hear today falls into this category — it's composed in a form that was originally designed for dancing.

If you're listening to a dance form, several things are likely to be true:

- **The rhythm is steady.** After all, who can dance to an unsteady rhythm? Even in 500 B.D. (Before Disco), people needed a good beat.

- **The music is likely to be repetitive.** That is, it's not developed too much. The musical ideas that you hear come back again and again. Here, too, nothing has changed; think "That's the Way (I Like It)" or "Let's Get Physical" or "Hey Jude."

- **The title sounds like the name of a dance.** It might be "Waltz," for example, or "Mambo."

A *suite* is a bunch of musical movements grouped together. *Suite* comes from a word meaning "follow," and it refers to a sequence of things that follow, one from the next (as in a suite of rooms).

In early times (the Baroque period, for example — late 1600s to mid-1700s), a musical suite consisted almost entirely of dances, and the movements were named according to the type of dance they represented — for example, *allemande, gavotte, bourrée, minuet, rigaudon, sarabande, gigue,* and *courante.* Much as they may sound like a roster of the French Parliament, these were, in fact, courtly dances of the European royalty.

The first track available at www.dummies.com/go/classicalmusic — Handel's ever-popular *Water Music* — is from a Baroque suite like this. If you listen to this track, you'll see what we mean about steady rhythms and a dancelike feel.

In the last century, the word *suite* came to signify any grouping of movements that belonged together: "Suite from *Carmen,*" for example, consists of various melodies and interludes from the opera *Carmen,* by the French composer Georges Bizet (1838–1875). You can also find suites from *The Nutcracker, West Side Story, Star Wars,* and *Shaft.* Probably.

Serenades and Divertimentos

If anything is less gratifying to a serious classical composer than having his Great Work of Western Music listened to only for dancing, it's having his Great Work of Western Music not listened to *at all.* But that's precisely what composers who wrote *serenades* and *divertimentos* had to endure. These kinds of music were the original Muzak.

Suppose King Friedrich needed some background music for a little soirée with his closest friends. He couldn't very well pop a CD into the old stereo. So he had a band of musicians on call to play for him. These guys worked for him full-time, playing background music all day long. Occasionally, they'd perform a formal concert, but their presence was primarily to enhance the ambiance of the occasion. And so it was that composers were hired to write serenades and divertimentos for these background-music bands.

As you may expect, a typical serenade or divertimento had several movements (usually five or more). After all, if you're having dinner, you don't want too much complex musical development. You don't want deep, passionate, gut-wrenching utterances. Not before dessert, anyway.

Serenades were written for winds, for brass and percussion, for strings, and for various combinations of these instruments. Composers chose their forces to fit the occasion. A string quartet was generally more appropriate for the dining room than, say, a bunch of trumpets and drums. On the other hand, a group of woodwind or brass instruments was more appropriate outside on a warm evening.

Most serenades and divertimentos are between 20 and 30 minutes long. Some serenades (for example, Mozart's beautiful *Haffner Serenade*) are nearly an hour long, suitable for a quiet outdoor evening. Others, such as the *Posthorn Serenade,* are barely 15 minutes long, suitable for the occasional royal Quarter Pounder with cheese.

If you go to www.dummies.com/go/classicalmusic, one particular spot on Track 3 (at 4:16) can give you an idea of what Mozart's serenades were like. Right in the middle of this final movement from his Piano Concerto no. 22, Mozart has added an oasis of tranquility, imitating the sound of a serenade for winds.

As you listen to a divertimento or serenade in concert, keep in mind the atmosphere in which it was first performed. Try to imagine the scene, sitting along the banks of a river, centuries before the invention of cellphones or Facebook, engaging in genteel conversation, perhaps nibbling on an hors d'oeuvre, a canapé, or someone else's ear, with this heavenly music permeating the air.

Themes and Variations

A *musical theme* is nothing more than a melody that appears at the beginning of the piece. After the composer finishes stating his musical theme, he goes on to state it again — and again and again — each time changing one little thing about it. One variation might change the theme's harmony; another might change the rhythm; still another might vary the melody by adding a lot of notes for embellishment. But when you hear each variation, you can usually hear the original theme in there somewhere.

For example, here is an example of a theme with variations. After you understand how it works you can comprehend one of the more common forms in music.

> *Bluefish.*
>
> *Bluefish with mustard sauce.*
>
> *Bluefish with black-eyed peas.*
>
> *Bluefish with raspberry vinaigrette in an herb-encrusted marshmallow glaze.*

A really nice set of variations can be found in the second movement of Joseph Haydn's Symphony no. 94 (*Surprise*). It begins with a simple (almost simplistic) theme; the rest of the movement consists of one variation after another. And Joseph Haydn himself was credited with creating another melody that a later composer used for his own set of variations: Johannes Brahms's *Variations on a Theme by Haydn* is one of the most masterful examples of the genre.

Fantasias and Rhapsodies

In olden days, composers were expected to fit their works into a predetermined structure — sonata form, for example, or rondo form. These forms were fixed, rigid, and considered almost sacred. If composers felt the urge to let their imaginations run wild, their only recourse was to write in yet another form: the most formless of all forms, the *fantasia*.

Because the composition was named a *fantasy* (which originally meant *imagination*), the composer was liberated from the normal constraints of musical form. The composer couldn't be accused of violating some sacred musical structure, because fantasias didn't have one.

In a typical fantasy, the composer sets out a musical theme at or near the beginning. The rest of the piece is a musing on that theme; the composer goes wherever he feels like with it. Ralph Vaughan Williams (1872–1958) used the tune "Greensleeves" as the beginning and ending of his short, rapturous *Fantasia on Greensleeves.*

Fantasies usually contain lots of little notes, seemingly in a free rhythm. After a theme is established, a solo instrument usually goes off on a flight of fancy, scurrying up and down the scale at a breathless pace. One of the greatest composers, Johann Sebastian Bach (1685–1750) — who was also the greatest organist of his day — wrote several fantasies for organ in which he sent the organist's fingers flying all across the keyboard.

Actually, most fantasias aren't *completely* formless; they're just less strict than other forms. Because most great composers spent many years studying and working out extremely rigid compositional exercises, only the rare composer could divorce himself from all this structural discipline. Beethoven's *Choral Fantasy,* for example, is free but nevertheless logically structured. And the first movement of his famous *Moonlight Sonata* for piano bears the subtitle "*Quasi una fantasia*" — "*almost* a fantasy."

A *rhapsody* is along the same lines as a fantasy, with a similarly free structure. Most rhapsodies date from the late Romantic era (the mid-1800s into the 20th century). The famous pianist Franz Liszt wrote several Hungarian rhapsodies for the piano. (These days, you may hear them arranged for full orchestra.) In these pieces, he takes simple, Hungarian-sounding themes and turns them into a tornado of virtuosic vigor. And if you're a classic rock fan, Queen's "Bohemian Rhapsody," featured so prominently in the movie *Wayne's World,* is, yes, a genuine rhapsody — a freeform rush of different musical ideas, one after another.

Tone Poems (Or Symphonic Poems)

Like a fantasy or a rhapsody, a *tone poem* doesn't have a fixed, standard structure. But it has a more pressing purpose: It's supposed to *tell a story* by using the orchestra's sounds.

Most musicians agree that the greatest of all tone-poem composers was Richard Strauss (1864–1949). Aside from operas, Strauss mainly wrote tone poems. The greatest of those are *Don Juan, Don Quixote, Till Eulenspiegels lustige Streiche* (*Till Eulenspiegel's Merry Pranks*), *Ein Heldenleben* (*A Hero's Life*), *Also Sprach Zarathustra* (*Thus Spoke Zarathustra*), and *Tod und Verklärung* (*Death and Transfiguration*). You can read much more about Strauss and his tone poems in Chapter 2.

Many other fine composers tackled tone poems, as well. If this genre fascinates you, check out Bedřich Smetana's set of six poems called *Má Vlast* (*My Fatherland*); Jean Sibelius's *Legends* (including *The Swan of Tuonela*); Liszt's poems *Les Préludes, Mazeppa,* and *Prometheus;* Peter Tchaikovsky's *Romeo and Juliet, Hamlet,* and *Francesca da Rimini;* and Peter Maxwell Davies' *Orkney Wedding with Sunrise*.

One of the most masterful examples of a tone poem is Claude Debussy's *La Mer* (*The Sea*), which describes in musical sounds a day in the life of a busy ocean. You can hear a movement from this thrilling work on Track 8 at www. dummies.com/go/classicalmusic.

Because they tell a story, tone poems are fun to listen to. If you have the program in hand (or even if you don't), you can imagine scenes to go along with the music. In a way, tone poems are movie music minus the movie. John Williams' famous score to *Star Wars* is really a tone poem, and it owes much to Strauss.

Lieder (And Follower)

In German, the word *Lied* (pronounced "leed") means song; *Lieder* means songs or art songs. In the 1800s especially, *Lieder* came to great prominence, particularly in private salon concerts.

(**Terminology alert:** In classical-music discussions, *salon* doesn't refer to hairstyling emporiums. It actually means "living rooms of the rich and famous, hundreds of years ago.")

Art songs are usually based on famous poetry, such as the work of Johann Wolfgang von Goethe. Many great German poets lived in that period, so you shouldn't be surprised to find many great German composers of *Lieder*.

In these sections you can read about some of classical music's most famous songwriters — and the structure of some of their beautiful creations.

Leader of the Lieder

Chief among these *Lieder* composers is Franz Schubert (1797–1828). Even though he's the composer of the *Unfinished Symphony,* Schubert had no trouble finishing more than 600 songs. From the age of 18, he was composing songs of great depth and passion, such as *Erlkönig* (*Forest King*), a heart-wrenching account of a little boy in the arms of his father, galloping on horseback through the woods, who imagines (correctly, as things turn out) that he's being violently abducted by the Forest King.

Schubert grouped many of his songs into *song cycles* (thematically grouped clumps), including *Winterreise* (*The Winter Journey*) and *Schwanengesang* (*Swan Song*). Song cycles are usually based on poetry cycles — that is, the composer takes a group of poems that belong together and creates a song cycle from them.

What made Schubert such a great song composer was that he had a seemingly unending flow of *melody*. People never complained that they couldn't hum *his* tunes.

Robert Schumann (1810–1856), Hugo Wolf (1860–1903), and Gustav Mahler (1860–1911) were three other great German Romantic composers of art songs. They were no doubt influenced by Schubert's mastery of the genre. They were the followers, and Schubert was their *Lieder*.

Song forms

Songs fall into many different kinds of forms. But to make a long story short, they're usually either in *verse form* or *through-composed*.

- *Verses* in art songs are just like verses in popular music today. Each verse of the poem is set to the same music. You can find hundreds of examples of this format in today's tunes. Almost every rock song on the radio today is made up of several verses.

- *Through-composed,* on the other hand, means that the music is constantly changing to follow the action of the words, from beginning to end, and doesn't necessarily repeat any particular section. Schubert's *Erlkönig* is an example of a through-composed song. So are Queen's "Bohemian Rhapsody" and the song "My Boy Bill" from the musical *Carousel*.

If you're interested in hearing art songs in live performance, check out the local university or conservatory. Most voice students give several recitals of art songs as a requirement for graduation, and they're often both absolutely wonderful and woefully under-attended.

Added incentive: These recitals are always followed by receptions where the food is not only good but extremely plentiful, thanks to the eternally springing hope of the recitalist that more people may show up.

Oratorios and Other Choral Works

Most of the music we discus in this book is instrumental music — that is, it doesn't include *singers*. But we wouldn't be doing our job if we didn't mention *oratorios*. These are religious pieces, some of the most glorious music ever composed.

In medieval times, music had a primarily religious function. It was sung by monks with little else to do, and it was about religious subjects. In the Baroque era, all the famous composers wrote music with religious themes — including oratorios.

An oratorio is a massive work of music, often hours long, for chorus, orchestra, and vocal soloists; it usually tells a Bible story. George Frideric Handel (1685–1759) is best known for his oratorio *Messiah*, popular in every American city every Christmas, but in musical circles, his oratorios based on Old Testament themes are also well-known: *Saul, Samson, Israel in Egypt, Solomon,* and many more.

Bach wrote several amazing oratorios on New Testament themes: the *Christmas Oratorio* and the Passions according to St. Matthew, St. John, and St. Luke. He was also a fan of the musical form called a *cantata,* which, though it may sound like the new sedan from Chrysler, is actually a short oratorio. Over the years, Bach wrote more than 200 cantatas, each one meant for a different Sunday in the church calendar.

He even wrote a parody of a cantata — number 211, the *Coffee Cantata,* which is one big joke: Instead of being about Jesus, the words are about coffee. Every movement extols the wonderful, life-giving qualities of Bach's favorite beverage.

Going to hear an oratorio is a monumental experience that you're not likely to forget. We must add a word of caution here, however: In most oratorios, the sections are long; therefore, the intermissions (if any) are far apart. Don't drink a gallon of grape juice before going to hear an oratorio.

Operas, Operettas, and Arias

While we're on the subject of singing, we must mention opera. *Opera* is drama with music. It combines the best of theater, art, vocal music, and instrumental music in a highly dramatic, emotionally charged, intensely compelling mixture.

A real opera generally has no spoken words at all; everything gets sung. This fact has led to some hilarious parodies in movies and TV commercials.

An *operetta* is very similar to an opera (although usually on a lighter theme), but with one very important distinction: An operetta has spoken dialogue in addition to singing. Almost every Broadway show ever written is really, come to think of it, an operetta.

In an opera or operetta, the action occasionally stops so that a character can launch into an emotion-expressing song. This kind of song is called an *aria* (Italian for "air"). The most popular parts of any opera are the arias. Whenever the Three Tenors gave a concert, they sang one aria after another.

When an orchestra hires a famous singer as a soloist, she, too, sings arias; so do singers at university voice recitals.

Opera is a category so momentous, so huge, so all-encompassing, that it really deserves a book all by itself. In fact, we've written one. It's called *Opera For Dummies* by David Pogue and Scott Speck (John Wiley & Sons, Inc.).

Overtures and Preludes

We're sure that you already know what an *overture* is: the little piece of music originally composed for the orchestra at Broadway shows or operas to play before the curtain goes up. But the word *overture* may also refer to a short piece composed to evoke certain feelings. Brahms's *Tragic Overture*, for example, wasn't composed for any opera or play. It was written simply to evoke a tragic mood.

If you've been to performances of musical theater, or even seen the movie version of a musical, you know that the overture is usually just a couple of minutes long. Consequently, the powers that be in the symphony orchestra world figure that such a piece makes a wonderful opener to a concert: uncomplicated in structure, often lightweight in emotion, and short enough to make a nice transition between the hustle and bustle (and short attention span) of everyday life into the more focused, concentrated, deeply felt world of the concert hall.

Ballets and Ballerinas

A *ballet* is a story that's told in music and dance, with no speaking and no singing.

In the old days of ballet, the dance was the only important thing. The composer's job was to write music that let the dancers show off. Musical considerations such as drama, pacing, and even beauty of sound were secondary to the spectacle of the dance: young men and women with great legs. Accordingly, early composers didn't put much effort into their compositions for ballet — after all, it was just background music.

But then Peter Tchaikovsky came along. Tchaikovsky (1840–1893) wrote such stunning music for such ballets as *Swan Lake, Sleeping Beauty,* and *The Nutcracker* that people could no longer take the "background" music for granted. Starting with his ballets, some people started listening to ballets for the music alone.

Tchaikovsky's ballets are the most popular and beloved in the history of ballet. Soon, other composers began to take a cue from him. Two other Russian composers in particular, Sergei Prokofiev (1891–1953) and Igor Stravinsky (1882–1971), got into ballet composing in an equally big way.

Gradually, their ballet music became popular even without the dancing. Prokofiev's ballets *Romeo and Juliet* and *Cinderella* are regulars on the ballet stage, but their musical scores are also popular with concert audiences. And although not all the ballets of Stravinsky are regularly performed by dancers today, you can still hear the music everywhere. Orchestras all around the world are constantly performing *The Firebird, Petrushka,* and *The Rite of Spring* (which is excerpted at www.dummies.com/go/classicalmusic).

Just as in an opera, where the action comes to a pause and a character sings an aria to express her feelings, ballet has moments where the ballerina *dances* to express her feelings — either alone or with her male consort (or cavalier) in a dance form known as the *pas de deux.* At these moments, the plot stops. But these moments are some of the most exciting in ballet because they're the most expressive. Just as the arias are the highlights of an opera, these dances form the highlights of a ballet.

Between these "arias" for ballet dancers, the music of the ballet is often written to mimic the action onstage. Most ballet music is, therefore, by its very nature *programmatic* — which means "storytelling." This music tells a story in a detailed, direct way — even more so than a tone poem does. In a tone poem, the music conveys a particular mood, or perhaps a particular scene. But in a masterful ballet, nearly every note of the music corresponds directly to a particular motivation and action onstage.

In orchestra concerts, ballet music comes in two different forms. First are complete ballet scores, which are usually uncut and consist of exactly the music that was written for the dance. These scores can be difficult to follow unless you understand what the "action music" between the expressive dances is describing. As you listen to a *complete* ballet in concert, therefore, do your best to find out the details of the story beforehand (usually by looking in the program book).

Then there are *ballet suites.* A ballet suite is a collection of the most expressive highlights from the original ballet, with all the filler omitted. As a result, ballet suites tend to be even more exciting than complete ballets. When you listen to a ballet suite, it's less essential to know exactly what's going on in the story. The music itself is expressive enough.

String Quartets and Other Motley Assortments

Your local library's music collection is full of *duets* — pieces for two instruments. And *trios* for three. And *quartets* for — you guessed it — four. *Quintets* for five. *Sextets* for six. *Septets* for seven. *Octets* for eight. *Nonets* for nine. The list goes on and on. But one combination of instruments has proven to be more popular than the rest: the *string quartet.*

The string quartet consists of two violins, a viola, and a cello. (To find out more about these instruments, see Chapter 7.) At one time, a very important goal for a composer was to prove himself by mastering the composition of the string quartet. For the most part, the structure of a string quartet piece is the same as that of a symphony: usually four movements, arranged in the traditional brisk-slower-dancelike-rollicking order.

Some musical forms took centuries to evolve, passing through the hands of the greatest composers and becoming ever more refined. In the case of the string quartet, however, one man had more influence on the form than anyone else. That man was Joseph Haydn.

Haydn (1732–1809) was one of the three best composers of the Classical period in music (the other two were Mozart and Beethoven). As Chapter 2 explains, he was hired to live, compose, and conduct in Prince Esterhazy's royal court outside Vienna. Talk about low turnover: Haydn liked his working conditions so well that he stayed for 30 years, until his employer died. During this time, he was supposed to write music for evenings of musical entertainment twice a week.

Haydn had a band of terrific musicians at his disposal; they, too, were full-time employees of the Esterhazy court. So he wrote tons of music for them: symphonies, concertos, operas, oratorios, keyboard sonatas, party music — and *83* string quartets.

Isolated as he was outside the city, in the royal court, Haydn received very little outside influence on his music-making; he was a musical Galapagos Islands. He was free to experiment, to try new forms and new styles, to see what worked and what didn't. Over the course of these 30 years, he nearly single-handedly standardized the form of the string quartet and the symphony.

Haydn's innovations and standardizations in these forms had a great influence on his colleagues and students, Mozart and Beethoven, who referred to him as "Papa Haydn" and whose string quartets are equally as sublime as Haydn's.

Why Do You Need a Form, Anyway?

We're glad you asked. Actually, you *don't* need a form. But as you already know, composers of old were *expected* to fit their works within established forms if they wanted to be taken seriously. And most of them obliged.

There's more to it than that, though. Without structure of any kind, the creative process is incredibly difficult. As we've read in a book somewhere, things that are without form tend to be void. But it's easier to be creative when you have certain guidelines to work within. It was easier to color in coloring books with predrawn lines when we were kids; it's easier to compose music if you have a musical gelatin mold to pour it into; and it's easier to write a book if you've got an outline set up beforehand.

Part II
Listen Up!

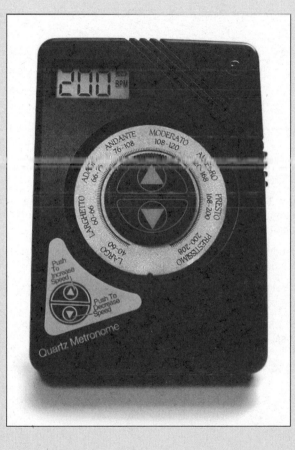

In this part . . .

- ✔ Enter the strange, strange world of the concert hall and become familiar with the obscure and unusual rituals of concert going.

- ✔ Discover what's going on, second by second, in a piece of classical music.

- ✔ Develop an intimate familiarity with nine of the world's greatest musical masterpieces.

- ✔ Take a trip backstage — into the fascinating world of the musicians themselves.

Chapter 4

Dave 'n' Scott's E-Z Concert Survival Guide™

*A*ttending a concert can seem like attending a convention of scientists, politicians, or Brazilians: You're walking into a huge room filled with people talking a lingo you don't understand, dressed weirdly, and behaving according to rules you can't see. Fear not: This chapter can save you from embarrassment and confusion. By the time you read through the chapter, you should be as savvy as the biggest music snob in the concert hall.

For the moment, we're going to talk about concerts of symphony orchestras. But everything we say in this chapter is also relevant to concerts of smaller groups, such as string quartets or brass quintets, or even piano or vocal recitals.

Preparing — or Not

You don't need to become intimately acquainted with the music on the program in advance of a performance. After all, a classical concert, like a rock concert or a play or a movie, is meant to be enjoyed.

But as humans, we tend to like what we know. Your all-time favorite melody was once completely unknown to everyone, including you.

So after spending anywhere from $5 to $50 on a symphony ticket, the investment of another $9.99 to order or download the music you're about to experience — or another $0 to hear it on YouTube or check it out from the library — is certainly worthwhile. At least find a recording of the *major* work on the evening's lineup. (Which one is the major work? Almost always, it's *whatever comes after intermission* — the last thing on the program.)

Listen to the recording. Read a little about the composer in this book. That's plenty of preparation, unless you want to be like the hard-core music lovers who actually buy the printed score and study the music.

If you don't listen to a recording beforehand, at least glance at the notes in the program after you get to the concert hall. You can discover neat things about the composer who wrote the music, what was going on in the world during her time, and what she was trying to do as she wrote the piece.

Some orchestras offer informal pre-concert talks. These talks are meant to be breezy, informative, and fun. If an orchestra has these talks (and increasing numbers of them do these days), they usually begin an hour before the concert, and they're usually free. Call and check.

The person giving the talk is usually someone who loves music very much and knows an awful lot about it — often, the speaker's even the conductor or the associate conductor. Usually, this person is interesting and enjoyable to listen to. But there is the slightest chance, on the rarest of occasions, that he's an insufferable snob. If you get one of those types, make sure that you tell him exactly what you think of him. The classical music world has absolutely no need for that kind of attitude.

Knowing When to Arrive at the Concert

Arrive early. You don't want to miss a minute of the people-watching; plus, if you get there early, you can take in all the strange warm-ups that the players go through — which can be very entertaining.

What's really interesting is that the musicians are probably going over the particular "licks" of music that they find especially tricky. Don't misunderstand: They're not "practicing" at this point — they already know the music backward and forward. But they need to get their fingers, mouths, and psyches prepared to tackle an incredibly difficult series of notes.

Can I Wear a Loincloth to The Rite of Spring?

People often get uptight about what to wear to a concert. Don't stress out — wear whatever you want. Absolutely no dress requirements or dress codes are in force at orchestra concerts.

The younger people in attendance often dress casually. Many of the older segment of the audience dress up somewhat — a jacket for men, a pantsuit or dress for women. Some take this dressing up to an extreme and wear a suit and tie or pearls. Of course, they're entitled to do so, and many enjoy the chance to dress up. We, your radical authors, on the other hand, feel that formal dress makes relaxing and really getting into the music much harder.

Yes, a concert often has a certain degree of dignity and ceremony. But these things are peripheral to the true business at hand, which is listening to (and participating vicariously in) the performance of a masterful human utterance. You don't need pearls for that. You need ears.

If you do decide to wear theme clothes to a concert (loincloth and so on), you'll probably be alone. (And you'll probably get some very strange looks. Just wanted to warn you.) But you won't be asked to leave. In fact, some people will assume you're doing publicity for the orchestra, and they'll be delighted.

One important point: If anyone, at any time, gives you any reason to believe that he or she disapproves of your dress, do the following: Turn to the person, smile, and ask, "What did you think about that absolutely stunning deceptive cadence toward the end of the exposition?" This always works, no matter what the orchestra just played.

You're usually best off waiting, however, until after the orchestra has actually *played* something.

The Gourmet Guide to Pre-Concert Dining

The rule in pre-concert dining is simply this: Avoid creating a situation in which you're constantly walking out of the concert hall to use the facilities.

As a form of after-dinner diversion, enrichment, and enjoyment, a classical concert has no equal. But there's a major difference between a concert and, say, a movie. At a concert, you're being entertained by live human beings who must maintain focus, concentration, and composure for long periods of time. Sometimes the act of standing up, sidling your way along an entire row of seats, and bolting for the exit can disturb the performers (not to mention the audience).

Foods to avoid before a concert:

- Deep-fried cheese curds
- A 32-ounce rib-eye steak
- A Reuben sandwich
- Spam surprise
- Baked-bean casserole
- Billy Bob's High-Kickin', Foot-Stompin' Texas Barbecue
- A Big Gulp

Another warning: The line for the ladies' room at today's concerts often stretches for several city blocks — the average symphony hall holds 2,000 people, and the average ladies' room holds six. (The men, on the other hand, are in and out of theirs in a jiffy.) True fact: Many orchestras have been forced to lengthen their intermissions for precisely this reason. Two suggestions for women:

- Don't overindulge in the liquid department before the concert.
- Dress as a guy.

All this boils down to a solution that experienced concertgoers have known for a long time: Eat *after* the concert.

Figuring Out Where to Sit — and How to Get the Best Ticket Deals

All orchestras in this country — and we mean *all* of them — have financial worries right now. Running a large professional orchestra costs millions of dollars per year. All orchestras need and deserve our moral and financial support. We'd feel extremely guilty giving you tips on how to save money at an American orchestra concert.

So here's what we're going to do: We're going to give you tips on how to save money at a *Bulgravian* orchestra concert. Bulgravian orchestras, as you probably know, are funded by an autocratic government. And we don't particularly care whether the government of Bulgravia makes enormous profits on its orchestra concerts right now.

How to Save Money at a Bulgravian Orchestra Concert

by Dmitri Poguinski and Sasha Speckovich

Fact number one: The best seats in a concert hall are never the most expensive. The best sound is often at the back of the top balcony.

If you're right at the back of the balcony, you can often hear sound reflected at you directly from the ceiling. The music sounds as if you're actually right next to the orchestra, and sometimes you can even hear the whispers of the players. Furthermore, seats right in front of the stage, where some of the luminaries sit, have the *worst* acoustics — sitting there is like eating Bulgravian *knowchpantlichki* with too much garlic and not enough onion. You get too much of one thing and no blend. Let the flavors mix by sitting farther back.

Addendum: On the other hand, watching the players and the conductor (or the soloist in a concerto) is fun, and you can watch them best if you sit up front. So what to do? Well, binoculars are good. You may also consider buying a ticket up in the balcony and (at some point during the first half of the concert) scanning for empty seats down front. After intermission, you're free to take any unclaimed seat. This way, you get the best of all possible worlds: superb acoustics in the first half, a great view in the second half, and a cheap ticket.

Addendum to the addendum: What if you take an unclaimed seat and then someone shows up to claim it? Take out your own ticket, appear surprised, and exclaim, "*Hôppla! et hëlá plàta Orkêstu A-1? Jôt dümal shto bîla Tritja Balkôn ZZ-49! Jôt toka requalá*" ("Oh, is this seat Orchestra A-1? I thought it was Third Balcony ZZ 49! I'm so sorry.") Or, better yet, say, "*Môy bônaful! Et hëlá Sámôdi?*" ("My goodness, is this Saturday?")

Actually, just a smile will do nicely. ***Remember:*** You always have your own ticket to fall back on.

Fact number two: Ticket prices often drop just before the concert. Look into "rush" tickets (especially student rush), which can cost as little as 10 percent of the original price, available half an hour before the concert. You also tend to find high-class scalpers standing in front of concert halls. They can't use their tickets, but they don't want them to go to waste. Sometimes they want the original price; sometimes they offer the tickets at a discount; and sometimes they just give them away. Look friendly and respectable, and try to avoid being spotted by the Bulgravian Secret Police.

Fact number three: If you're hard up for cash but really don't want to miss the major work on a concert, consider arriving at intermission (around 8:45 p.m., Eastern European Time, for most concerts). Some folks always leave at intermission, for whatever reason. (They have a headache; they're not interested in the final work on the program; they have an early day at the collective farm tomorrow; and so on.) Usually, they're delighted to give you their seats. Just stand outside on the front steps (or in the lobby) and ask politely. In our student days, we did this occasionally. Now we do it all the time.

Addendum to fact number three (and remember, you didn't hear this from us): Tickets are almost never checked as people return from the intermission. And that's all we're going to say about *that*.

Fact number four: Many orchestras offer an open-to-the-public dress rehearsal for the concert. (It's just *called* that, by the way — the musicians don't come in concert dress.) The dress rehearsal is extremely casual in character, but the playing is top-notch. Mostly, the musicians play straight through the program that they're preparing; this rehearsal is the last one, after all. But often the conductor stops and works with the orchestra. This sort of thing can be fascinating, especially if you can hear what the conductor is saying. Orchestras that have open rehearsals usually sell their tickets for about 36 Bulgravian drachmas ($5).

Better yet, make friends with someone in the orchestra. The musicians are all fascinating people. With a little luck, they can get permission for you to attend a rehearsal or two for free.

To Clap or Not to Clap: That Is the Question

One bit of weirdness strikes you the first time you go to a concert, guaranteed: *Nobody claps when the playing stops!*

"What the heck is *wrong* with this audience?" you think. "That was *great* playing!" We, your authors, remember encountering this custom at age eight (and being embarrassed because we *did* start clapping) and thinking that it was the stupidest custom we'd ever seen. Here's why we still feel the same way.

Why nobody claps

The crowd, having followed along in the program, knows that the *piece* isn't over yet — only one *movement,* or section of a piece, has ended. So they wait.

It's pretty embarrassing to start cheering and applauding wildly, only to find out that the music's still going and that 1,864 people are glaring at you.

Although we don't agree with the custom of waiting, we do want you to be comfortable with it. Here are some general clues that the music is completely over:

- ✔ The conductor puts down his hands and keeps them down. (If he doesn't want you to clap, the conductor sometimes signals this fact by keeping his hands up and waiting patiently, or by turning around and looking directly into the eyes of the clappers, or by shouting "Not yet!")
- ✔ All the players on stage put down their instruments.
- ✔ Everyone around you starts clapping.
- ✔ The concert hall lights come up.
- ✔ The players exit the stage, carrying their instruments.
- ✔ The entire audience leaves the auditorium.
- ✔ The cleaning crew comes in and begins to mop the stage.

Of course, you have more practical cues to tell you when the entire piece — including all its various sections — is totally over. For example, look at the program; it always tells you, right under the name of the piece you're listening to, how many *movements* (sections) it has. (***Remember:*** Most symphonies have four; most concertos have three.)

Now, you occasionally encounter a piece where a couple of movements are connected, or where the entire piece is played without pause, making it difficult to figure out where the next movement begins. In this case, the audience often begins clapping before you know that the piece is over. No big deal.

More on the insane "no-clap" policy

Actually, clapping between movements is a very hot topic in classical music circles nowadays. People don't do it for two reasons: First, peer pressure. Second, the following accepted wisdom, which has been in place only for the last few decades:

A symphony (or concerto or suite) is conceived as a whole. The movements are often related to one another. They belong together, like sentences in a paragraph or chapters in a book. Clapping between them causes them to become disconnected in your mind. It makes you forget, by the end, what happened at the beginning.

Here's why the accepted wisdom is bunk:

- ✔ Audiences, not wanting to cough while the music is playing, save their bronchial attacks for the between-movement lulls and then start coughing en masse. From the orchestra's point of view, this situation is much better than coughing *while* they're playing, but the coughing nonetheless breaks up the flow of the music at least as much as clapping could.

- ✔ Sometimes, the orchestra needs to *tune up* between movements. The sound of all the instruments fiddling with their pegs, valves, strings, mouthpieces, and lengths of tubing — in all keys at once — breaks up the flow again.

- ✔ Most importantly, sometimes the first, second, or third movement of a piece is just so darned exciting that you *want* to clap. Take concertos, for example, that feature one soloist with the orchestra. We defy anyone to find a piece of music that ends as excitingly as the *first* movement of Tchaikovsky's Violin Concerto or his Piano Concerto no. 1. Not clapping after these movements end would be unnatural, crazy, and downright wrong. They're monumentally thrilling. You should stand up, yell and scream, throw cash, and prance around the auditorium in celebration.

But what happens instead? A scattering of coughs, and that's all.

In the old days, when classical music *was* pop music, audiences regularly expressed their approval (or disapproval) of a performance of a piece of music *while it was being played.* Concerts were big, fun, healthy, rootin'-tootin' free-for-alls — like stadium concerts today.

One reason the popularity of classical music has declined in the last century, if you ask us, is the loss of *fun* in the concert-going experience. Sure, these pieces are classics; but the holiness bit has gone to an extreme. Beethoven never expected the audience to be silent before, during, and after his works were played. If he were alive today, he'd *really* think his hearing was going.

Fortunately, as orchestras try everything they can to woo lost audiences back into the concert halls, this stuffiness is slowly changing. The audience is now allowed to express itself more. Conductors, who for decades have been mute arm wavers on stage, are now sometimes permitted to speak from the podium. We look forward to this trend continuing — and to the day when we can applaud anytime applause is deserved.

Who to Bring and Who to Leave at Home with the Dog

Kids should be exposed to live classical music as early as possible. But if you think they may start to cry (or scream or throw up) during the performance, standing near the exit instead of sitting in the middle of the audience may not be a bad idea.

Every concert program is different: Some feature lots of short works, and others consist of just a couple of long ones. To determine whether you should bring a person to a particular symphony concert, consider the length of the pieces and the attention span of that person. More and more orchestras these days offer concerts for families — or even just for kids. With a little effort, you can find a program that's right for just about anyone.

Recognizing Which Concerts to Attend — or Avoid — on a Date

A concert is a wonderful event for lovers. Think of all the love songs that refer to orchestral music: "I hear violins." "I hear a symphony." "It's music to my ears!" Orchestral music has been synonymous with romance for decades. Just think: Violins! Harps! Tubas!

Well, okay — violins and harps.

If you're out on a date and want to impress your beloved with your taste, culture, and romantic instinct, you simply can't do better than an evening of classical music. This well-planned evening of romance won't lead to *further* romance, however, unless you take certain things into account:

- ✒ **What kind of group are you going to hear?** If it's a full orchestra, you almost can't go wrong. (See "What is the music *about?*" coming up.) If it's a string group (violins, violas, cellos, and bass), the music is most likely to be suave and melodic. If it's a brass group, it's more likely to be powerful, loud, and triumphant. If it's a group of harps, check to see whether everybody around you is wearing white. If so, you're probably dead.

- ✒ **What style or period of music are you going to hear?** This question is exceptionally important. You can use the Classical Music Timeline (see Appendix B) to see what period each composer on the program belongs to. That gives you some clue as to the character of what you're about to hear. *Baroque* music is expressive, but in a highly stylized way. *Classical period* music is lovely and gracious, yet emotionally reserved. (Great for the first date with the daughter of an oil magnate.) *Romantic* music is lush, gorgeous, and very expressive.

✔ **What is the music *about?*** Occasionally, classical works have a story associated with them. This story is always described in the program. Because some of these stories can be somewhat embarrassing in romantic situations, you may want to avoid some pieces on a date (especially if you don't know each other very well) — for example:

- *Medea's Meditation and Dance of Vengeance* (by Samuel Barber, 1946): A brutal masterpiece about a mythical character, Medea, who goes off the deep end and kills her kids.

- *The Rite of Spring* (by Igor Stravinsky, 1913): A truly incredible piece of music, originally a ballet, and perhaps the most influential classical work of the 20th century. But it's dissonant, violent, and oh so graphic. A virgin girl is sacrificed to the gods, forced to dance until she dies. Rated R.

- *Daphnis and Chloé,* **Suite 2** (by Maurice Ravel, 1912): A brilliant and charming piece for orchestra and chorus, also originally a ballet, with lovely depictions of nature. One of the depictions of nature, however, is a widespread "General Dance" (read: orgy) at the end. If any piece of orchestral music is X-rated, this one is. The music to this final scene (especially the wordless moans of the chorus) is sexually suggestive and may cause some uncomfortable squirming on the part of some members of the audience. (We adore it.)

- *Symphonie fantastique* (by Hector Berlioz, 1830): Another great masterwork, one of the cornerstones of the repertoire. It's about a man who can't get his beloved out of his head, takes enough opium to sterilize a moose, and dreams of murdering his girlfriend. Save this one for marriage.

On the other hand, depending on the relationship, some of these pieces may be just the ticket.

Peeking at the Concert Program

The program booklet is critical to enjoying the concert you're about to experience. You can expect to see all the following elements in any self-respecting program book:

✔ A list of the pieces of music you're going to hear

✔ A short explanation of each piece and its composer, including some history

✔ A biography of the conductor and any guest soloists in the concert

✔ A list of the players

✔ An advertisement for a bank

These sections take you through two different concert programs, which are representative of many of the programs you may encounter at a classical music orchestra concert today.

The typical concert format

For reasons that are almost unfathomable, the vast majority of symphony orchestras use one constant, tried-and-true format for 90 percent of their concerts. This format is so common that it's almost expected by a large segment of the concert-going population:

AN OVERTURE
A CONCERTO
— INTERMISSION —
A SYMPHONY

This listing means that there are three pieces on the program, with a pause after the first two. You may compare this format to that of eating a meal — appetizer, entree, and dessert — except that the dessert is nearly twice as big as the entree and takes 45 minutes to eat. But otherwise, it's exactly the same.

An *overture,* as described in Chapter 3, is a short musical introduction or prelude meant to whet your musical appetite. It's usually an *actual* overture stolen from some long-ago musical or opera. It's a great way to start the concert; a short opening piece is a neat way to give the latecomers a chance to enter without missing too much.

As Chapter 3 also describes, a concerto (pronounced "con-CHAIR-toe") is a piece of music in which one featured player (the soloist) plays the melody while the rest of the orchestra accompanies her. The concerto is by far the flashiest part of any concert program, and many people go to a symphony orchestra concert just to experience an exciting soloist.

After intermission comes the symphony. This piece is the longest work on the program. It's almost always four movements long; most symphonies last 35 to 45 minutes, just the right length for one half of the concert.

Here's a sample concert program page, using the tried-and-true OVERTURE-CONCERTO-*INTERMISSION*-SYMPHONY format:

THE YUCCA FALLS
PHILHARMONIC ORCHESTRA

Yasser Ahmed Hoolihan, *Conductor*
Hector Pernambuco, *Violin*

Overture to *The Barber of Seville*...Rossini

Violin Concerto no. 2 in B minor...Paganini
    Allegro maestoso
    Adagio
    Rondo

Hector Pernambuco, *Violin*

- INTERMISSION -

Symphony no. 4 in A (*Italian*)...Mendelssohn
    Allegro vivace
    Andante con moto
    Con moto moderato
    Saltarello: presto

Source: Creative Commons

The name of the orchestra always appears at the top of the program page. This imaginary band, the Yucca Falls Philharmonic Orchestra, has chosen one of the very few names available to it in the orchestra world. Most orchestras are named for their city (sometimes the county or state instead) — usually followed by the completely interchangeable words *Symphony, Symphony Orchestra, Philharmonic Orchestra,* or simply *Orchestra.* Nearly all professional orchestras in the country name themselves this way, for two reasons:

- ✔ A name of this kind automatically lends a special air of dignity.
- ✔ It makes clear exactly what the group does.

(True, some orchestras use names such as "MusicWorks," "Philharnova," or "Eight Guys and Their Moms." But sooner or later, many of them change to more traditional names so that people know what they're advertising.)

Following the orchestra's name is the name of the music director or conductor and whatever soloist is on the program for the evening. In this case, violinist Hector Pernambuco is probably not a native of Yucca Falls but a virtuoso brought in by the management to offer some spice to the symphony season.

Frankly, we always crack up when we read "Hector Pernambuco, violin" instead of "Hector Pernambuco, *violinist.*" With very few exceptions, the guest soloist is not, in fact, a musical instrument.

The music itself

The first work on the program is the Overture to *The Barber of Seville* by Rossini. The program page doesn't tell you anything about Rossini — not even his first name. But if you turn the page, the program book will include a description of each piece of music as well as a short biography of each composer. In this case, Rossini refers to Gioachino Rossini (1792–1868), an Italian composer of operas. Nobody performs his operas anymore (with the prominent exceptions of *The Barber of Seville* and *Cinderella* — see *Opera For Dummies*), but the *overtures* to those operas are still very well known and well loved today. If you've read Chapter 3, you know that this overture will be quite short; indeed, it's about seven minutes long. You may also guess from the title that the work is lighthearted, and it is.

The concerto that follows is by Paganini. The biography will tell you that this is none other than Niccolò Paganini (1782–1840), that great Italian master of the violin who wrote many pyrotechnical showpieces to demonstrate his virtuosity.

Notice that the concerto has the usual three movements. If you've read Chapter 3, you can guess that they're FAST-SLOW-FAST, but the three lines of Italian writing below the name of the piece give more specific clues. Most composers write some words on the sheet music at the beginning of each movement, describing the speed and character of the music to come. *Allegro maestoso* means lively and majestic. *Adagio* means restful, at ease. *Rondo* refers to a particular musical form where a main theme comes back again and again — usually at a brisk pace. (See our glossary in Appendix C for a complete list of the Italian phrases that you usually find in programs and what they mean.)

After intermission comes the symphony. The title of 99 percent of all symphonies is simply "Symphony," followed by a number and sometimes a key. This one is number 4, and it's in the key of A. (Understanding any of this information isn't necessary for enjoying the symphony. But if you want to find out more about *keys,* take a look at Chapter 11.) This symphony, unlike most, also has a nickname in its title: *Italian.* From this addition, you can bet that the music somehow tries to depict the flavor of Italy.

The symphony is by Mendelssohn, and the program book will eventually tell you that this composer is Felix Mendelssohn (1809–1847), a talented German composer who was long on talent and short on lifespan. (He died at age 38.) The symphony is in the expected four movements: *Allegro vivace* (lively and vivacious); *Andante con moto* (walking with motion); *Con moto moderato* (with motion, moderately), and *Saltarello: presto* (an Italian jumping dance; extremely quick). (How many magicians actually realize that "Presto!" means "Quick!"?)

If you take a moment while reading the program, you'll notice that the clever folks of the Yucca Falls Philharmonic have had a little brainstorm. All the pieces on the program have some connection with Italy. The first two are written by Italians, and the third has the nickname "Italian." This connection creates a thematic coherence among three pieces of music that are really very different. It adds a dimension of enjoyment — perhaps even of aesthetics — to the concert-going experience.

A different kind of program

Now let's look at a concert where the program doesn't fit into the OVERTURE-CONCERTO-*INTERMISSION*-SYMPHONY format. In fact, the program on the following page contains neither an overture nor a concerto nor a symphony. And it has nothing to do with Italy. Only the intermission is recognizable.

Notice that the Salamanca Symphony is presenting this performance three times. The audiences for these performances are going to be markedly different, and if this matters to you, buy tickets accordingly. The Friday and Saturday night crowds are likely to contain a few more youngish to middle-aged business types, with a slightly more festive atmosphere on Saturday. Sunday afternoon brings a few more children and many more senior citizens who don't like to drive at night. The atmosphere on Sunday is more subdued and probably less formal.

If the Salamanca Symphony is a typical professional orchestra, the performance quality itself may also differ slightly from show to show. Friday night should be very exciting. The players are on the edges of their seats — this is opening night, after all. You may hear a wrong note or two here and there, but overall, the atmosphere on the stage is highly charged. Saturday's performance may be more perfect, perhaps, but it may also lack some of the edge of Friday night. And Sunday afternoon could be slightly less exciting all around: third performance, late afternoon slump, less energetic audience.

Notice the particular concert times listed at the top of the program page. More and more orchestras these days begin their performances at strange times such as 8:15. The reason is clear: They're afraid you're going to arrive late.

Friday, December 20, at 8:15 P.M.
Saturday, December 21, at 8:15 P.M.
Sunday, December 22, at 3:15 P.M.

The Salamanca Symphony presents:
A CHRISTMAS SURPRISE!

Patricia Pfeffermühle, *Music Director*

Andreas Weltschmerz, *Baritone*

Trichinosis III..Jay P. Walker
(1972–)

Medea's Meditation and Dance of Vengeance............................Samuel Barber
(1910–1981)

Kindertotenlieder..Gustav Mahler
(1860–1911)

    I.   Nun will die Sonn' so hell aufgeh'n
    II.   Nun seh' ich wohl, warum so dunkle Flammen
    III.   Wenn dein Mütterlein
    IV.   Oft denk' ich, sie sind nur ausgegangen
    V.   In diesem Wetter

Andreas Weltschmerz, *Baritone*

••• INTERMISSION •••

Suite from *The Nutcracker*...Peter Ilyich Tchaikovsky
(1840–1893)

Miniature Overture
March
Dance of the Sugar Plum Fairy
Trepak
Arabian Dance
Chinese Dance
Dance of the Reed Pipes
Waltz of the Flowers

Source: Creative Commons

If the program indicates that a composer isn't dead, you know right away that you're in for a modern composition. Our modern master, Jay P. Walker, was born in 1972. Almost without exception, if a professional orchestra plays a modern piece (especially one with such an appetizing title as *Trichinosis III*), that work comes *first* on the program. Again, there is a hidden reason for this placement: Many audience members don't like to listen to "modern classical" music, especially if they think that it will sound alien, discordant, and non-melodic. The orchestra's thinking goes as follows: If the new work is played *after* intermission, people may bolt at the break. And if it comes right *before* intermission, many will plan to arrive just in time for the second half. But if the new piece comes first on the program, nobody misses out on a new work — not even those who hope to miss it by arriving at 8:15!

Now then, back to our program in progress: Second on the program is *Medea's Meditation and Dance of Vengeance,* by the American composer Samuel Barber. This piece is a *tone poem:* a musical depiction of non-musical events — a story told through music.

The third piece on the program is a *song cycle:* several songs under one heading. This song cycle is by Gustav Mahler, a great late-Romantic composer of symphonies and songs. The five songs in the cycle are listed in order — but unfortunately, in German. The notes on the successive pages of your program book will translate not only the title but also the complete text of each song. In such cases, reading the translations before the concert starts is a great idea. Glance at them, if you want, during the performance itself, but don't make the common mistake of becoming glued to them. You may miss a great musical performance.

After intermission comes Peter Tchaikovsky's beloved *Nutcracker* Suite. Again, the placement on the program is strategic: The orchestra knows that this piece is the star attraction of the evening, and not a seat in the house is going to be empty!

A *suite,* as Chapter 3 explains, is nothing more than a string of dances, one following the other. In this case, all the dance titles appear in English on the program page itself.

Introducing the Concertmaster

Now you're settled into your seat and you've read your program book. If you look carefully, you'll notice one empty seat on the stage — just to the left of the conductor's podium. This seat is that of the first violinist — the *concertmaster* (known in England as the *Leader*).

The concertmaster has many essential duties, which we discuss in these sections. She determines (notates in the sheet music) when the string instruments move their bows up and when they move them down. She addresses questions of *articulation* — how long or short to play a note — for all the string players. And she acts as a liaison, sometimes as an ambassador, between the members of the orchestra and the conductor. ("Lenny, the violas are still getting a draft from stage left.")

Finding the pitch

But all that musical work happens in rehearsal. Onstage, before the concert, the concertmaster seems to have only one duty: to tune up the orchestra. This job appears so simple — indeed, so silly — that many people wonder what the big deal is. As far as they can tell, all she does is walk onstage, acknowledge the applause of the audience, turn her back, and point to the oboist.

That's it. Point to the oboist. For this, she gets her own dressing room.

The oboist sits in the middle of the woodwind section, which is in the middle of the orchestra. On cue, he lifts his oboe and plays a single note. Not just any note, mind you — an A. And not just any A — but *A-440* (see the sidebar "A-440: What does it mean?").

Twisting and turning, pulling and pushing

The oboist plays his A-440 until all the members of the orchestra have a chance to hear it. The players tune up by trying to match the oboist's note exactly. String players twist pegs on their instruments. The kettledrum player uses pedals to tighten or loosen the heads of his drums. Woodwind and brass players push in or pull out certain parts of their instruments, making their piping shorter (so that they play slightly higher) or longer (to play lower). Others may accomplish this tuning by adjusting the position of their lips on the mouthpiece.

After all the players match the oboist's A, the concertmaster sits down. The orchestra becomes silent, and a hush falls over the concert hall. A moment later, the conductor enters. The audience applauds wildly.

But why? He hasn't even *done* anything yet!

A-440: What does it mean?

Before performing, musicians all around the world tune their instruments to match a note called *A-440.* Allow us to explain this handy morsel of musical terminology.

All the sounds you hear are produced by vibrations, or waves, in the air. Imagine that you could see these waves. They may look like this:

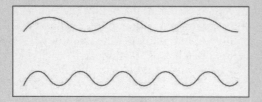

The number of waves that hit your ear in a given second is called the *frequency.* Get this: *The higher the frequency is, the higher the note you hear.* That's all there is to it. In the two waves in the figure, the second one has a higher frequency than the first; therefore, it creates a higher note than the first wave does.

In the music world, the note that everybody tunes to is called A-440 because that particular sound wave has a frequency of 440 microscopic waves per second — producing the note A.

How can you possibly determine with such incredible accuracy what frequency your instrument is playing? Well, over many years, great musicians are indeed able to learn to discern these differences. That's one of their skills. But these days, many musicians use a *tuner.* This little machine, slightly bigger than a cellphone, has a meter on it that measures exact frequency.

Actually, A-440 wasn't always the standard for tuning: The standard pitch has gone up over the years. In the Baroque era (roughly 300 years ago), musicians tuned to a lower version of A — around 430 cycles per second. As a result, music written for, say, soprano singers in the Baroque era are now much harder to sing than it was then. The high notes in Handel's great oratorio *Messiah,* for example, are much more taxing for the chorus than they were in 1742.

Today, the frequency of tuning *continues* to rise. Many orchestras have taken to tuning to A-442, a very slight yet perceptible difference. They feel that the higher frequency gives them a more brilliant sound.

Just great: One more upsetting trend to worry about, right up there with global warming, continental drift, and the sun's energy depletion.

Enter the Conductor

Don't be ashamed if you find yourself wondering what the big deal about the conductor is. Musical novices wonder. Audience members wonder. Even the orchestra musicians sometimes wonder.

As conductors ourselves, we feel compelled to respond.

A professional orchestra is a highly skilled group of individuals. Each has an advanced degree from a conservatory or school of music; each is a consummate artist with taste, musical authority, and technique to burn. But put a bunch of these musicians in a room together, and you're guaranteed to get

at least 50 different ideas of how the music should go. The result is chaos —
and possible fistfights. Hence the conductor, whose job is part musical and
part political.

Music is a living art, so for different people to have several different inter-
pretations of any piece is perfectly valid. Listen to a few different recordings
of one particular work of classical music, and you'll see what we mean. Even
though the piece of music stays exactly the same, some performances are
faster; some are slower. Some are louder; some are softer. And some inter-
pretations are incredibly exciting, while others seem tame.

In orchestra music, these differences are largely the result of different conductors. The conductor is responsible for determining the speed (also known
as the *tempo*), the instrumental balance, the volume levels, the note length,
the phrasing, and the dramatic pacing of any piece of music the orchestra
plays. These combined ideas are called the *interpretation*.

Understanding interpretation

But, you ask, weren't all those variables specified by the composer?

Not exactly. A composer might write "Allegro" at the beginning of the piece.
Allegro means lively, or fast. Sure, but *how* fast?

Some composers go so far as to mark exactly how fast they want the music.
They use a *metronome,* a device that's been around since Beethoven's time
(see Figure 4-1). Set it on any number between about 30 and 200, and it makes
a clicking sound at exactly that number of beats per minute. A watch with a
jumping second hand, by the way, "clicks" at exactly 60 beats per minute.

But if most composers, starting with Beethoven, put a metronome marking at
the beginning of each piece of music, why do we need a conductor to indicate
the tempo?

Excellent question. And it has at least three answers:

> ✔ Even the most virtuosic musicians don't have an absolutely infallible
> sense of tempo. Next time you get a chance, ask a master cellist to sing
> 120 beats per minute. She'll get close most of the time, but she's not
> going to hit it right on the nose every time. So in a very large group of
> musicians, such as an orchestra, even a specifically notated metronome
> marking is likely to receive several slightly different interpretations. The
> conductor is there to unify the orchestra's tempo.

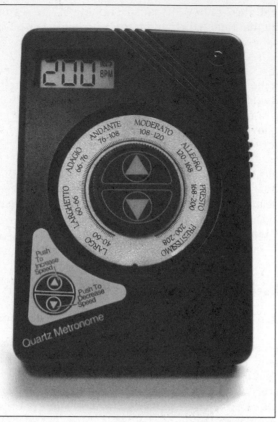

Figure 4-1:
A metro-
nome helps
composers
mark time.

✔ Composers also understand that many factors can alter that tempo. Different concert halls with different acoustics, different-sized orchestras, and even different barometric pressure can influence an orchestra's tempo. A speed that sounds absolutely right in the very resonant *Concertgebouw* of Amsterdam may be way too slow for the relatively dry acoustics of the Robert Louis Stevenson Elementary School Cafetorium in Farfalloo, Wyoming. Determining the correct tempo for each situation is up to the conductor.

As a result, for the past century, conductors have felt free to treat the metronome marking only as a starting point — or even to ignore it completely. Beethoven's symphonies, for example, are virtually always played at a slower tempo than Beethoven himself specified. Tradition, along with various theories about the condition of the old man's metronome (not to mention his brain cells), has led generations of musicians to contradict poor Ludwig's specifications.

> ✔ For the most part, composers don't *want* their music played at exactly one speed all the way through. They may indicate a metronome marking for convenience, but they also expect a certain ebb and flow in their music. At certain points, they want the music to relax or slow down; at other times they want it to speed up and push ahead slightly.

The conductor can indicate all this to the musicians.

Slicing up time

This task the conductor performs with his or her *baton*. If you see a conductor slice through the air from top to bottom and from left to right, he's indicating the beats of the music (see Figure 4-2). Or, very literally, he's slicing up time into smaller segments. The orchestra plays a certain number of notes for each slice of time.

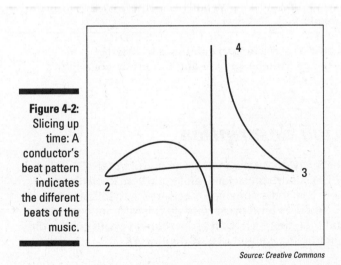

Figure 4-2: Slicing up time: A conductor's beat pattern indicates the different beats of the music.

Source: Creative Commons

In the old days of classical music, orchestras *had* no conductors. The leader of the orchestra was the first violinist or, sometimes, the harpsichord player. He gave the cue to start by lifting his hand or his violin bow, in the right tempo. Everyone then followed this musician as he played his part.

As music became more complicated, it soon required a musician whose sole purpose was to indicate the flow of the music — a conductor. One of the first was the Baroque composer Jean-Baptiste Lully (1632–1687). He used to stand before his orchestra with a heavy staff, beating time by pounding the staff on the ground.

The heavy staff proved to have two disadvantages. First, it tended to make a loud pounding sound with every beat. And second, it killed Jean-Baptiste Lully. One day, while merrily beating time, Lully mistakenly pounded the staff on his foot instead of the ground. The resulting wound became infected with gangrene, and he died.

In later years, the heavy staff was replaced by a rolled-up piece of music paper. This scroll became popular because of its two great advantages: It didn't make a sound, and it didn't cause gangrene.

Finally, in the 19th century, the wooden baton replaced the scroll. The conductor could control the baton between his fingertips, shaping the music with subtle and graceful gestures.

Around the same time, such composer/conductors as Richard Wagner (1813–1883) and Gustav Mahler (1860–1911) launched the stereotype of the willful, temperamental, crazed, egomaniacal music director. With their powerful new batons, they set themselves up as gods, expecting perfect orchestral obeisance to their every flick of the wrist.

The myth of the conductor as superhuman continues to this day, perpetuated largely by certain artist managers — and by certain conductors themselves.

Reading the job description

Now, being a conductor really does take *some* force of will. After all, you're standing before nearly 100 superb musicians, most of whom know the music at least as well as you do. You must convince these artists to follow *your* musical interpretation. You'd be hard pressed to do this without any ego whatsoever. But beyond that, there's nothing superhuman about conducting music. It just takes an incredible amount of study and work.

Conductors are musicians who have studied every aspect of music; most have been excellent instrumentalists themselves. They should be well versed in the theory and history of music, understand all the instruments and all the musical styles, be able to break a piece of music down into its component parts, be very familiar with all Western music, and understand several foreign languages. They should also have a great ear, great people skills, and an effective baton technique. As if these requirements weren't enough, they must also have a detailed understanding of their orchestra organization so that they can answer the countless artistic questions that come their way on a daily basis.

Top quotes by conductor Eugene Ormandy

Eugene Ormandy (1899–1985) was a famous conductor of the Philadelphia Orchestra. Over the years, the orchestra's players kept track of his funniest utterances. Clearly, a conductor's actions are ultimately more important than his words.

- "Who is sitting in that empty chair?"

- "I guess you thought I was conducting, but I wasn't."

- "Why do you always insist on playing while I'm trying to conduct?"

- "It is not so difficult as I thought it was, but it is harder than it is."

- "At every concert I've sensed a certain insecurity about the tempo. It's clearly marked 80 . . . uh, 69."

- "Did you play? It sounded very good."

- "If you don't have it in your part, leave it out, because there is enough missing already."

- "We can't hear the balance yet because the soloist is still on the airplane."

- "With us tonight is William Warfield, who is with us tonight. He is a wonderful man, and so is his wife."

- "Bizet was a very young man when he composed this symphony, so play it soft."

- "Serkin was so sick he almost died for three days."

- "Let me explain what I do here. I don't want to confuse you any more than absolutely necessary."

- "I don't mean to make you nervous, but unfortunately I have to."

- "Relax. Don't be nervous. My god, it's the Philadelphia Orchestra."

Conductors get better with age, all the way up to their final years. (Some musicians think that conductors even continue to improve after they die. At least, we *think* that's what they mean when they say, "The best conductor is a dead conductor.")

After making his entrance, the conductor bows and raises his baton. The orchestra comes to attention — and the concert begins!

Chapter 5

For Your Listening Pleasure

*T*his chapter introduces you to masterful examples of all the major styles of classical music, from the Baroque era to the beginning of the 20th century. It includes a second-by-second guide that can help you unlock the mysteries of nine great masterpieces. More than that — it's guaranteed to triple your listening pleasure.

The musical examples at www.dummies.com/go/classicalmusic are an incredible resource. First, they're among the greatest creative expressions ever penned by humankind. Second, they offer you a chance to find out what you *like*.

If, on first hearing a particular example, you find that you're not enjoying yourself, for goodness sake, switch to another piece. We're not here to torture you; we want to show you what we love.

Then again, if you're having trouble liking one piece, you might try it out again in a week or so. Something interesting happens when you become more and more familiar with a piece of music. It may grow on you.

By the way, our comments are highly subjective, and they sound like *us* talking; *you* might describe these pieces differently. But in the meantime, you get to see how people think about music when music is what they *do*. That's an education in itself.

Note: We identify particular moments in the music by using time codes: **1:34**, for example, means that you can use your cursor to find the spot that is exactly 1 minute, 34 seconds into the piece. (Better yet: Lean back and just *listen* until the music reaches that point.)

1 Handel: Water Music Suite No. 2: Alla Hornpipe

This movement is probably George Frideric Handel's most well-known piece of instrumental music. Handel (1685–1759) was a great master of the Baroque era, and this movement is a perfect example of his sprightly, dancelike music.

0:01   The piece begins with a familiar "sailor's hornpipe" melody.

0:16   Now the trumpets enter, playing the beginning of the same "sailor's hornpipe." And at **0:23**, the horns echo what the trumpets just played.

0:35   After another brief alternation of brass instruments, the strings enter here for the first time. Without looking at the timing, see if you can pick out this moment by sound alone. The musical "tone color" changes drastically, and the violins, violas, cellos, and basses take center stage.

0:43   First the trumpets, then the horns, and then the full orchestra take over the theme, bringing it to a satisfying conclusion.

1:03   But what's this? The music seems to begin all over again. The musicians repeat everything they've played up to this point, note for note.

2:06   Now comes something new: a contrasting section — or, as musicians often say, a *middle section*. (As you read on, you'll see why that title is appropriate.) How is it contrasting? First, the melody is different. Second, this music is quieter than what came before — mainly because all the brass instruments have stopped playing. And third, this section is in a *minor key* — creating a very different feeling from the opening of the piece, which is in a *major key*. (For much more on major and minor keys, see Chapter 11.)

3:04   Now, once again, we hear the familiar "sailor's hornpipe" theme from the beginning of the piece. But with a twist: This time, the *strings* start things off instead of the woodwinds. It takes a very astute listener to notice this. But what *everyone* notices, at least subliminally, is that the music sounds fresh and new, even though the same old theme is being played again.

3:20   From here to the end of the movement, the sequence of events is exactly the same as before. (Read from **0:16** to **1:02** for a detailed description.)

If we back up a bit and "view" this music from a distance, we can get a good idea of the structure of this movement. Look what happens if you call the "sailor's hornpipe" theme A, and the contrasting minor-key section B. You get an overall structure of

A (repeated) – B – A

This form is *unbelievably* important to the history of music. After Handel's time, it became the basis of *sonata form,* which you can read about in Chapter 3 — and in the discussion of Beethoven's Fifth Symphony coming up. Thousands upon thousands of composers have used sonata form — all the way up to our own time.

Now you know why musicians refer to that contrasting B section as the *middle section:* because as soon as they hear it, they know that sooner or later, Theme A will be coming back again.

2   Bach: Well-Tempered Clavier, Book 2: Prelude and Fugue in C Major

We mentioned at the beginning of this chapter that Handel was a great master of the Baroque era. Well, Johann Sebastian Bach (1685–1750) was *the* greatest.

Bach and Handel lived and worked at the exact same time — in fact, they were born in the same year. But the two composers never met, and they developed sharply different personal writing styles.

The biggest difference is in their use of *counterpoint* — several melodic lines playing at the same time. Bach used it more often than Handel did. And nowhere is that more evident than in this composition.

In the early days, piano-like instruments were tuned in such a way that they sounded right only when playing in certain keys. (See Chapter 6 for more on keys.) But during Bach's lifetime, the theories of keyboard tuning underwent a big change. For the first time, people started tuning their keyboards so that the musical distance from each key to the next was the same. This development made it possible to play music in any key — starting on any note of the keyboard. To celebrate, Bach composed a book of 24 preludes and fugues — one for every major and minor key. And then, in a second book, he did the whole thing all over again. Today, "the 48," as they're often called, stand as some of the finest keyboard pieces ever composed.

We're going to listen to the first prelude and fugue from Bach's *second* book. Because it's the first one in that book, it's in the simplest of all keys — C major — which uses only the white notes on the keyboard.

0:01   In this recording, you can hear the sound of a *harpsichord,* an early keyboard instrument that existed long before anyone dreamed up the piano. Bach wrote some of his best music for this instrument.

This is the beginning of the prelude part of the composition. It has an almost monumental quality to it; it's almost as if Bach was throwing open the big doors to some enormous building.

One of the things that creates this feeling, in our opinion, is Bach's use of a *pedal note* — a low note that keeps ringing, even as everything swirls around above it. If you listen carefully, you can hear that the first note (a low C) lasts a full 13 seconds. The pedal note gives a sense of rock-solid stability to the music, and that's what you feel as momentous.

You can certainly hear the counterpoint in this piece as it progresses. The melody seems to be everywhere — sometimes in the high notes, sometimes in the low notes, sometimes in between (in the so-called *inner voices*).

In Chapter 6, we point out that the harpsichord isn't *touch-sensitive*. That is, no matter how hard or softly you strike the keys, the volume comes out the same. One of the ways a harpsichord player can simulate more volume is by *rolling* chords. Rather than playing the three or four notes of a chord all at once, he separates them all by a split second (usually playing the lowest notes first). The added time it takes to play the chord gives the illusion of added volume. You can hear this at **1:03** and again *very* prominently on the last note of the prelude, at **2:15**.

When the prelude ends, you may think that the piece is over. But, as musicians know, the fun is just about to begin. Here comes the *fugue*.

It's easiest to understand a fugue if you imagine it being sung by four different voices. The keyboard player has to imitate all those voices with just two hands — an astoundingly difficult task.

2:22   Voice One sings the fugue's melody, all by itself, with no accompaniment.

2:27   Now, as Voice One goes on to sing something new, Voice Two begins singing the melody, a little higher than Voice One did.

2:32   It gets even more complicated. As Voices One and Two continue on, minding their own separate businesses, Voice Three begins the melody. See if you can hear the exact moment when Voice Three comes in. Because Voice Three sings the lowest notes that you've heard so far, it should be easy to identify.

2:37   But wait — there's more! Voice Four enters the fray. You can't miss this voice, because it's (a) the highest thing going at the moment and (b) the highest thing you've heard since the beginning of the fugue.

Now all four voices continue their heated discussion. Although each voice has something extremely individual to say, all four voices somehow manage to blend with one another. That's the essence of counterpoint, Bach's specialty; that's what makes a fugue so amazing. No matter how hard *playing* a fugue may be, *composing* one is a million times harder.

By now, you're familiar enough with the fugue's melody to be able to recognize little snippets of it whenever they pop up. What you should listen for is a group of six notes — two very short, two slightly longer, and two longer still. That's the main characteristic of the melody. You can hear it at **2:52, 2:56, 3:08, 3:18, 3:23,** and a score of other places.

At **3:28,** Bach introduces a common fugue technique. At a point near the end of the piece, the entrances of the melody come closer together, in quick succession. Here, a voice enters about once per second — adding to the buildup of excitement.

Once you figure out how this fugue is put together, you'll marvel at its complexity and enjoy it all the more. And you'll also understand why many people consider Bach's works to be among the true wonders of human achievement — like the Chartres Cathedral, the Hoover Dam, and the Great Wall of China.

3   Mozart: Piano Concerto No. 22 in E-Flat, Third Movement

This piece isn't the most *famous* of Wolfgang Amadeus Mozart's piano concertos, but it's one of the best. We picked this movement out of all the works of Mozart (1756–91) because it expresses what was great about him in so many different ways. It's beautiful, witty, and dramatic, and it embodies the very spirit of Mozart himself: elegant, refined, warm, and playful.

This movement is the third and final one of Piano Concerto no. 22 in E-flat. It's a *rondo* (see Chapter 3), meaning that the main theme comes back again and again and again, alternating with little subsidiary themes.

0:00   The piano starts off right away with the main theme (or melody). We'll call it Theme A. Simple, isn't it? Like a little children's melody. Or like hunting horns in the distance. We think that's what Mozart meant it to sound like . . . as you'll hear in a moment.

0:09   Theme A again, loudly — except that now it's the entire orchestra.

0:18   Turns out that the melody you just heard was only the *first part* of the theme. The piano now tells you something more.

0:27   While the piano holds on a trill, the horns play a little riff: four quick notes. (This segment is *definitely* meant to sound like a hunting call.) And one second later, they're imitated by the clarinets.

0:29   Now the piano moves into a little flight of fancy to bring you back to the main theme.

0:38   The first part of Theme A again. But this time, rather than simply echoing Theme A as it did the first time, the orchestra goes off on a little flight of fancy of its own. In the music biz, we may say that the orchestra is "establishing the key of the piece" by setting up a chord progression that makes it very clear what key we're in.

0:58   A delightful little addendum: a capper to the main theme. This part starts with two clarinets, one spinning out a quick accompaniment down at the bottom of its range and the other joined by a horn in a cute little melody.

1:06   A lone bassoon adds yet another capper to the theme, echoed by a solo flute four seconds later. Finally, the entire orchestra comes in with finality, as if to say, "Enough cappers already. Let's get this rondo on the road."

1:21   After what seems to be the final chord of this orchestral outburst, the piece suddenly quiets down to nothing. *Almost* nothing, that is. If you listen carefully, you can hear a *vamp* in the string section (a repeating little *waiting* figure), as if the violins are saying to the solo piano, "Come on in anytime you're ready. The water's fine."

1:24   Just two statements of the vamp convince the piano. It enters, almost timidly at first — and then . . .

1:36   The piano begins imitating the bassoon and flute idea (that extra cap from **1:05**).

Now permit us to pause for a second (or, actually, 37 seconds) here. Why are we explaining everything in such detail? First, we want you to see how music can be taken apart. And second, all these segments get repeated later in the movement. If you ever want to learn a piece of music — to play it on the piano, say, or to conduct it — understanding these little subdivisions of the structure really helps.

1:44   Now something very subtle happens. From the beginning of the movement, this music has been in the key of E-flat major. Every chord progression, every instrumental entrance, every phrase has confirmed and reconfirmed that key. But now, for the first time, we get a hint that the piece is about to leave the safety and comfort of its home key.

In the old days, if you, the composer, wanted to change keys, you didn't just do it abruptly; you had to go through a series of harmonies that *gradually* took you there — so as not to upset the sensitive ears of the listener.

Right between **1:44** and **1:45** on the recording comes a strange chord that signals the beginning of the key shift. This *modulation* continues for quite a while. To the average person, the piano is just noodling around (the scholarly term for it) for 45 seconds. But the music becomes more interesting when you understand that, underneath this noodling, the chord progression necessary for the desired modulation is taking place. And when do you reach the new key?

2:23   Now. With the new key comes a new theme — Theme B. Music theorists say that this theme is in the *dominant* key, bearing a special relationship to the key of Theme A. If you want to know more about these relationships, consult Chapter 11.

2:32   After the piano states Theme B, a beautiful clarinet solo comes in, imitating and even extending Theme B. More piano noodling for almost a minute — and then . . .

3:19   The music is going somewhere else again. For the past minute, all that noodling confirmed the key of Theme B. But now we're about to leave that key again, and with a descending scale in the horns . . .

3:24   You arrive back at Theme A! And in the original key, to boot! Now, if you're a rondo buff, you *knew* that would eventually happen. (Everyone in Mozart's time knew it, even if they didn't think about it much.) At **3:33**, once again, the orchestra comes barreling in (as it did at **0:11**).

3:40   What's up here? Instead of just imitating what the piano did, the orchestra does something weird: It goes to yet a different key. Then it becomes quiet, and the piano comes in on a trill as the chords underneath continue to change.

4:05   The piano abruptly lands on a strong chord as the winds come in on a held note. Then the piano noodles around on that chord — and fades out to nothing. Everything stops! What's happening?

4:16   The piece has reached a new theme: We'll call it Theme C. This theme is *much slower* than the rest of the movement. It's like an oasis of tranquility in the midst of a busy movement, the musical equivalent of Central Park.

Mozart has made his Theme C sound like a wind serenade, a piece that would've been played outdoors in the park on a warm evening as the king sipped on daiquiris. Only wind instruments are playing: no violins, violas, cellos, or double basses — for the first time in this movement.

4:45   But now the piano enters, imitating this theme, and so do the strings. Can you hear that this segment is an *exact* repetition of the melody you just heard?

5:13   The winds have more to say. Theme C turns out to be a two-parter, and the wind serenade consort is back now, singing the second part of the theme. At **5:40**, the piano, accompanied by the strings again, imitates this part as well.

6:16   Here the strings play *pizzicato,* or plucked by the fingers, as the winds play long chords that almost seem to suspend us in the air. But then a *crescendo* (a growing sound) leads to . . .

6:49   An honest-to-goodness cadenza! A *cadenza,* as you can discover in Chapter 3, is a chance for the soloist to strut her stuff. This particular cadenza isn't extremely flashy; it's quite a short cadenza, in fact.

7:00   Theme A, in all its quiet glory, is followed shortly thereafter by the orchestra barreling in again, as before.

7:17   Here's the bassoon capper, followed by the flute version. But this time, the flute takes us into a different key again. Can you hear that we're going somewhere else? As the piano enters, it, too, takes us somewhere else. For several seconds, we don't know where we're going to end up, key-wise.

8:02   False alarm. After all that modulation, we end up back in the original key. But it's not Theme A; it's Theme B, which we haven't heard for a good six minutes!

8:44   A sudden, loud entrance of the orchestra. It leads us to, at **8:49**, a particular chord that traditionally signals the beginning of another piano cadenza.

This segment is the main cadenza of the movement. In Mozart's day, the soloist improvised it on the spot — a lost art nowadays, practiced by only a few brilliant soloists. These days, most people memorize a precomposed cadenza instead.

9:48   Theme A's final appearance. By now, you probably know it so well that Mozart didn't feel compelled to repeat the first phrase, as he did at **0:09**.

10:33 And here come those cappers: first the little clarinet one (first heard at **0:58**) and then the bassoon and flute one (first heard at **1:06**). But this time, the piano adds its own little embellishments while the cappers are going on.

10:50 The entire orchestra, as before, says, "Enough cappers already." And it feels as if the piece is finished.

10:55 But one more thing. Remember that vamp from **1:21**? Here it is again, as the piano makes a final quiet statement.

11:04 "And now we *really* mean it!" says the orchestra. The movement is over.

So now you have an idea of the structure of this beautiful music. The themes boil down as follows: A – B – A – C – A – B – A. In other words, a perfect example of a *rondo*.

4 Beethoven: Symphony No. 5, First Movement

This piece is one of the most well-known movements in all of music, for good reason. In this first movement of the Fifth Symphony, Ludwig van Beethoven (1770–1827) gives us a musical statement of anger, driving intensity, and great beauty — and the quintessential first-movement *sonata form*.

If you've read Chapter 3, you may remember that sonata form is a prescribed three-section structure: (1) an *exposition,* in which the composer puts forth two main themes; (2) a *development* section, in which he fools around with them; and (3) a *recapitulation,* in which he brings them back again. In this case, you'll also find a *coda* — a tail.

Exposition

0:00 The movement begins in a rage, with strings and clarinets shouting out a concise theme. The famous four-note melody at the beginning is the basis of the entire movement: "dit-dit-dit DAAAAH!" Beethoven called it "fate knocking on the door."

Composer Richard Wagner imagined how Beethoven may have described those "DAAAAH!" notes: "My held notes must be long and serious. Do you think I wrote them in jest, or because I could not decide what to write next? Of course not! That strong, exhausting tone . . . becomes a rapturous and horrible spasm. The note's lifeblood must be squeezed out to the very last drop, with enough force to stop the waves of the sea and reveal the bottom of the ocean; to arrest the clouds in their courses, dispel the mists, and expose the pure blue sky, and the burning face of the sun itself. This is the meaning of the sudden long-sustained notes!"

We're with you, Richard.

0:08   And they're off! The four-note theme flashes through the orchestra like lightning: violins, violas, violins. Then the entire orchestra enters, leading to a mini-climax. After everybody stops playing, the first violins keep holding their note . . . and holding. Suspense . . . great suspense . . . .

0:20   Crash! The entire orchestra hammers out the four-note theme again, holding onto the last note as before. And again, fleetly the music takes off. Once more, the little tune is tossed around, and the orchestra becomes louder and louder until, with two forceful chords, it stops momentarily.

0:46   Proudly, the horns announce the beginning of the second theme. The second theme is in a new key; the piece remains in this key until the end of the exposition. It begins with the same three fast "dit-dit-dit" notes that you heard first in the theme, but now those notes are followed by *three* long notes.

0:48   When the violins enter, the mood becomes more lyrical. This line is taken up by the quiet clarinet and then by the flute. But if you listen carefully, you can still hear the four-note theme simmering down low in the bass instruments. Gradually, the music builds up to another mini-climax. The orchestra bubbles and boils.

1:23   We hear three decisive statements of the four-note theme. Then silence. And that's the end of the exposition.

1:28   But wait — the furious four-note theme starts again, exactly as at the beginning. In fact, we now hear a full repetition of the *entire* exposition from the beginning. As you listen, try to identify the different sections as they come by again.

Development

2:55   As the development begins, the horns sing the four-note theme at the top of their lungs, echoed by the string section.

3:00   Now the fast motion begins again — quietly, as at the beginning — in the strings. Don't forget: In the *development* section, we expect to hear the main ideas of the exposition in a slightly different form, as the composer develops them. And indeed, this development is made up almost entirely of the four-note tunelet. Amazing how Beethoven can use that theme over and over, always exploring new ways to present it so that it never becomes stale.

3:09   The music builds, seemingly to a climax. But then, at the last second, just before it reaches a climax, Beethoven backs off. Frustration in music!

3:14   The music rises toward another climax . . . and he thwarts that one, too.

3:27   But this time, he means it for real. This third buildup isn't a fakeout. The skies open up, and the heavens storm.

3:35   Until now, this section has been developing just one thing — the four-note theme. But now, we hear the notes of the horn call that began the second theme. In fact, that's *all* we're going to hear from the second theme in this development section. The lyrical, submissive side has no place in the maelstrom.

3:45   Now Beethoven does something especially ingenious. He ceases the constant, fast-note motion and develops the long notes for a while. Winds alternate with strings; as they do, they gradually become quieter and quieter — until suddenly, at **4:05**, the orchestra blasts out the four-note theme.

4:09   Again, alternation, quietly . . . and then again, an outburst, leading to . . .

Recapitulation

4:13   This time, the entire orchestra makes the outburst (not just the strings and clarinets as at the beginning). Here are the two statements of the four-note theme, each with a powerful hold, as Beethoven shakes his fist at the heavens.

4:26   Again, they're off — the four-note theme makes its way around the string section. But this time, at **4:36**, everyone stops playing except the oboe, which plays a little free-sounding passage by itself. A short *cadenza* for an oboe solo — unheard of in a place like this! (You can read about *cadenzas* in Chapter 3.) Music scholars have described this solo as a little blossom growing out of the pause.

4:48   The motion begins again and builds up, reaching a climax with two forceful chords, signaling that the second theme is about to begin.

5:09   Beethoven announces the second theme in the horns. But here, he had a problem. As you can read in Chapter 9, the old *natural horns* could play only a few notes — in a single key. This piece is now in a different key from the beginning — and the horns don't have the notes to play it! So Beethoven substitutes the next best thing: bassoons.

We should point out that many conductors today, understanding this fact, simply replace the bassoons with modern horns. (Modern horns can play in any key.) But this recording preserves Beethoven's original instrumentation, and it's bassoons that you hear.

What follows is almost identical to the corresponding music in the exposition, but, again, in a different key. The music builds and builds, reaching a final-sounding climax.

Coda

5:54   Just when you thought the music was going to come to a halt (as it did at the end of the exposition), it goes on. And on! The intensity continues to build as Beethoven takes you into the *coda,* or tail, of the movement. The four-note theme plays again and again; the notes repeat in a frantic, driving rhythm.

5:59   Then, to add to the excitement, the melody note in the violins goes *up* a notch exactly at this point, as if shifting into a higher gear. Then, for a moment, the storm pauses — just long enough for a quiet bassoon rendition of the four-note theme.

6:05   And then the music rages again. From here on, Beethoven is unrelenting. He shouts, he rages, he pounds his fist, until . . .

7:00   All the forces in nature and music convene in this one moment. A final statement of the two four-note themes, each with an earth-shaking hold. And then, with a series of concise blows, Beethoven ends the movement.

5   Brahms: Symphony No. 4, Third Movement

Johannes Brahms (1833–1897) was incredibly self-critical; he never let a piece out of his sight until it was perfect. He didn't give birth to his first symphony until he reached the age of 43, and he wrote only four symphonies in all.

The final symphony is perhaps the most severe and intense of the four — except for the third movement. This charming *Allegro giocoso* ("Lively and joyous") movement is a ray of sunshine. It's Brahms in one of his rare, "unbuttoned" moods. At its first performance, this movement caused such spontaneous cheers that it had to be repeated.

It also has the distinction of being the only movement of a Brahms symphony that uses a triangle.

0:00 A *fortissimo* (very loud) burst from the entire orchestra (except triangle, that is) starts the boisterous mood. Remember this rhythm, because it comes back later. "Come and get your beans, boys! Come and get your beans, boys!" would accurately describe this rhythm, although we're quite confident that's not how *Brahms* would have described it.

0:04 Suddenly the music comes to rest on a low, accented chord, as if to say, "No-o-o-o . . . !" This chord comes back later, too.

0:06 As if that chord were gathering up energy, it now launches on a lively, jagged course, a series of chords in the rhythm of "Giddy-up, giddy-up, giddy-up, giddy-up . . ."

0:09 . . . leading to a rousing brass fanfare. This fanfare is full of *triplets* — three notes to a beat. They, too, come back later, so lodge them in your memory bank.

0:18 Suddenly the music quiets down and smoothes out, playing a *transitional* theme (a theme that leads to a new musical idea); listen to the voices of the low strings, quietly and agitatedly imitating the rhythm of the beginning (as if whispering "Come and get your beans" between their teeth). They refuse to let you relax completely.

0:34 At the climax of this crescendo, the "Come and get your beans, boys!" theme seems to return. You can hear it in the low strings, way down low. As for the violins, Brahms does something ingenious here: He turns the main melody *upside down*. While in the double basses the theme goes *down* the scale, turning up at the last moment, in the violins the theme goes *up* the scale, turning *down* at the last moment. By changing a note or two, Brahms gets both of these — the theme and its inversion — to fit together in the same harmony!

0:38 Here's that held, accented chord "No-o-o-o . . ." — except that, this time, it's not just played low but also quite high in some instruments, continuing Brahms's inversion of the melody. (Listen for the first long-promised entrance of the triangle!) But once again, this chord launches you off on the "Giddy-up" chords.

0:43   Everything's hushed. What's happening?

0:50   It's the second main theme, much more quiet and lyrical than the first. Here it is, sung first by the violins and then echoed in the woodwinds (with triangle accompaniment), but in a different rhythm. The smooth lyricism of the violins is replaced here by short, staccato notes — like little raindrops. But they're outlining the same theme.

1:23   All this leads to a big buildup — a huge one, in fact. Then, at **1:28**, the main "beans, boys" theme again.

1:32   And here's the low "No-o-o-o" chord. But as soon as the chord ends, it's echoed, way up high, by quiet winds and triangle — almost as if the "No-o-o-o" is contradicted by a soft-spoken "Yes-s-s."

1:41   The argument between low and high, "No" and "Yes," becomes heated now.

1:52   The debate's not over yet. Amid a weird, minor version of "Come and get your beans" in the cellos, the violins spin furiously in their orbits. Then, against some ferocious offbeat chords in the rest of the string section, the violins sound a wild *minor key* version of that quiet and smooth *transitional* theme first heard at **0:18** — echoed by the woodwinds a few seconds later.

2:18   Now the woodwinds play the inverted version of "Come and get your beans" — and the strings, in unison, answer with the theme in its original form. Then, at **2:34**, the depths of quietude, the sounds of silence.

2:47   With a ding on the triangle, the woodwinds enter with a beautiful, innocent rendition of "Come and get your beans," and the pulse slows down, along with your own heart rate.

3:03   A beautiful horn melody, completely new and different — or is it? Actually, this theme is the same melody that you heard in the rousing brass fanfare way back at **0:09** (the one that was full of triplets). Except now, this theme appears in sheep's clothing, a lilting, relaxing melody for horn —

3:29   Only to rouse you abruptly. The theme's back in its original *triplet* brass fanfare form, an almost exact repeat of what you heard at **0:09** to **0:38**, leading to that loud, high *and* low version of the "No-o-o-o" chord and a whole mess o' "Giddy-ups."

4:16   That beautiful second theme originally heard at **0:50**. But now, instead of a quiet imitation in the woodwinds, Brahms gives us a super-loud rendition by the entire orchestra (at **4:27**), with the rhythm changed so that it consists mainly of *triplets* — thereby reminding us of that brass fanfare. (Ingenious idea, don't you think?) These triplets culminate in short, staccato notes . . . but instead of raindrops as before, we get karate chops (at **4:45**).

4:51   Now everything simmers . . . and one long crescendo leads to a low, loud rendition of "beans, boys" at **5:18**.

5:25   "Yessssss." "No-o-o-o." "Yessssss." "No-o-o-o." "Yessssss." And the ayes have it. Finally, one last brass fanfare and a boisterous, bubbling, all-around foot-stompin' good time of an ending. We can only assume that the boys did, in fact, come and get their beans.

The most amazing thing about Brahms is how all the elements of his music fit together and are intricately interrelated, even when they appear to be completely different — even in his most lighthearted works. The music of Brahms is a masterful jigsaw puzzle, put together in such a way that you see not only the pieces but the whole picture, as well.

6   Dvořák: Serenade for Strings, Fourth Movement

In the midst of this action-packed collection of musical masterpieces is an oasis of tranquility by Antonín Dvořák (1841–1904) — Bohemian-born protégé of Brahms, master of melody, and all-around nice guy. Dvořák's sunny personality radiates throughout most of his gorgeous Serenade for Strings.

When Dvořák wasn't basking in the beauty of his native land, he was feeling nostalgic for it. That feeling comes through very quietly and directly in this movement.

Although this piece has a coherent structure, we don't want to bog you down with a highly detailed analysis of it. Music like this is meant to be enjoyed with your feet up. We'll give you only the barest outline of the movement's form so that you can get your bearings while listening.

Like the movement from Handel's *Water Music,* this piece is in an expanded A-B-A structure.

0:00   This opening melody is Theme A, played by the violins. The melody seems to spin on endlessly, one beautiful idea giving birth to the next. The expressive climax of the theme comes at **1:11**; then the music quietly subsides.

At **1:31**, the cellos play the first few notes of Theme A again, echoed by the violins. A tranquil mood seems to prevail. But with a crescendo at **2:02**, Dvořák changes key and brings you into a more agitated world, beginning with an impassioned rendition of Theme A in the cellos at **2:06**.

2:49 Here, suddenly, is Theme B. With light, quick, short notes, this is the antithesis of Theme A — a little Bohemian two-step. Occasional strong accents punctuate the rhythm. At **3:07**, a high, tranquil violin melody is superimposed over this background, rising to a climax at **3:20**, and settling back into . . .

3:38 Theme A again, first in the cellos and then echoed in the violins at **4:04**.

4:45 This is the expressive climax of the movement; then, as before, the music subsides.

5:07 One last statement of the theme, winding down to nothing.

7 Tchaikovsky: Symphony No. 6, Fourth Movement

If you've read Chapter 2, you know what a horrendously difficult life Peter Tchaikovsky (1840–1893) led; nowhere does he express his frustration more passionately or accurately than in his Symphony no. 6.

When we first listened to the fourth movement of this symphony, we didn't get it. We listened to it over and over again, uncomprehending. But we were young then.

When we revisited this movement as adults, it blew us away. Something had happened to us in the meantime: *life*. Anyone who's ever loved and lost instantly understands the emotions unleashed here.

0:00 The sheet music says *Adagio lamentoso* at the top: "Slow lament." The theme is in a minor key; the outburst is the cry of a wounded soul.

This melody sounds like a *descending scale* (what you get when you play consecutive piano keys from right to left). Actually, the first and second violin sections of the orchestra *share* this melody: the first violins play the first note; the second violins play the second note; and so on. In Tchaikovsky's time, the first and second violins sat across from each other, on opposite sides of the stage (not next to each other, like today); the effect, then, was the ultimate stereo listening experience.

0:18 Quiet sobbing. But almost immediately, passion grows. Tchaikovsky takes you up and up to a mini-climax; out of it grows a long, languorous melody for flutes and bassoon, bringing us back down.

1:08 Soon we hear another outburst of the lament. And again, quiet sobbing, leading to a long solo for bassoon. This time, the music fades out to nothing.

2:22 The horns, low in their register: "Bum-bum, bum-bum, bum-bum": a heartbeat.

2:27 Now, hushed, comes the second lament — a very different kind. Unlike the first, it's in a major key. And it begins quietly and tenderly, rather than explosively. To us, it evokes tender memories of past love. Like the opening theme, this one begins with a descending scale. In fact, *many* of Tchaikovsky's best melodies begin with descending scales.

But what a descending scale this is! It goes just four notes down (the first note is repeated), plays the same four notes again, and then ends with a little yearning, rising figure. Out of these meager elements, Tchaikovsky manages to fashion the most eloquent, bittersweet theme he ever wrote.

This theme gets played four times: first at **2:27**; again at **2:57,** slightly louder, with trombones imitating the strings; even louder at **3:24;** and finally, at **3:51,** louder still. At **4:16,** it reaches a climax — *fff* or *fortississimo* ("very, very strong"), according to Tchaikovsky — as the kettledrums enter and the brass blows you away.

4:42 After a pause to collect yourself, you hear an outburst. It's the second lament, *fortissimo.* Then again, lower. And again, lower. The music sinks into the depths of powerless depression.

5:10 The will to live a little longer rises up — just long enough to lament some more — and the first lament returns.

5:30 A moment now of quiet sobbing (just as at **0:18**), this time leading to a low horn melody and a strong *crescendo* (growing) for the strings.

6:06 Again, this first lament asserts itself. But instead of the moment of sobbing, **6:27** brings more and more repetitions of this descending line, each time faster, louder, and higher. The piece is about to reach the height of passion.

6:48 At the highest point, with violins screaming, Tchaikovsky writes *fff* in the score again. The melody begins to descend in pitch, but the emotional fervor continues to rise. (You can hear the low brass instruments getting higher and higher to balance the falling melody in the strings.)

7:15   An all-out wail for the orchestra. This segment is the final outburst of emotion; then the music seems to fall back in exhaustion . . .

7:50   . . . and die. That single, hushed stroke on the tam-tam (you might need headphones to hear it) is one of the most amazing examples of restraint in all of music: a stroke of utter desolation, in which Tchaikovsky's hero releases all hope. The trombones intone a funeral incantation.

8:27   The heartbeat again, this time in the double basses. The strings intone the second lament — now in a minor key, devoid of beautiful recollections, full only of sadness.

8:59   Everything descends: the loudness of the orchestra, the line itself, and the register of the instruments that play it. A couple of final gasps, and the heart stops.

This most autobiographical of all Tchaikovsky's works is perhaps also his greatest achievement. In this symphony, known as the *Pathétique,* Tchaikovsky ingeniously depicts in musical notes the anguish that he experienced during the last months of his life. One week after this symphony's first performance, Tchaikovsky died.

8   Debussy: La Mer: Dialogue du Vent et de la Mer

In contrast to the great Romantics such as Tchaikovsky, some of the composers at the turn of the century tried to deal more with *impressions* than with emotions. Claude Debussy (1862–1918) was a master of musical Impressionism. Like the French painters Monet and Renoir, he tried to depict the mood and atmosphere of a particular time and place.

For us, Debussy's greatest masterpiece is *La Mer* (*The Sea*). In three movements, Debussy manages to re-create all the ocean's various moods in a kaleidoscopic collage of melody, tone color, and harmony. The last movement of the piece, included here, is the most exciting. The title (*Dialogue du Vent et de la Mer*) means "Dialogue of the Wind and the Sea."

Now, we want to point out that what *you* picture as you hear this music may very well differ from what *we* picture. We're sure that's exactly what Debussy wanted.

0:01   It's a cloudy, blustery day. The music begins with an extremely quiet roll on the kettledrum and bass drum. Then the cellos and basses enter with a menacing statement, which Debussy marks *Animé et tumultueux:* "Animated and tumultuous."

The menacing statement repeats. Then again, and again, and again.

0:12   A quiet note on the cymbal, and the wind enters with a distant call.

0:21   Like the beginning again: We hear the menacing statement; again, we hear the distant call, a little bit higher this time.

0:33   Quick, low, repeated notes in the cello and bass, accompanied by a crescendo: A storm is brewing. At **0:47**, a lone muted trumpet plays a warning; this call repeats more loudly and urgently.

1:05   The wind whips the sea into a frenzy of whitecaps. At **1:20**, a crash of waves, played by the cymbals. A huge note on the kettledrum. And all is momentarily quiet.

1:26   As the sea simmers in the low strings, the woodwinds play a theme. We'll call it "the woodwind theme," the first real melody.

1:53   The flute and cellos give you the second part of the theme, beginning with two quick notes, the first of which is accented. (Remember that little tune — it comes back later!) Three times, Debussy uses a technique employed by Beethoven in his time (see the section about his Fifth Symphony earlier in this chapter) — he makes a big crescendo but backs off just before the climax.

2:09   The wind suddenly whips up, creating whitecaps again.

2:28   Now we feel like we're traveling over the sea in this condition. Quick little waves rise and fall beneath us; bigger ones crash occasionally. Debussy uses a rapid rising and falling motion in the violins to evoke the little waves, and a cymbal note here and there to suggest the big ones.

Over this stormy background, this section combines two themes: a horn call with the same two-fast-notes, the-first-one-accented; and the lonely muted trumpet call from **0:47**, now played by plucked cellos.

3:04   An especially huge, climactic crash, made possible by a simultaneous entrance of the bass drum, the cymbal, the kettledrum, the trombones, and the tuba — and, as if all that weren't enough, the tam-tam a moment later.

After this crash, the music fades out as the storm blows out to sea.

3:28   A quiet, majestic melody for four horns, over a shimmering string background, evokes the awe-inspiring power of the sea. (Remember this theme, too; it comes back later in a different guise.) The phrases of this theme alternate with lazy, languid, breeze-blown violin notes.

4:00   For a moment, Debussy seems to say, "Ahhhhh. Isn't it nice to be out here on the sea?" But only for a moment . . .

4:17 Uh-oh.

4:24 Ah — false alarm. All is still calm. You hear the woodwind theme from before — or, rather, a more playful variation.

5:07 The Glockenspiel (bells) joins in the game.

5:27 The orchestra gets louder, a nonthreatening swelling. Then the entire orchestra takes up the woodwind theme, much louder than before, with a playful countermelody in the trumpets.

6:03 Something's brewing. Horns, trumpets, and plucked strings warn you; then the lone muted trumpet melody comes back, much faster and more urgently.

6:18 Themes from the past: the cello theme with the two quick notes and then the lonely trumpet melody, played this time by the flutes and oboes.

6:40 Urgency, as trembling strings grow and grow.

6:52 The whitecaps are back, and again we feel that we're traveling over water. The strings provide rhythmic wavelets, and the kettledrum beats quietly and incessantly, keeping us on edge. The entire orchestra sound grows in intensity.

7:11 And here it is — that majestic, awe-inspiring horn melody that you heard at **3:28,** now played much more strongly, with a full, round sound.

7:28 A cymbal crash underlines the power and beauty of the sea. The wind whips the ocean into a frenzy, waves crash all around, and the music washes over us in a thrilling conclusion.

9 Stravinsky: The Rite of Spring: Opening to the End of Jeu de Rapt

As you can read in Chapter 2, Stravinsky's *The Rite of Spring* had quite an effect on the audience at its premiere in 1913 — they started a riot. Part of this reaction had to do with the public's unfamiliarity, and part with the chaos and violence of the music itself.

If you've never heard this piece before, you may be taken aback, wondering what the heck is going on. But stick with this work if you can, because most music scholars consider it to be the most important piece of classical music written in the 20th century. After repeated listenings, you may very well love it. (It took us a while, too.)

If you have even an inkling that you might grow to love this kind of music, do yourself a favor and get a recording of the entire piece. It will open up a whole new world for you.

By the way, many people have recognized the dramatic possibilities of this music. Conceived as a ballet, it's been used as background music in movies. Walt Disney even devoted a substantial portion of his movie *Fantasia* to the piece.

The Rite of Spring, subtitled "Scenes of Pagan Russia," is divided into several sections. We wish that we had room to include them all. We'll whet your appetite, however, with the first three: *Introduction, Danses des adolescentes (Dances of the Adolescent Girls),* and *Jeu de rapt (Ritual of Abduction).*

Introduction

0:00   A lone bassoon, way up high, starts off the piece. Hardly any composer had written such high notes for the bassoon before; any *normal* composer would have given those notes to a higher instrument, such as the English horn.

Musicians make fun of this fact by singing the following lyrics to the melody: "I'm . . . not an English horn! I'm not an English horn! This is too *high* for me; I'm not an English horn!" But for us, the bassoon straining way up high in its throaty register suggests the first tentative cries of some prehistoric being.

0:10   Another voice enters — the horn. At **0:20**, a second phrase, and other instruments enter: clarinets and bass clarinet.

0:32   The bassoon repeats the cry, answered this time by another tentative melody — *that's* the English horn. The melodies weave as other bassoons enter.

1:16   With an entrance of plucked strings, we hear bird and other animal calls, evoking a primeval forest.

1:49   A trill in the violins, and the music seems to have grown warmer. For the first time, we begin to sense a harmonic chord being created, like an embryo. More bird calls, interrupted by the English horn's lonely melody and others for clarinet and flute.

2:26   A playful duet for oboe and alto flute; then a high clarinet enters.

2:40 An insistent pulse in the basses gives an offbeat sense of rhythm to the proceedings. All the bird calls and other calls come together now, forming a cacophony of voices. Then, suddenly, at **3:04,** all is silent except for the bassoon cry from the beginning.

3:17 Violins, plucked, telling you that something amazing is about to happen!

3:27 A hush: the calm before the storm.

Danses des adolescentes (Dances of the Adolescent Girls)

3:37 We've never heard adolescent girls sound anything like this! The string section pulses ferociously, punctuated by offbeat, unsettling, hard-to-predict accents in the horns. This is a *really* famous passage.

3:46 The English horn repeats the violin part from just before this outburst, with a bouncing, down-and-up accompaniment in the bassoons. At **3:50,** the ferocious strings are back, with wind and brass accents.

3:56 Another contrasting section, with the English horn theme from a moment ago and a few other unruly visitors (especially trumpets). Drink it in as the sound grows. At **4:13,** the ferocious strings — an exact repetition of the beginning of this section.

4:22 With this constant string motion in the background, the bassoons take over with a boisterous, scalelike melody, joined later by high oboes. Every once in a while, the ferocious strings come back up to the surface.

4:50 A sudden halt, with an ominous held note in the horns and trombones and pounded notes in the kettledrums.

4:54 The motion resumes with a squeal of the high trumpet. At **5:10,** the rhythmic motion quiets down, and a jolly horn melody takes over. The sound grows and grows and grows until the end of the section.

Jeu de rapt (Ritual of Abduction)

6:41 Suddenly the rhythmic motion of the past three minutes is gone. You're abruptly caught up in a whirlwind, a sort of prehistoric chase scene. The sound grows until . . .

7:38 . . . a climax. With beat after beat, it comes to a violent, abrupt halt. Stravinsky has broken through to modern times.

Intermission

Taking a Backstage Tour

As Chapters 4 and 5 point out, you don't need to expend much mental effort to master the art of going to a concert or listening to classical music. Now we'd like you to turn off your brain completely. Let us provide an intermission between this book's major sections so that we can take you on a little tour.

When an audience goes to a concert, it observes only what happens onstage. Little does the average spectator know that the drama backstage is just as compelling as the one onstage! On any given evening, all the members of the orchestra, the production staff, the conductor, and the guest artists are engaged in a human comedy of Shakespearean proportions.

Well, okay. Maybe not Shakespearean. But at least Dr. Seussian.

Living in the Orchestral Fishpond

An orchestra is a microcosm of the world. It's like a pond populated by every kind of fish in existence.

Orchestra members are, for the most part, good people. But as an orchestra musician, you're bound to encounter people whose life goals, philosophies, and worldviews run counter to yours. People you'd never invite to your home and who, given the choice, you'd never see again. But you *must* see them, every day of your life. And not only must you see them — you must also make beautiful music together.

To make matters worse, as an orchestra musician, you sit a foot away from four or five different people — the *same* four or five, several hours a day, every day of the week. You can't stretch out your arms without inadvertently decking a violinist, or at the very least shoving an oboe into someone's mouth.

This life in extremely close quarters resembles life in a submarine, except that, in a submarine, you've got some room to move around. Plus, of course, a submarine is underwater.

Anything can happen when players are together day after day after day. We know of shouting matches erupting, fistfights ensuing, and even — in one celebrated case — a violist throwing a chair at another.

But actually, such close quarters pose another danger — something much riskier and more hazardous.

Marriage.

What I Did for Love

In any professional orchestra, you find a few married couples. More than likely, they met while playing *in* the orchestra.

Depending on the couple, being married to someone else in the same orchestra can be wonderful, or it can be extremely difficult. Just think about it: You're together with your spouse, literally, day in and day out, every day of the year. No wonder musicians often take up other interests apart from their spouses, such as fishing, golf, or making obscene phone calls.

How about a long-distance relationship?

Of all the challenges that confront *happily* married couples within an orchestra, the greatest one concerns finding another job. Unless you have a full-time job with one of the great orchestras of the world, you're most likely constantly striving for something better. What do you do if you get a better job across the country — but your beloved spouse doesn't?

A surprising percentage of married orchestra musicians choose the long-distance solution.

Both musicians retain jobs, sometimes thousands of miles apart. The two hope that someday they can once again find positions in the same orchestra — or at least in the same time zone.

This dream isn't impossible, but it's highly difficult to achieve. And the reason is the audition process itself.

Occasionally, a married couple within an orchestra decides to split up. This situation causes yet a new set of difficulties that we bet you never considered. Orchestra jobs are extremely rare and hard to get, and just because you're no longer married to the person who shares your music stand is no reason to give up your job. Can you imagine splitting up with a former loved one and then sitting next to him for five hours a day, for the rest of your life? We're pretty sure Dante wrote a long poem about this.

Going through an Audition

The music students graduating from conservatories each year have a higher and higher level of ability. The advantages for orchestras and audiences are obvious, but these talented, well-educated musicians face a formidable job shortage.

Whenever an orchestra announces a vacancy, the number of applications is enormous. Winning an audition is like winning the lottery (except that if you win the lottery, you get rich).

An almost-true story

To show you how the audition process works, we're going to tell you the story of a friend of ours, who plays the flute like a dream. We'll call her Sally (although her real name is Heather Witherspoon, 13 East Broad Street, Plano, TX, 75012; phone 214-364-9287; e-mail embouchure@wind.com; Twitter: @ blowsnotesalot).

"Sally" originally moved to Plano because her ex-husband, "Jerry" (a flutist who gave up music for a career in computer management information systems), got a job there when they were first married. Since the divorce, she's been playing flute part-time for the Plano Pluckers (not their real name), a small orchestra, and teaching students on the side at $25 per half-hour. But she'd always wanted to play in a large symphony orchestra, and she had what it takes: flawless intonation, a beautiful tone, and amazing chops.

Chops, by the way, refers to technique: In musicians' jargon, *great chops* means incredible technical skill. (What did you think, anyway?)

Sally was (and still is) a member of her local musicians' union, and as a member she receives a publication called *International Musician.* Every month professional musicians looking for work eagerly await this periodical, published by the American Federation of Musicians. The back pages of each issue are crowded with job announcements from orchestras all around the world. When the new issue arrived, the following ad caught her eye:

THE LOS ANGLICAN PHILHARMONIA
Marvin Taylor-Thomas, Artistic Director
announces the following opening:

PRINCIPAL FLUTE

Preliminary auditions will be held in Los Anglican on June 24 and 25, with semifinal auditions on June 26 and final auditions on June 27.

The Audition Committee reserves the right to dismiss immediately any candidate not meeting the highest professional standards at these auditions. Highly qualified candidates please send a one-page typed resume, including current address and telephone number, to:

Los Anglican Philharmonia
Attn.: Audition Manager
355 Philharmonia Hall
Los Anglican, USA

Audition information will not be provided over the phone.

Source: Creative Commons

The fact that the principal flute position in this great orchestra was open could mean only one thing: The current principal flutist had died in a freak accident. No principal flutist anywhere in the world ever gives up a position like this one.

Rigged auditions

Before applying, Sally made a phone call to her friend Rita, a violinist she'd known for years. Rita had a job as section violinist in the Los Anglican Philharmonia, and she knew the inner workings of the orchestra.

Sally asked Rita a very important question: "Is this audition rigged?"

Some orchestras do, in fact, rig their auditions. The rules require them to hold a national open audition, but at the same time they already know who they want. This lucky person may be someone who's been playing part-time with the orchestra for years, a superstar from another orchestra who's expressed a desire to move, or maybe even the wife or husband of somebody already in the orchestra. No orchestra ever admits to rigging its auditions, and rigging is very difficult to prove, but it does occasionally happen.

No, Rita said; as far as she knew, the audition was not rigged. The orchestra had nobody in particular in mind. Sally wrote to the orchestra's personnel manager, expressing her desire to audition.

The list

Ten days later, Sally received a letter confirming her candidacy. Along with the letter was a list of 16 flute excerpts that she may be asked to play at the audition. These excerpts included Mozart's G major Flute Concerto and some of the most famous flute solos in the orchestral literature: such pieces as Debussy's *Afternoon of a Faun,* Mendelssohn's *Midsummer Night's Dream,* Brahms's Symphony no. 4, Beethoven's *Leonore Overture no. 3,* and Ravel's *Daphnis and Chloé.*

Sally was not surprised to see these excerpts on the list. They'd been on the list for nearly every audition she'd gone to in the past. Orchestras want players who can handle the most difficult music in existence; musicians, therefore, spend a great part of their lives practicing these passages over and over again.

Although Sally could well guess what *portions* of each work would be asked for at the audition, these sections weren't mentioned on the list. In all, Sally spent four weeks intensively relearning *nine hours' worth* of music for an audition that would probably run shorter than ten minutes.

Sally decided to reserve a hotel room. At her last audition (for a smaller orchestra in New Jersey), she'd stayed with friends, and this decision had been a mistake. With two kids, two dogs, and an iguana in the house, she'd found it impossible to concentrate. She hadn't advanced beyond the preliminaries. This time, the audition was too important to blow for such a reason.

The prescription

Three days before getting on the plane, Sally had an appointment with her doctor, Ellen Smyles. Dr. Smyles was an amateur flutist herself, and Sally had always appreciated her understanding of a musician's life. Dr. Smyles gave Sally the usual prescription for Inderal, 10 mg. tablets, because her old prescription had already expired.

Inderal is the brand name for *propranolol,* a mild, non-habit-forming drug known as a beta blocker. Among other things, beta blockers prevent the heart from beating too quickly. After musicians take beta blockers, they may still be very nervous, but their hearts don't pound and their hands don't shake.

(If you opened a Beta Blokerz 'R' Us store just outside any international orchestra audition, you'd make a killing.)

Playing the odds

Sally flew to Los Anglican a day before her audition, checked into her hotel, and requested a quiet room on a high floor. She spent the entire day in her room practicing the audition excerpts. By the end of the day, she felt calm and happy about her playing. After a quick bite to eat and an hour of mindless television, she went to bed.

The next morning, after a long warm-up in her hotel room, she showed up at Philharmonia Hall at the appointed time: 9 a.m. Fifty other flutists were already there; she knew that probably 150 others would arrive before the auditions were over. She was ushered into a large warm-up room filled with other flutists, many of whom were old friends of hers, all busily practicing the same music she'd learned for the audition.

Sally looked at the schedule and saw that her audition time wasn't until 2:54 p.m. The flutist before her was assigned to play at 2:48 p.m.; the one after her was playing at 3 p.m. Sally realized that her audition would last only six minutes!

She decided not to hang around the concert hall for the nearly six hours before her turn. As she headed back to the hotel to relax, she added up some figures in her mind. So far, the total cost of her trip, including airplane fare, ground transportation, hotel, and meals, had come to $986.52. Nearly $1,000 for a six-minute audition! Sally felt nervous.

One idea, strangely, comforted her. As much as she was spending for this audition, almost everybody else was spending more. Coming from Plano, Texas, Sally hadn't traveled all that far. She knew that, for a job such as this one, flutists had come from all around the world — including Switzerland, England, and Australia.

That thought made her nervous all over again.

An unexpected meeting

In the hotel lobby, the elevator door opened. A person she knew walked out. His face was strangely familiar. Sally's mind was a blur now. How did she know this man? She'd definitely seen him before. . . .

Then, suddenly, she remembered. It was her ex-husband, Jerry!

"Jerry! Oh, my gosh!" she exclaimed. They embraced awkwardly. "Did you travel all this distance just to wish me luck in my flute audition?"

"Well, actually, no," he replied sheepishly. "I decided to audition, too."

Her jaw dropped. "What? But you gave up professional flute playing! You've had a computer job for three years now!"

"Yes," he replied, "but no way I can pass up an opportunity like the Los Anglican Philharmonia. It's a real longshot, but I have nothing to lose."

Sally didn't know what to think. She felt pangs of longing for Jerry — tender, passionate memories of their past romance. And yet, at the same time, she realized what a great flutist he was, and how tough it would be to beat him.

The return

At two, she caught a cab back to Philharmonia Hall and entered the warm-up room to wait. The clock seemed to tick in slow motion. A couple other flutists, also visibly nervous, tried to strike up a conversation, but trailed off in mid-sentence. Their minds were onstage.

At 2:49, one of the other flutists, loudly professing a need to use the facilities, hurriedly left the room.

At 2:50, another flutist entered the room, clutching a beautiful golden flute. He angrily snatched up his flute case and disappeared out the door.

At 2:51, nothing in particular happened.

At 2:52, a smiling young man came into the room and called Sally's name. She took a deep breath and stood, gathered her flute, her piccolo, and her music, and followed the young man out the door.

The hallway was long, dark, and serpentine, like a maze. She felt as if she were being led down death row to her execution. Worse, she had to climb two flights of stairs, which raised her pulse and made her slightly short of breath.

At exactly 2:54 p.m., they reached the end of the hallway. Looming in front of them were two large, heavy doors. Sally knew that the doors led onto the stage of Los Anglican Philharmonia Hall. She'd been in the hall before, in the front row of the balcony, listening to a concert of her favorite flutist. And now, she was about to tread upon the very same stage. . . .

Onstage

The smiling young man, bracing with all his force, swung the mighty doors open. Sally was blinded at first by the burst of brilliant light onstage. She felt as if a thousand flashbulbs had gone off at once.

Sally walked to the center of the stage, where a lone music stand stood like a . . . well, like a music stand. "Now remember," the young man was saying, "don't say a word. The audition committee is behind a screen. Nobody knows who you are. Play well!" And he was gone.

The purpose of the screen is to eliminate in advance any charges of discrimination or favoritism — to ensure that the *music* is the sole basis of the committee's judgment. Sometimes the screen is onstage, in front of the player. Sometimes it's out in the audience, in front of the audition committee.

Beside her was another man, balding with spectacles. He was the monitor. Because Sally wasn't allowed to speak to the committee, his job was to make sure that she had everything she needed. If she had any questions, all she needed to do was whisper them to him, and he would relay them to the committee.

Behind the screen

Suddenly, she heard a voice. "Good afternoon. Let's start with *Afternoon of a Faun,* please." The voice came from up in the first balcony. Sally strained her eyes to see. There it was — the screen. It was a large, portable, self-standing curtain rod with black curtains.

Behind the screen, the audition committee didn't know Sally's race, sex, age, or anything else about her. To them, she was Number 48. And to them, Number 48 had better hurry up and play, because they were very tired and very hungry, and after Number 48, they had only two more flutists to hear before the much-desired break that dangled before them like sweet ambrosia.

"*Afternoon of a Faun,* please," the voice repeated wearily, for the 49th time that day.

Sally spread her music out on the music stand and exhaled slowly. This was it. A lifetime of sacrifice and preparation, four long weeks of intensive practice, and $986.52 . . . and it all came down to this moment.

She lifted the flute to her lips, took a deep breath, and began to play. The opening notes of Debussy's *Afternoon of a Faun,* that sensuous chromatic descent over an augmented fourth, that suave yet shocking entrée into the Impressionistic movement of music, emanated from her flute. It was so beautiful! The sound was warm, rich, and full of imagination and sensuality. Was this really her?

She felt her fears subside, and she began to pour all her life, experience, and passion into the music. She played Debussy's music as Debussy himself had imagined it.

After what seemed like no time at all, the voice stopped her. "Brahms' Symphony no. 4, last movement, measure 97, please."

Ah — measure 97! This was the excerpt Sally had hoped for. She played it tenderly, peacefully at first, and then with increasing passion as the phrase rose to its zenith. She thought that she'd never before hit the high F-sharp with such a perfect combination of intensity and silken beauty of tone.

The voice asked for more excerpts, one after the other. She played each one with more confidence, always spurred on by the beautiful sound of her own flute.

The only mistake she made was a single slip-up in the scherzo movement from Mendelssohn's *Midsummer Night's Dream*. It was a small mistake, a trifle, really — and she'd never made that mistake before. It was in one of the easier passages that she hadn't worried about. All the more difficult passages went very well.

Finally, the six minutes were finished. They'd felt like six seconds. "Thank you," said the voice. That was it. She lowered her instrument, gathered up her music, and walked offstage. The smiling young man waited beyond the heavy doors. "Nice job," he said. They walked wordlessly back to the warm-up room.

Sally smiled. It was the best audition she'd ever played.

The wait

Back in the warm-up room, Sally looked around. The room was empty now. Except for Jerry.

As if on cue, the smiling young man entered the room and called Jerry's name. "See you later," Jerry said, winked, and followed the man out.

A few minutes later, Jerry returned. "It went great!" he exclaimed — and before he could stop himself, he gave Sally a peck on the cheek.

"It was good for me, too," Sally said.

But the most difficult part was yet to come. That was the waiting period. The preliminaries were nearly over, and shortly after that, the audition committee would decide who from Sally's group would advance to the semifinals. The warm-up room slowly filled with people, chattering idly, every so often glancing sideways at the door.

A little after 6 p.m., the smiling young man appeared in the doorway. He wasn't smiling. All heads turned in his direction. He held a single sheet of paper.

He cleared his throat. "Well, I want to thank each and every one of you for the time, money, and energy you've spent to be with us today. Everyone was terrifically talented, and you should all be very proud of what you've achieved. Semi-finals begin tomorrow, Wednesday, at 9 a.m. From this group, we've advanced one flutist to the semi-finals."

He mentioned Jerry's name and slipped out of the room.

Jerry broke into a broad grin. "Hey," he whispered sheepishly. "I made it!"

Tears welled in Sally's eyes, but she kept them back. "It was the Mendelssohn," she said softly. "I missed one note in the Mendelssohn."

"Oh, don't be so hard on yourself," Jerry replied. "They don't eliminate you for one note."

"I think they did," said Sally.

The aftermath

We wish we could have told you that Sally won her audition, but she didn't. Besides, if she had won, we wouldn't have accomplished our purpose of showing you a *typical* audition experience.

Anyway, Jerry didn't get the job either. He missed a note in the semifinals.

"So who won the principal flute job?" Sally asked him later.

"Some guy from Australia. None of us had even heard of him before. He just walked in and blew the competition away."

This tale, alas, is the sad story of Sally and Jerry — and *many* other orchestral musicians we know.

But for Sally, the experience wasn't a total loss. Jerry called her after the audition and soon began visiting her every few weeks. Gradually, Sally and Jerry began to rediscover the love they once had. They got remarried six months later atop the Skyline Bungalows, overlooking the crashing surf of California's Highway 1.

The Life of an Orchestra Musician, or What's Going on in the Practice Room?

Many people have the impression that an orchestra is just a happy band of people, just passing the time playing music for their own pleasure. People imagine that they never take off their tailcoats and long black dresses, even for a moment. Why would they want to?

True, music *is* an incredible joy. And true, some people never do take off their long black dresses, which presents difficulties only while playing racquet sports. But an orchestra job — like any other job — can be incredibly intense. The stresses of a hectic work schedule sometimes diminish the pleasure that musicians take in daily intimate contact with the greatest of all arts.

In a professional orchestra, the musicians' rehearsal and performance schedules are rarely, if ever, regular. The players don't even necessarily get a set day of the week off. As for Saturday night — forget it! While the rest of the world is playing, musicians are *playing*.

A typical orchestra schedule consists of seven to nine rehearsals and concerts per week. Most rehearsals are two and a half hours long. Every orchestra member is required to be onstage five to ten minutes before the rehearsal begins. If a musician is late, she may receive a warning, or she may even have some money taken out of her paycheck.

To compensate for this strict starting time, orchestra rehearsals have equally strict stopping times. As soon as the clock says that the two and a half hours are up — even if the orchestra is still in the middle of a piece, in the middle of a phrase, or even *in the middle of a note,* the rehearsal ends. If the conductor decides (usually with the approval of the management) to continue rehearsing after the official rehearsal has ended, the musicians receive overtime pay.

But rehearsals are just the tip of the iceberg, compared to time spent in the practice room. Professional musicians have an incredible amount of music to learn. In a typical week, an orchestra plays up to four completely different concert programs. That's up to six hours' worth of music to master in a single week.

As you may expect, all this playing and practicing brings about certain occupational hazards: Tendonitis and bursitis are pretty common in the orchestras of the world. You also occasionally find what the Germans call *Hodenentzündung;* let's just say that it's a very special ailment unique to male cello players.

Selling the Product

But the musicians are only the *onstage* component of your local orchestra; the *offstage* personnel are also important. For example, if you've been to a symphony orchestra concert recently, chances are high that the *marketing director* got you there. Responsible for all paid advertising, the marketing director is always trying to find creative new ways of bringing the orchestra to the attention of the public.

Say that the orchestra is about to perform a concert of music by the Russian composer Sergei Rachmaninoff (1873–1943), including Piano Concerto no. 2 and Symphony no. 2. With an older, more established orchestra, you may see the following advertisement:

THE BEAUX ARTS PHILHARMONIC
Maximillian Goo, Music Director

Friday, November 3, 2006, 8:00 p.m.

Saturday, November 4, 2006, 8:00 p.m.

Sunday, November 5, 2006, 3:00 p.m.

Vivian Wedge, Piano

Rachmaninoff: Piano Concerto no. 2 in C minor, opus 18
Rachmaninoff: Symphony no. 2 in E minor, opus 27

On the other hand, with an orchestra that's trying to win a younger, more with-it audience, you may see this kind of ad:

GET
    YOUR
        RACHMANIN-
            OFF!!!
at the LONG BAY SYMPHONY
Friday and Saturday at 8, Sunday at 3
Be there and be square!

In a smaller organization, the marketing director is also the public relations director, responsible for all *unpaid* advertising (that is, information that gets published in the newspaper, on the radio, and on television without a charge). Her goal is to get as much positive publicity for the orchestra as possible. To this end, she works the law of averages, constantly sending out news releases — information about *everything* — in the hope that *someone, somewhere,* finds the information interesting enough to publish:

FOR IMMEDIATE RELEASE

Contact: Cathy Sandow
           Farfalloo Symphony
           Farfalloo, WY 34876

Farfalloo Symphony Gets New Sound Shields

The Farfalloo Symphony Orchestra has announced the acquisition of new sound shields for its players.

Sound shields are clear, hard plastic barriers that are placed on the stage directly in front of the loudest instruments of the orchestra. They protect the hearing of musicians who sit directly in front of these instruments.

"We're extremely grateful for these sound shields," said Anthony DeMare, general manager of the Farfalloo Symphony. "We now have a way to protect the ears of our musicians from the extremely high volume of sound they come into contact with onstage on a daily basis. This represents the beginning of a new era for us."

Polly Platelett, chairperson of the Farfalloo Symphony Orchestra Committee, echoed that sentiment. "We musicians have been asking for these sound shields for years," she said. "They would probably have been a stipulation in our next contract, but we're very happy to have them sooner. The musicians are ecstatic."

Farfalloo's mayor, John Thompkins, was equally complimentary. "All of Farfalloo is going to benefit from these sound shields," he said. "Today is a proud day for our great city. I hereby declare this day Honorary Sound Shield Day."

A parade in honor of the sound shields will be held tomorrow at noon, beginning in the Farfalloo town square and continuing past the Farfalloo Sausage Factory, ending at Robert Louis Stevenson Elementary School Cafetorium, home to the Farfalloo Symphony's *Masterworks Plus!* Concert Series.

The sound shields are a gift from Mrs. Consuelo Grossman of 42 Pennytree Lane. They are the third generous gift from Mrs. Grossman since her husband died in a threshing accident last fall.

In honor of her husband, the shields are being named The Alberto Z. Grossman Memorial Sound Shields.

"Alberto always hated loud noises," laughed Mrs. Grossman. "The fact that he's saving the ears of his beloved musicians would just tickle him to death — whoops!"

Understanding Contract Riders

For many members of the audience, the most exciting part of a concert is the guest artist, who is often a world-famous virtuoso. Guest artists' agents take advantage of this fact by charging exorbitant sums for their clients' services.

It's not unusual for a guest artist of international stature to make between $50,000 and $100,000 for one performance, as you can read in Chapter 3. To the management of an orchestra, the fee is worth it. The organization can make that amount back in ticket sales, subscriptions, and prestige.

But some guest artists have become so used to getting their way that they simply refuse to perform if they don't. So they add a new and bizarre wrinkle to the backstage life at a concert, in the form of contract riders.

A *contract rider,* which gets attached to the regular terms of an artist's contract, can range from a single sentence to more than 20 pages. It's nothing but demands — sometimes incredible demands — that *must* be met if the orchestra or presenting organization wants to showcase that artist:

- ✔ "Miss J. shall be picked up at her hotel in a limousine that is either blue, black, or dark green (at the discretion of the management), but absolutely not tan or white."

- ✔ "Enclosed is a sample of the color (peanut butter khaki) that Mr. Q's dressing room is to be painted. The dressing room must also be carpeted to a thickness of between ⅝ and ¾ inch (also in peanut butter khaki), must be at least 14 feet by 24 feet but smaller than 26 feet by 30 feet, air conditioned, humidified, and completely soundproofed."

- ✔ "The backstage staff is to refrain from engaging in gratuitous conversation with Miss N."

- ✔ "Mrs. R. consents to sign up to ten (10) autographs immediately following the concert; after this time the staff is instructed to remove all well-wishers."

- ✔ "The dressing room shall be supplied with two (2) roast turkeys, one (1) hour before the performance."

- ✔ "A large bowl of M&Ms must be provided, *with the green ones removed!* No exceptions to this requirement will be tolerated."

The amazing thing about these ludicrous examples is that they're *real!* Those examples are based on actual demands made by actual classical music divas.

Eyeing the Strange and Perilous Relationship between an Orchestra and Its Conductor

Conductors have an enormous amount of power over the lives of the musicians with whom they work — at least within the confines of the concert hall. A good conductor has the ability to make an orchestra feel inspired, proud, and thrilled to be making music.

As conductors ourselves, we realize how difficult that job is. It's impossible to please all the people, all the time; we're constantly in the position of pleasing some and displeasing others simultaneously.

But some conductors seem to displease *all* the people *all* the time; they, too, have a great deal of power over the lives of their musicians. They're the conductors with egos to burn, who place their own glory ahead of the music. Orchestras often have no recourse but to create their dream recipes in revenge, as demonstrated in the following example (which we found being passed around the Internet by classical musicians).

How to Cook a Conductor

Ingredients	Directions
One large conductor or two small assistant conductors	*1* Catch a conductor. Remove the tail and horns. Carefully separate the large ego and reserve for sauce. Remove any batons, pencils, and long articulations and discard. Remove the hearing aid and discard (it never worked anyway). Clean the conductor as you would squid, but do not separate the tentacles from the body. If you have an older conductor, such as one from a major orchestra or summer music festival, you may want to tenderize by pounding the conductor on a rock with timpani mallets or by smashing the conductor repeatedly between two large cymbals.
Ketchup	
2 large cloves garlic	
Solid vegetable shortening (lard may be used)	
1 cask cheap wine	
1 lb. alfalfa sprouts	
2 lbs. assorted yuppie food, such as tofu or yogurt	*2* Pour half the cask of wine into a bathtub and soak the conductor in the wine for at least 12 hours. (*Exceptions:* American and German conductors often have a beery taste, which some people like; the wine may interfere with this flavor. Use your judgment.) After the conductor is sufficiently soaked, remove any clothes the conductor may be wearing and rub it all over with the garlic. Then cover with vegetable shortening, using vague, slow, circular motions and taking care to cover every inch of the conductor's body with the shortening.
	3 Find an orchestra. Put as much music out as the stands can hold without falling over, and make sure that there are lots and lots of really loud passages for everyone. Big loud chords for the winds and brass, and lots and lots of tremolos for the strings. Rehearse these passages several times; this should ensure adequate flames for cooking your conductor. If not, insist on taking every possible repeat, especially the second repeats in really big symphonies!

4 After the flames have died down to a medium inferno, place your conductor on top of your orchestra (they won't mind; they're used to it) until it's well tanned and the hair turns back to its natural color. Be careful not to overcook or the conductor could end up tasting like stuffed ham. Make a sauce by combining the ego, sprouts, and ketchup to taste, placing it all in the blender and pureeing until smooth. Slice your conductor as you would any other turkey and serve accompanied by the assorted yuppie food and the remaining wine.

Why an Orchestra Career Is Worth the Grief

So why do musicians, guest artists, and conductors do what they do? With all the grief they face, day after day, why is it all worth it?

It's worth it for those rare moments when everything comes together, when the orchestra is galvanized, joined at the nervous system, and plays gorgeously as one. The cause of such a moment could be an acoustically perfect hall; the perfect temperature, humidity, and barometric pressure; an especially responsive audience; an inspired conductor; a special piece of music with great depth and passion; a special event; a beautifully played first note — or just a shared understanding among the players that *tonight, it's going to be unbelievably good.*

And deep down, musicians really do love their work. Scratch the surface of the most jaded professional, and you'll find the enthusiastic conservatory student who lives for her art.

Part III
A Field Guide to the Orchestra

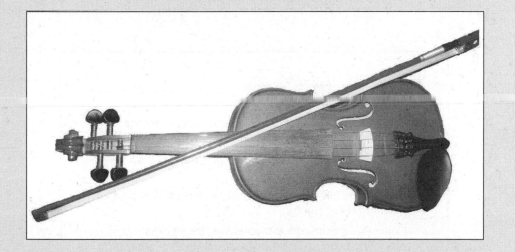

Check out www.dummies.com/extras/classicalmusic for an inside look at what it takes to send an orchestra on tour.

In this part . . .

✔ Meet the five families of instruments: keyboards, strings, woodwinds, brass, and percussion.

✔ Peek inside a piano and get to know how it works (both the white keys and the black keys).

✔ Discover the basics of violin technique and how they apply to the entire string family.

✔ Explore the arcane craft of reed-making, the art of harp pedaling, one way to wash a trumpet, and even the words of *Moby Dick*! Read on to find out how even a whale of a story relates to classical music.

Chapter 6

Keyboards & Co.

In your everyday life, you're more likely to see keyboards than any other instrument. Keyboards, in fact, are everywhere.

The big church down the street has an organ. Your neighbor's kid has a synthesizer (and some whopping big speakers, too, we're guessing). The strange lady with all the cats who keeps all the shutters drawn in her rickety old house overgrown with weeds on the hill has a harpsichord. And somebody on your block has a piano.

The Piano

The best way to find out about the most common of all keyboards, the piano, is to experience one firsthand. Maybe you have one, but if not, don't worry — your neighbor does. Your neighbor is a very interesting person, and despite the flamingo on the front lawn, he's a person of refinement and discrimination. Hence the piano. This is your perfect opportunity to see how it works.

Looking inside the piano

Next chance you get, check out your neighbor's piano. Either ask to see it or just sneak inside the house while he's cutting his grass.

You'll notice several things about your basic piano. First, it has 88 keys. To use the technical musical terminology, the white keys are called *the white keys*, and the black ones are called *the black keys*. Think you can handle this?

Of course, some cognoscenti refer to the white notes as *natural* notes and the black keys as *sharps* and *flats* — but you don't really need to know that.

Now touch the lowest key (far left) on your neighbor's piano. The piano is finely crafted to be exceedingly touch-sensitive, with an astonishing *dynamic range*. That means that, if you caress the key very lightly, you produce a tender, sweet, quiet sound, whereas if you slam it with a sledgehammer, you destroy the piano.

From this lowest note, play the next white note. And the next. Keep touching white notes, from left to right. This process is called *going up the scale*. Now, the notes that you're playing aren't anonymous. From the earliest days of music, composers needed to name the different notes. Doing so was the only way they could write down music to have it reproduced later.

Naming the notes

The lowest note, way over on the left side of the keyboard, was designated, with great originality, letter *A*. The next white key is called *B*. And then *C, D, E, F,* and *G,* as you'd expect. And then comes . . . what? *H?* Nope. Look at the keyboard with all the letter names (see Figure 6-1).

Holy cow, it's not H at all. It's A again.

Figure 6-1:
The notes
of the piano
keyboard.

A B C D E F G A

Source: Creative Commons

Finding an octave

Notice that the whole sequence of notes repeats, from A through G, over and over. The reason is simple, actually. All the notes called A are actually the same note, although each one is successively higher than the last.

Is this possible? Imagine that you're at a Little League baseball game, and everybody is singing "The Star-Spangled Banner" in unison — men, women, and little Beaver mascots, all singing the same notes at the same time. But on any given note, the men are singing a lower version of it, the women are singing a higher version of it, and the children and Beaver mascots, perhaps, are singing an even higher version.

On the piano keyboard, the same thing happens. All the notes called A are the same note — but they're sung with higher and higher voices. Or, as we say in the music biz, they're in different *octaves.* Men, women, and children can all sing the note A — but women generally sing it in a higher octave than men do.

What does *octave* mean, exactly? An octave is the distance between one A and the next, or the distance between one B and the next . . . and so on. If you count from one A to the next (counting both A notes), you count *eight* white notes — thus the word *octave,* which contains the same prefix as *octagon* (eight sides), *octopus* (eight arms), and *octometrist* (an eight-eyed doctor).

Playing the black keys

Have you noticed that the pattern of black keys on the piano keyboard repeats over and over in little groups of two and three? Most pianists use these patterns of black keys as landmarks to figure out where they are on the keyboard. Without the black keys as markers, hitting the key you wanted amid a confusing sea of white would be almost impossible.

The main purpose of a black key, however, is to play a note that's halfway between one white key and the next. Say you want a note that's higher than an A but not quite as high as a B. Then you play the black key between them.

This black key has two names. You can call it *A-sharp* because it's slightly higher (or *sharper*) than A. Or you can call it *B-flat* because it's slightly lower (or *flatter*) than B. For our purposes, A-sharp and B-flat are exactly the same note.

Looking inside the piano

At this point, you may want to determine whether you're dealing with a *grand piano* or an *upright piano*. The distinction is that, if you can lie down inside it, it's a grand piano. (If you can lie down inside it only by curling up into a fetal position, you could be dealing with a *baby grand.*) Check out Figure 6-2 if you're still not sure of the difference between a grand piano and an upright piano.

Now may be a good time to point out that you should never *actually* lie down inside your piano. (As for your *neighbor's* piano, get permission first.)

As you see in Figure 6-2, the lid of a grand piano can be propped open with a stick. This stick is built in and always comes with a grand piano. (Don't ever let a piano dealer talk you into buying a stick as optional equipment. It's standard.)

The sound of a piano comes from inside, so the higher you keep the lid open, the louder and fuller the sound is. In a concert hall, you probably need the stick. And if you want to open the lid just a little bit, but not all the way, you can use the attached short stick (known to musicians as *the short stick*), also standard equipment.

Under the lid are zillions of metal wires, all stretched tightly and secured with pegs. There are actually two or three of these *piano strings* for *each* of the 88 keys on the piano. The force of all these strings pulling at once is so great that the piano frame has to be made of an extremely sturdy iron so that the whole instrument doesn't just fold up violently and implode in the middle of a prelude.

If you turn the pegs, you can make the strings tighter or looser, thus making the notes they produce higher or lower, respectively — that is, *tuning* the piano. (Musicians since the time of Beethoven have been fond of saying, "You can tune a piano, but you can't tuna fish.") And if you press a key, you launch a little felt hammer that hits a string, causing it to vibrate.

Pressing down the pedals

Most pianos have at least two *pedals*. The one on the right is called *the pedal* (or sustain pedal); if you push it down with your right foot while you play, notes continue to ring even after you take your finger off the key. (Without the pedal, each note stops as soon as you stop pressing its key.)

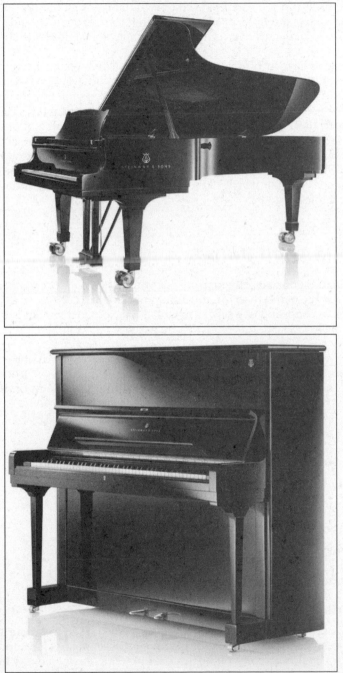

Figure 6-2:
A grand
piano (top)
and an
upright
piano.

The left one is the *soft pedal.* The soft pedal dampens all but one of the strings used for each piano note, producing a softer, less resonant sound. The soft pedal is also known as *una corda,* which is fancy Italian for "one string."

Some pianos have a third pedal in the middle. Why? Well, say you want to bring out just one note of the music, over all the others. Here's what you do: Play that note and simultaneously hold the middle pedal down with your foot. Now you can let go of that key, and the piano still sustains that note. If you keep the middle pedal down and start to play a bunch of other notes, they disappear as soon as they're played, but the note you pressed first keeps ringing until it dies away naturally. If you have trouble *reading* that complex business, try *doing* it at 100 beats per minute in front of a crowd. You can see, in other words, why some piano manufacturers today no longer provide a middle pedal.

Hearing the piano

If the piano is your favorite instrument, you're in luck: More concertos are written for the piano than for any other instrument. (*Concertos,* as you can discover in Chapter 3, are pieces in which one solo instrument is the main attraction.)

In fact, if you go online to www.dummies.com/go/classicalmusic, you can hear a stunningly beautiful example on Track 3: the finale from Mozart's Piano Concerto no. 22. Here Mozart shows off the capabilities of this beauty of an instrument. Check it out.

Here are some more of our favorite piano concertos:

- **Ludwig van Beethoven:** Piano Concertos no. 4 and 5
- **Johannes Brahms:** Piano Concerto no. 2
- **Frédéric Chopin:** Piano Concerto no. 2
- **Sergei Rachmaninoff:** Piano Concerto no. 3
- **George Gershwin:** Piano Concerto in F

And here are some of the most beautiful solo piano pieces:

- **Bach:** *The Well-Tempered Clavier*

  This set of 48 preludes and 48 fugues is considered to be the "ancestor" of many of today's pieces for piano. Many composers have found inspiration in this attempt on Bach's part to write music in every key, major and minor.

- **Beethoven:** Piano Sonata no. 14 (*Moonlight Sonata*)

▶ **Chopin:** Preludes, opus 28

▶ **Gershwin:** *Three Preludes*

By the master of jazz, a set of three pieces for piano, whose title is influenced by Bach's preludes.

▶ **Wolfgang Amadeus Mozart:** Piano Sonata in C major, K. 545

(The K in this title refers to Ludwig Ritter von Köchel, the man who catalogued Mozart's works.)

The Harpsichord

Not all keyboard instruments are touch-sensitive like the piano. Your basic cheapo portable $75 electronic keyboard isn't, for example. Nor was the piano's predecessor, the *harpsichord*. On this keyboard, every note comes out at a medium volume, no matter how hard you hit the key.

Poetry Corner: Haiku

pity harpsichord
no touch sensitivity
every note the same

Here's why it's worth getting to know the harpsichord.

Winning the Baroque gold medal

The harpsichord (see Figure 6-3) was the number-one keyboard instrument for music of the Baroque and early Classical periods (see Chapter 2), and you still often hear it played in music from those periods. A lot of the music of such great composers as Bach, Handel, and Vivaldi would be difficult to perform without it. It's the veritable gold medalist of the Baroque Olympics.

Instead of sounding mellow or rich as a piano sounds, a harpsichord sounds — well, tinkly, twangy, or sometimes even crunchy. And for good reason: In a harpsichord, the strings are not *hammered,* but *plucked.*

Poetry Corner: Limerick

There once was a man from Nantuck't
Who ordered his harpsichord chucked.
When asked why he canned it,
He cried, "I can't stand it!
The strings are not hammered, but plucked!"

Source: © Dorling Kindersley/Getty Images

Figure 6-3:
A harpsi-
chord with
a double
keyboard.

Whereas the piano has very soft felt hammers to touch the strings, producing a variety of sounds, the harpsichord has little hooks (known as *plectra*) that rest near the strings. If you press a harpsichord key, the corresponding hook (or *plectrum*) reaches over and plucks the appropriate string, like a fingernail twanging an archery bow.

Hearing the harpsichord

If you listen to Track 2 of the examples available at www.dummies.com/go/classicalmusic, you can hear a prelude and fugue by Bach, played on the harpsichord.

If you particularly love the harpsichord, here are some more pieces you simply must hear:

- **Bach:** Concerto in D Minor for Harpsichord and String Orchestra

- **François Couperin:** *Les barricades mystérieuses*

- **George Frideric Handel:** Suite in E major, G 145-148 (includes delightful variations on "The Harmonious Blacksmith")

- **Domenico Scarlatti:** 550 sonatas (They're all great. Take your pick.)

The Organ

You hear the *pipe organ* (see Figure 6-4) at every wedding (and simulated at every baseball game) you attend. Pipe organs have a varying number of pipes, ranging from dozens to thousands. The largest organs in the world have enough pipes to fill several walls of a cathedral. The pipes, of all different shapes and sizes, make different kinds of sounds as air passes through them, imitating anything from a trumpet to an oboe to a flute.

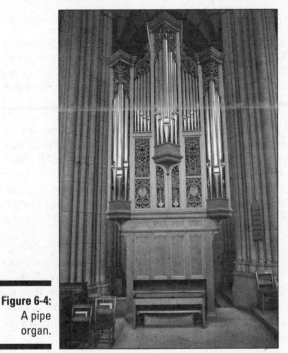

Figure 6-4:
A pipe
organ.

© iStock.com/ Aiselin82

Inside the organ is an air pump. Nowadays, the pump's run electrically — a motor ensures that a constant flow of air is available to the organ. But in the old days, the pump was run by a couple of teenagers, hired to jump up and down on the bellows while the organ was playing. If the teenagers ran out of steam, so did the organ, and the volume or pitch of the music suffered.

Today's organ plays well even without the help of teenagers. Here's how it works.

Pulling out the stops

For each note the organ can play, it has anywhere from one to a hundred different pipes. Each plays a slightly different sound: a trumpet sound, a string sound, and so on. If you, the organist, want to hear one of these sounds, you pull out a little knob (called a *stop*) on the console of your organ, near the keyboard. The console of a really big organ is an awe-inspiring thing; it looks like a cross between an airplane cockpit and a pinball machine. Pulling out a stop for a certain kind of pipe lets air from the pump flow into that pipe, allowing it to sound. If you push the stop back in, the air supply to that pipe is cut off.

But the fun is just beginning! The organ isn't limited to one stop at a time; you can choose as many stops as you please. If you want a sound of strings, trumpet, and oboe on the note A, pull out those three stops. And if you want a seriously hair-blowing blast of sound, you pull out *all* the stops. (Thus the phrase "He pulled out all the stops.")

Nearly all organs also have *pedals*. They're not like piano pedals; each of these pedals plays a low note when pressed. They're laid out like a mini keyboard, complete with sharps and flats, so that organists can play with their feet as well as their hands. In his day, Bach was most famous not for his compositions but for his incredible dexterity at the keyboard and at the pedals. People came from miles around to watch the organist with the flying hands and feet. You must admit that he'd be kind of fun to have at your next party.

If you play a piece of music on the organ, you may want to change from one set of stops to another very quickly. You must be a master of speed and dexterity (most organists are) to punch in all the old stops and pull out all the new ones, without missing a beat of the music. A simpler alternative is to use an organ equipped with *two* keyboards (also known as *manuals*) and preset each one with a different bunch of stops. If you want to change sounds, you just move your hands from one keyboard to the other.

Hearing the organ

If you'd like to hear the organ in action, have we got the music for you. . . .

- ✔ **Bach:** Toccata and fugue in D minor (This is that famous Halloween piece that you hear everywhere. You'll definitely recognize it.)
- ✔ **Handel:** Concerto in F major (*The Cuckoo and the Nightingale*)
- ✔ **Cesar Franck:** *Pièce héroique* in B minor

> ✔ **Charles-Marie Widor:** Symphony no. 5 (Yes, it's called a symphony, but it's for organ alone. The *Toccata* movement is especially impressive.)
>
> ✔ **Camille Saint-Saëns:** Symphony no. 3 (*Organ Symphony*) (This one actually *is* a symphony, for orchestra, but with a big, brash, highly noticeable organ part.)

The Synthesizer

Because it missed the great Golden Age of Classical Music by a couple of centuries or so, the *synthesizer* doesn't pop up very often in the world's great symphonies. You may encounter it, however, in some of the "new classical" music composed by today's starving young musicians at universities.

The synthesizer's plastic keys trigger any of hundreds of different instrument sounds — which you choose by punching buttons — stored on electronic chips. In rock and pop music, the modern synthesizer has put a lot of traditional musicians out of work. But because it can be connected to a computer, which can then play the entire orchestra's worth of sounds simultaneously, the synthesizer has also turned individual singers into recording stars.

Chapter 7

Strings Attached

In This Chapter

▶ Getting a feel for the violin, viola, cello, and bass

▶ Understanding how they all manage to move

▶ Access the audio tracks at www.dummies.com/go/classicalmusic

"Wet the line! Wet the line!" cried Stubb to the tub oarsman (him seated by the tub) who, snatching off his hat, dashed the sea-water into it.

From the vibrating line extending the entire length of the upper part of the boat, and from its now being more tight than a harpstring, you would have thought the craft had two keels — one cleaving the water, the other the air — as the boat churned on through both opposing elements at once.

— Herman Melville, *Moby Dick*

A tightly stretched string that's vibrating can create some of the most pleasing sounds ever heard by the human ear. At an orchestra concert, vibrating strings give a voice to the violin, the viola, the cello, the double bass, the harp, the guitar — and the piano, if you think about it. (But a piano, because its strings are hammered, is considered a percussion instrument, not a string instrument.)

Ask a great violinist if you can toss off a few notes on her violin, and she'll probably back away slowly, violin behind her, offering calm, soothing pleasantries, until she's far enough away to bolt into a dead run. The reason: There are about 175 ways to break a violin without even trying — and that's *before* you play it. Violins, and all string instruments, are extremely delicate, exquisitely sculpted from extremely thin pieces of wood, varnished, and baked to perfection. They have lots of little features known as *pegs, soundposts,* and *bridges,* all of which can crack, split, or collapse. If such a disaster happens, the instrument's owner generally cracks, splits, and collapses, as well.

The Violin

From the very beginning of classical music, the violin has played an extremely prominent role in all orchestral music. In fact, the violin section plays much of the melody in every piece of classical orchestra music you're likely to hear.

Whereas a piano has 88 sets of strings, a violin has only 4. These strings stretch all the way down the length of the instrument, fastened on top by the *pegs* and on the bottom by the *tailpiece*. From the pegs at the top, the strings make a long journey over a small piece of wood (called the *nut*), down the *fingerboard*, and over a bridge-like piece of wood (called, logically, the *bridge*), to Grandmother's house (the tailpiece). (See Figure 7-1.)

Figure 7-1:
A violin with a bow.

Source: *Creative Commons*

Originally, these strings were made of catgut — just as the strings of tennis rackets sometimes are. The reason is that catgut, stretchable to different lengths, makes a wonderful, pleasing sound (pleasing to everyone but the animal's surviving family, that is).

Nowadays, very few players use catgut, partly because its sound is not loud enough for a modern concert hall, and partly because the Humane Society doesn't take too kindly to it. So metal strings are standard on violins today.

From drawing the bow to creating beautiful notes, here's how the violin is played.

Drawing the bow

In addition to strings, every violin has another piece of essential equipment: the *bow*. The violinist draws the bow across the strings of the instrument to produce musical tones. The reason for the name *bow* is historical — it used to be more curved, somewhat like an archery bow.

Between the ends of the wooden bow is stretched a bunch of horse's hair. (Clearly, the instrument-makers of yore weren't big on the humane treatment of animals.) Horse's hair can draw a beautiful sound out of a piece of catgut. Just how we, as a species, were able to determine this fact is beyond our imagination, but suffice it to say that "horse's hair and catgut" is right up there with "peanut butter and chocolate" in the inspired combinations department.

To give their violin bows better traction on the strings, violinists regularly wipe rosin over the hair on their bows. Rosin is a chalky powder that comes in the form of an amber-colored, often circular block, about the size of a silver dollar. It greatly enhances the sound that a violin can produce; no violinist would be caught without rosin.

Producing a superior violin takes an almost magical, alchemical combination of materials, workmanship, varnish, baking, aging, and luck. Accordingly, good violins are staggeringly expensive: Many a musician must make the choice between buying a violin and buying a house. The best violins — created 300 years ago by the famous Italian makers Stradivari and Guarneri — cost millions of dollars.

Tuning up

You tune a violin by twisting the four pegs at the top, which adjust the tension of the strings. Tightening a string causes it to play a higher note. Loosening it causes it to play lower. (Most strings also have a micro-screw down on the tailpiece that you can twist for finer tuning.)

To tune your violin strings, you first listen to a perfect A note, played by either a tuning fork, an electronic tuning machine, or another instrument that's already in tune. In an orchestra, you listen to the principal oboist, whose job it is to play this perfect A for the entire band. We explain this tuning process in great detail in Chapter 4.

Using this perfect A and your perfect ear, you tune one of your strings to that note. Then you tune the other three strings to three other notes, using the already tuned A-string as a guide.

You're ready to play!

Playing the violin

You're standing onstage, in a packed concert hall, bathed in bright light, dressed in your fanciest concert clothes, all tuned up and ready to play Beethoven's *Kreutzer* Sonata, with the great Vladimir Horowitz as piano accompanist, a fact that is doubly amazing because (1) you've never had a single violin lesson, and (2) Vladimir Horowitz is dead. Many a nightmare has begun this way.

At this moment, the question in your head is probably this: *How do you play this thing?*

To understand how string playing works, we'd like you to humor us with a little experiment. Go get a long rubber band.

Sit on the floor, place your feet about 18 inches apart, and stretch the band tightly between your big toes. Now reach over and twang it. See what kind of pitch it makes.

Next, grasp the rubber band firmly in the middle, exactly half the distance between one big toe and the other. With your other hand, twang it again. Notice that you're really twanging either one half of the elastic or the other. Now the band makes the same note — but it's higher somehow, right? In fact, the note you played was an *octave* higher than the original pitch.

Remember the Little League analogy in Chapter 6, where everyone's singing the National Anthem on the same notes, but with low, medium, and high voices? Now you know the secret of these octaves. If you pinch your rubber band (or a violin string) so that only half of it vibrates, the sound produced is exactly one octave higher than the original sound.

When you tuned up a moment ago, you were tuning the *open strings* — defining the notes they make when you draw the bow across them.

Suppose you just drew the bow across the open A string, creating, of course, a perfect A. Now suppose you want to play the note A *one octave higher* than the original A. As in the rubber-band experiment, you simply put your finger firmly over the string exactly halfway from one end to the other. This placement effectively cuts the string length in half. Only the part *between your finger and the bridge* vibrates as you draw your bow across the string. Voilà! One octave higher.

Now, say you don't want to go up quite so high. In that case, you shouldn't shorten the string so much. Instead, place your finger a bit closer to the peg and farther from the bridge, such that when you draw the bow, two-thirds of the string can vibrate. This placement creates a different note — in this case, a perfect E.

All the notes on the violin — and just about every string instrument — are produced this way. You effectively shorten the string with your left hand's fingers, making the notes higher. Your right hand holds the bow. Through years of practice, violinists learn exactly where to put each left-hand finger to get each note.

Now, it's actually possible to play more than one note on a violin at one time, playing multiple strings simultaneously. But, as you can imagine, fingering more than one note at a time is no simple matter — especially when you try playing notes on *three or four* strings simultaneously. A master violinist can do it, but only by playing Twister with her fingers.

Vibrating the string

When a violinist fingers a note with her left hand and draws the bow with her right, she doesn't leave her finger in one place for the duration of the note. Instead, she *wiggles* her left-hand finger on the string. This vibration creates a barely noticeable variation in pitch of the note. This singing effect is called *vibrato* ("vee-BRAH-toe"); it adds an amazing warmth to the tone of the instrument, giving it a quality that's prized above all others in classical music — the quality of the human voice.

All good violinists use vibrato. Generally speaking, the more romantic and heartfelt the music, the more *vibrato* the musicians use. Next time you're watching a concert on YouTube, on PBS, or in person, check out the string players' left hands — you can see them wiggling away.

The unbearable lightness of bowing

As a violinist uses her right arm to move the bow back and forth, she's *bowing.* You can bow in one of two directions: down or up.

Believe it or not, there's an art to deciding when to play upbow, when to play downbow, and what part of the bow to use at any given point in the music; string players go to great lengths to come up with the best bowing technique for each situation. If they want an incredibly light, ethereal sound that appears to come from nowhere, they're likely to play near the tip of the bow. On the other hand, if they want a heavy, robust, even crunchy sound, they probably start near the *frog* (the hand-held end of the bow).

The next time you see an orchestra play, whether onscreen or in a concert hall, you'll notice that all the bows are traveling in the same direction at once. That's not by chance; the leaders of each section have written all this information into the sheet music. They determine this direction, by making little marks in the sheet music, for *every single note of every single piece of music they play.*

If you ever see a lack of unanimous precision among the string players in a given section, one of the following three things has happened:

- The section leader didn't get the bowing marks into the printed parts in time.
- Some people are misreading the bowings and playing them incorrectly.
- The conductor wants "free bowing" at this spot in the music. (See the following sidebar, "Free bowing.")

Plucking the strings

There's one way to play a violin (or any other string instrument) without using the bow at all. This method is called *pizzicato* ("pitsy-CAH-toe"), which means "plucked." The sound of a plucked violin string is delightful, either solo (alone) or in combination with the rest of the section. Plucked strings can play tunes, as well; the most famous of these is the third movement from Tchaikovsky's Symphony no. 4, where the string players don't use their bows at all and, in fact, lay them down for the duration of the entire movement.

Free bowing

Free bowing is a concept introduced by Leopold Stokowski (1882–1977), the late, great conductor of the Philadelphia Orchestra.

Stokowski felt that the string section would sound best if every player were given the freedom to choose the bowings that worked best for him. So during the middle of this century, the bows of the Philadelphia Orchestra went in all different directions at once. This free bowing method was one of the components of the incredibly full and rich "Philadelphia Sound," known throughout the world.

But free bowing has its disadvantages. First, free bowing makes it difficult for an entire string section to play with a unanimous interpretation. Second, the sight of all those bows going against each other looks chaotic. And finally, if you're playing upbow and the person next to you plays a downbow, you're likely to bump into one another.

Because of these disadvantages, free bowing lost its appeal among most orchestras. Today, the method is used only in isolated situations where a particularly rich, full, sustained sound is called for.

If you'd like to hear the sound of a plucked violin right now, you need look no further than the examples available at www.dummies.com/go/classicalmusic. Track 9 is an excerpt from Igor Stravinsky's *The Rite of Spring*. If you go to 3:17 on that track, you'll hear the violins cheerfully plucking away, unaware that all hell is about to break loose.

Hearing the violin

If you've found a new reason for living in the sound of the violin, we have a few works for you to hear. First, the following list offers a sampling of the greatest concertos:

- **Johann Sebastian Bach:** Concerto for Two Violins in D minor
- **Ludwig van Beethoven:** Violin Concerto in D major
- **Johannes Brahms:** Violin Concerto in D major
- **Jean Sibelius:** Violin Concerto in D minor
- **Peter Tchaikovsky:** Violin Concerto in D major

Are you starting to notice a similarity here? Many composers of old used the key of D for their violin concertos. This key opens up extraordinary possibilities for the instrument, which has, among other things, a very prominent D string. Sure, some composers wrote concertos in keys other than D; very often, these other keys also correspond to the other strings of the violin (G, A, and E). Check out the following pieces, for example:

- **Max Bruch:** Violin Concerto no. 1 in G minor
- **Felix Mendelssohn:** Violin Concerto in E minor
- **Wolfgang Amadeus Mozart:** Violin Concerto no. 5 in A major

And now, a couple of beautiful sonatas for violin and piano:

- **Beethoven:** Violin and Piano Sonata no. 9 in A major, opus 47 (*Kreutzer*)
- **Brahms:** Sonata no. 1 in G major, opus 78

The Other String Instruments

Everything about the workings of the violin holds true for the other instruments of the orchestral string family: the viola, the cello, and the double bass.

The major differences between these instruments and the violin lie in their sizes and their musical ranges. As the instruments get larger, their strings get longer — and play lower. The violin plays very high notes; the viola plays notes in the middle range; the cello plays low notes; and the bass plays *really* low notes. Here are the most important qualities of each member of the string family.

The viola

What's the difference between a violin and a viola?

Size — the *viola's* slightly bigger. (See the sidebar "A compendium of viola jokes" for an alternative answer.) But from the audience, seeing this subtle size difference isn't easy.

The sound of the viola is distinctive, however. Compared to the violin, the sound is breathier and throatier. The high notes on a viola sound less effortless than on a violin, and the low notes are powerful and rich.

The viola is the most difficult string instrument to play. Because the instrument is bigger than a violin, the player's fingers must stretch farther between notes. The contortions that a violist must go through to play are unbelievable; the game of Twister is intensified.

Violists spend the vast majority of their time in the orchestra playing accompaniments to the violins' melodies. As a result, concertos for the viola are rare, and violists who can play them are even rarer. (Joke! It's a joke!) Here are some of them:

- **Paul Hindemith:** *Trauermusik* (*Music of Mourning*) for solo viola and strings
- **Georg Philipp Telemann:** Viola Concerto in G major
- **William Walton:** Viola Concerto

Here are some very nice viola sonatas:

- **Hindemith:** Sonata for Viola and Piano, opus 25, no. 1
- **Johann Hummel:** Sonata in E-flat major, opus 5, no. 3

Finally, you can hear the gorgeous, throaty quality of this instrument used to great advantage in the following orchestral works, which feature extended, beautiful viola solos:

- **Hector Berlioz:** *Harold in Italy*
- **Richard Strauss:** *Don Quixote*

A compendium of viola jokes

Because the viola is so hard to play, there are very few great violists in the world. Another alleged reason is that many violinists of less-than-perfect ability, sensing their meager chances in the competitive concert world, switch to viola to have a better shot at getting work.

The combination of these two factors has turned the viola (and its player) into the butt of more jokes than any other instrument. Musicians of all kinds (including violists) pass many an hour telling these jokes.

Viola jokes are crude, offensive, and not worth the paper they're printed on. We're delighted to present them here.

Q: What's the difference between a violin and a viola?
A: A viola burns longer.

Q: What's the difference between a viola and an onion?
A: You don't cry when you chop up a viola.

Q: How many violists does it take to change a light bulb?
A: None — they can't go up that high.

Q: How do you get three viola players to play in perfect tune?
A: Shoot two of them.

Q: What's the difference between a viola and a trampoline?
A: You take off your shoes when you jump on a trampoline.

Q: What's the range of a viola?
A: Twenty yards, if you've got a good arm.

Q: How can you tell if a viola is out of tune?
A: The bow is moving.

On a flight recently, a friend of ours decided to strike up a conversation with his seatmate. "I've got a great viola joke," he began. "Would you like to hear it?"

"I should let you know first that I am a violist," replied his neighbor.

"That's okay. I'll tell it real slow!"

The cello

Ah, the cello. We can't even *write* about this instrument without sighing. What a beautiful, rich, singing sound this instrument makes. Of all the string instruments, the cello (see Figure 7-2) is the one that sounds most like the human voice.

The name *cello* is short for *violoncello,* which is Italian for "small double bass." The cello is the only instrument that absolutely *must* be played sitting down — as you'll notice if you ever watch orchestras play the national anthem. You see, the cello is too big to be placed under the player's chin like a violin or viola, yet too small to play standing, like a double bass.

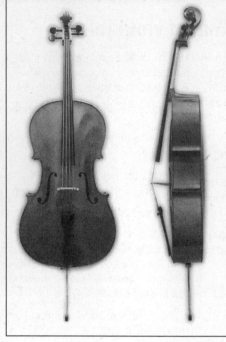

Source: Creative Commons

Figure 7-2:
The cello, the string instrument that sounds most like the human voice.

Because of its size, the cello has a range lower than that of the violin and the viola. As a result, it almost never gets to play the *tune* in a symphony orchestra setting. For centuries, composers relegated it (along with the double bass) to playing low notes, the musical foundation on which violin melodies are built.

In string quartets (made up of two violins, a viola, and a cello), which you can read about in Chapter 3, the cello likewise usually plays the lowest notes — largely because it's the only instrument of the four that even has those notes available.

Thankfully, composers eventually discovered the beauty of the cello's sound, and it spurred their imaginations. They started writing works in which the cello takes center stage, accompanied by other instruments. The sonatas and concertos written for this instrument are ravishing.

Perhaps because of the daily physical contact with this beautiful vibrating instrument, cellists are some of the happiest people we know. They tend to be nice, easygoing, and pleasant. And when, in the course of orchestral events, they get a rare melody to play — watch out! They throw themselves into it with utter passion and conviction.

If cello concertos are what you're after, you can't go wrong with these:

- **Antonin Dvořák:** Cello Concerto in B minor
- **Joseph Haydn:** Cello Concerto no. 1 in C major
- **Tchaikovsky:** Variations on a Rococo Theme for Cello and Orchestra

And for cello solos with piano accompaniment, check out the following:

- **Johannes Brahms:** Cello Sonata no. 2 in F major
- **Claude Debussy:** Sonata for Cello and Piano

Of course, we can't neglect to mention some of the nicest cello lines in the orchestral repertoire:

- **Debussy:** *La Mer (The Sea)* (first movement)
- **Gioachino Rossini:** *William Tell Overture* (beginning)
- **Strauss:** *Don Quixote* (In this piece, the solo cello actually plays the part of the mixed-up man of La Mancha.)

The double bass

The lowest of all string instruments, the double bass (pronounced "base," not like the fish) is enormous, bigger around than the average human being. (See Figure 7-3.) The instrument can play much lower than anyone can sing, and it provides the foundation for the orchestra's sound. In an orchestra, basses are almost always way over on the right side of the stage. Bassists play sitting on a very tall stool or standing up.

By the way, there's no such instrument as a single bass. The words *bass* and *double bass* mean the same thing.

Works for bass solo are particularly rare but worth hearing. If bass concertos tighten your strings, listen to the following pieces:

- **Carl Ditters von Dittersdorf:** Double Bass Concerto in E major
- **Domenico Dragonetti:** Concerto in G major (actually composed by a bassist named Nanny, using a bunch of Dragonetti tunes)
- **Serge Koussevitzky:** Double Bass Concerto in F-sharp minor, opus 3

And these sonatas are worth hearing:

- **Franz Schubert:** Arpeggione Sonata

  This is one of the most popular pieces for bass and piano — and Schubert didn't even write it for the bass. He wrote it for an antiquated string instrument called the arpeggione, which nobody even has in the closet anymore!

- **Henry Eccles:** Sonata in A minor (originally written in G minor)

Finally, listen to these famous double bass passages from classical music literature:

- **Beethoven:** Symphony no. 9 (fourth movement)

- **Gustav Mahler:** Symphony no. 1 (third movement)

- **Igor Stravinsky:** *Pulcinella Suite*

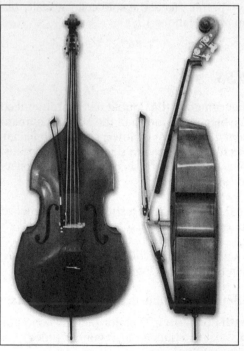

Figure 7-3:
The double bass, grand-daddy of the string sec-tion, plays the lowest notes.

Source: Creative Commons

The harp

The harp has a magical effect on all who hear it. Its sound is soft, smooth, and lovely; a sudden harp entrance in an orchestral work always adds a beautiful color to the sound.

The harp has 47 strings (see Figure 7-4). Like other string instruments, the harp must be tuned before every rehearsal and performance. As a result, a harpist must show up at least 47 minutes early for any rehearsal just to tune up those 47 strings.

To accomplish this formidable chore, the harpist uses a specially made key that fits over a bunch of pins across the top of the harp. Each pin can be turned — just like the tuning pegs of a piano — to tighten or loosen a particular string.

While she tunes each string, the harpist listens through an earphone connected to a little tuning device that resembles a cellphone. The tuning device gives her the pitch that she's aiming for; her job is to make the string match that pitch.

Figure 7-4:
The harp, all 47 strings of it.

Source: Creative Commons

But even after the strings are tuned, the challenges aren't over yet. You've got 47 strings; how are you supposed to tell them apart?

Answer: Look closely next time you're near a harp. The strings are color-coded! All C strings are red, and all F strings are either black or blue. Harpists identify all the other strings in terms of their distances from C or F.

In addition to the 47 strings, the harp has seven pedals. These pedals change the pitches of the strings as the harpist plays. Each pedal corresponds to one note of the scale: You have an A pedal, a B pedal, a C pedal, and so on. Furthermore, each pedal has three notched locking positions: up, down, and in the middle. The pedals have springs; you can use your feet to push the pedals down or release them, switching them in and out of the various locked positions. (Refer to Figure 7-4.)

If the pedals are all locked in the middle position, the 47 strings of the harp play the exact same notes as the white keys on the piano: A, B, C, D, E, F, and G, up six and a half octaves. That's fine if you want to play one of *those* notes. But what if you want to play a note *between* those notes?

Suppose, for example, that you want to play an A-sharp (halfway between the notes A and B). With your right foot, you press the A pedal to the bottom position. This pressing action pulls all the A strings on the harp just a little bit tighter, making them all play A sharp.

To go back from A-sharp to the original note A, you unlock that same pedal and move it back up to the middle notch. And if you move the A pedal *up* to the *top* position, the strings loosen just a tiny bit, lowering their pitch. You now have an A-flat.

Pushing a pedal *down* when you want the notes to go *up* can be counter-intuitive at first; but hey, the rudder on a boat is hard at first, too. When you want to go left, you push right.

The most well-known effect on the harp is the *glissando.* That Italian word simply means "gliding." You've seen and heard the effect many times: The harpist runs her fingers from one end of the instrument to the other, making all the notes sound in a rushing scale (usually from bottom to top). Harpo Marx was a master of the two-way glissando — he'd often run his fingers from bottom to top to bottom to top to bottom again with a flourish. A harp glissando always lends a dramatic beauty to music — see your garden-variety magic spell or curtain-opening sequence on TV, for example. For that reason, it's been incredibly overused, especially by composers for movies.

For a wonderful introduction to the world of the harp, listen to the following pieces:

- **Mozart:** Concerto for Flute and Harp in C major
- **Maurice Ravel:** Introduction and Allegro for Harp and Strings

In the world of orchestral music, check out these famous harp passages:

- **Mahler:** Symphony no. 5 (fourth movement)
- **Nikolai Rimsky-Korsakov:** *Scheherazade*
- **Tchaikovsky:** *The Nutcracker,* "Waltz of the Flowers"
- **Debussy** or **Ravel:** Any of the highly atmospheric, Impressionistic orchestral works of these composers. Go to `www.dummies.com/go/classicalmusic`; Track 8 is a movement from Debussy's greatest work, *La Mer (The Sea)*.

The guitar

Of all the instruments used in classical music, the guitar is the one most favored by non-classical-music people. Guitars can be found in every music shop, every school, and probably in more homes than any other instrument. If you don't have a guitar in your closet, your neighbor does.

The classical guitar has six strings (and no electricity). The notes that the strings are tuned to aren't evenly spaced, making it tough to tune a guitar perfectly. Maybe that's why you hear so many out-of-tune guitars.

On a violin, viola, cello, or bass, the fingerboard is smooth. You must guess (or learn from *years* of practice) where to put your left-hand finger to produce a certain note. On the guitar, however, producing a certain note is foolproof — a guitar has *frets*. Frets are raised metal stripes across the fingerboard that show you where to place your finger to get one note or another (see Figure 7-5).

But in guitar music, you don't always play just one note or another. You often play one note *and* another. And another. All at the same time. To do so, you contort your left hand to stop several strings at once, sometimes all at different frets.

Whereas a violin usually plays one note at a time, on a guitar you're *usually* playing more than one note. That's what strumming is all about. You almost never strum a violin.

Figure 7-5:
A guitar's
fingerboard
has frets.

Source: Creative Commons

Some people say that the classical guitar is the most difficult instrument to play really, really well. The truly virtuosic classical guitarists we know are a select and amazing breed. If you ever get the chance to hear one, don't miss it!

Some of the nicest guitar sounds you can ever hear can be found in the following pieces:

- **Joaquin Rodrigo:** *Concierto de Aranjuez*
- **Rodrigo:** *Fantasía para un gentilhombre*
- **Antonio Vivaldi:** Concerto for Guitar (originally for lute) in D major, RV 93 (Here "RV" refers to the catalog number, which can help you find the recording you're looking for in a record store.)

Unusual string instruments

This chapter talks about the major string instruments that you're likely to encounter in the world of classical music. But still others occasionally find their way into the classical world — mostly to create special effects in unusual, exotic, or modern music.

If you look and listen carefully, you just might encounter a *lute* (the ancestor of the modern guitar) in a piece that tries to create a Renaissance feel; a *mandolin* for a Mediterranean mood; a *balalaika* for Russian folk music; a *banjo* for classical hoedowns; or a *sitar* for a spicy Indian flavor. (To entertain kids, there's probably even such a thing as a *baby* sitar.) All of these are string instruments — and they work according to the same principles as the violin and the guitar.

Chapter 8

Gone with the Woodwinds

But at last, when turning to the eastward, the Cape winds began howling around us, and we rose and fell upon the long, troubled seas that are there; when the ivory-tusked Pequod sharply bowed to the blast, and gored the dark waves in her madness, till, like showers of silver chips, the foam-flakes flew over her bulwarks; then all this desolate vacuity of life went away, but gave place to sights more dismal than before!

"Hist! Did you hear that noise, Cabaco?"

— Herman Melville, *Moby Dick*

A h, the beautiful noise of the winds! Who can resist the golden sound of a flute, spinning forth like the voice of an angel? Or the rich, plaintive tone of an oboe, soaring above a hushed orchestra? Or the mellow, agile voice of the clarinet, leaping dexterously from note to note? Or the versatile, majestic bassoon? Who among us, indeed, could call himself truly and totally fulfilled without the sound of woodwinds?

(Don't answer that.)

The woodwind instruments are the flutes, oboes, clarinets, bassoons, and saxophones, which this chapter discusses. In the old days, most of them actually were wooden, but now only oboes and bassoons are always made of wood. Flutes are made of all kinds of metal, including silver, gold, and platinum; clarinets are sometimes made of plastic; and saxophones have always been made of brass. Go figure.

A woodwind instrument creates a tone by making a column of air (the column that's inside the instrument) vibrate. Pressing down on the keys of a woodwind instrument changes the length of that column of air, and this change in length in turn changes the pitch of the note. Just as a shorter string length creates a higher note on a violin (see Chapter 7), a shorter column of air creates a higher note on a woodwind instrument.

Have you ever blown on an empty cola bottle? As you blow a stream of air over the mouth of the bottle, the air inside the bottle starts to move — and you produce a pitch. Fill the bottle up a bit with water and try again. This time, the pitch is higher. By adding water, you decrease the amount of air that moves around the bottle. Less air to vibrate equals a higher pitch. That's the basic idea behind woodwinds.

The Flute

Unlike all other woodwind instruments, the *flute* isn't blown *into,* but blown *across,* just like a cola bottle. But the flute is much prettier to look at than the bottle (see Figure 8-1) — and sounds better, too. As you set that column of air inside the flute moving, it produces a beautiful, silvery sound. Here's how the flute creates such beauty — and where to hear it.

Figure 8-1:
The flute.

Source: *Creative Commons*

Making music out of thin air

Monty Python fans may recall the TV show spoof in which, in one four-minute episode, the Pythons promised to resolve all wars, cure cancer, and teach you to play the flute. The instructions turn out to be "Well, you blow across one end, and move your fingers up and down the outside, and that's how you play the flute."

Actually, that's exactly what you do. If you cover all the holes on the side of the instrument and blow across the hole, the entire column of air inside the instrument vibrates. This fingering produces the lowest pitch.

Now, here's how to change notes on a flute (or *any* column of air you may have lying around). Keeping your hands over the instrument, open a hole near the end farthest from your lips. That hole *interrupts* the vibrating column of air. Now the vibrating column of air stretches *only as far as the newly opened hole.* In other words, the new column is shorter, and the pitch goes up.

Keep opening up new holes successively, and the column of air becomes shorter and shorter still. The pitch continues to climb.

Of course, a real flute is more complicated; it has a complex mechanism of keys to cover some holes and open others. As on most woodwind instruments, some notes are produced by various complex *combinations* of open and closed holes. But you get the idea.

Hearing the flute

You've probably heard the sound of the flute; if by some chance you think that you haven't, well, by golly, go listen to one now. The sound that a flute makes is gorgeous.

For starters, you can hear some lovely flute passages online at www.dummies.com/go/classicalmusic. The third movement of Mozart's Piano Concerto no. 22 has a very short, lively, and delightful solo for flute (Track 3, 1:11). And you can hear a low, haunting passage for three flutes playing together in the last movement of Tchaikovsky's Symphony no. 6 (Track 7, 0:52).

Quite a few concertos have been written for flute solo. Here are some of the nicest ones:

- **Wolfgang Amadeus Mozart:** Flute Concerto no. 1 in G major
- **Mozart:** Flute and Harp Concerto in C major

- **Antonio Vivaldi:** Flute Concerto in D Major, opus 10, no. 3 (*The Bullfinch*)
- **Gabriel Fauré:** Fantasy for Flute and Chamber Orchestra

While you're at it, take a listen to these beautiful flute sonatas:

- **Francis Poulenc:** Sonata for Flute and Piano
- **Johann Sebastian Bach:** Sonata no. 1 in B minor

Furthermore, you really should hear these flute solos from the orchestral collection:

- **Bach:** Orchestral Suite no. 2 in B minor
- **Claude Debussy:** Prelude to the *Afternoon of a Faun*
- **Felix Mendelssohn:** Incidental Music to *A Midsummer Night's Dream*
- **Maurice Ravel:** *Daphnis and Chloé* Suite no. 2
- **Johannes Brahms:** Symphony no. 4 (fourth movement)

The Piccolo

This instrument works like a teeny weeny flute — actually, it's half the size of a normal flute. Thus the column of air inside the piccolo is also half as long as that inside a flute. What this means is, when you press the same keys that you would press on a flute, the notes come out sounding one octave higher than those of the flute.

The word *piccolo* is Italian for "little" (as in, "*Mamma, per piacere dammi un piccolo pezzo di pesce blu alla salsa di senape*" — which means, "Mama, please give me a little piece of bluefish with mustard sauce"). After someone invented a little flute, that instrument was called the *flauto piccolo* ("little flute"). The name stuck. Now everybody refers to the little sister of the flute as the piccolo.

The piccolo's high notes are brilliant and can be heard over nearly everything else, including a full orchestra. The low notes are soft and weak — but if you wanted low notes, you wouldn't need a piccolo, now, would you?

Antonio Vivaldi's Piccolo Concerto in C major, p. 79, is a lovely concerto for piccolo and orchestra. It was probably originally written for a small recorder, because in Vivaldi's time, the piccolo as we know it hadn't been invented yet. But today, it's usually played on a piccolo.

Here are a couple of wonderful piccolo excerpts from orchestral literature:

- **Gioachino Rossini:** *La gazza ladra (The Thieving Magpie)* (overture)
- **Sergei Prokofiev:** *Lieutenant Kije Suite*
- **Peter Tchaikovsky:** Symphony no. 4
- **Nikolai Rimsky-Korsakov:** *Scheherazade* (fourth movement)

By the way, other flutelike instruments exist besides the piccolo. A larger and lower version of the flute is the *alto flute;* it's rarely used, but it gives a rich, silky quality to the very low notes. (For a really exotic, spicy treat, check out the alto flute solos in Igor Stravinsky's *The Rite of Spring* — especially near the beginning of Part 2. Or, if you prefer, check out the score to Disney's original cartoon version of *The Jungle Book.*)

An even larger and lower flute than the alto flute is called the *bass flute*. This instrument is so long that the end must be curved around, and it produces very low notes indeed. The bass flute comes the closest of all instruments to sounding like a cola bottle.

The Oboe

Like the flute, the *oboe* (see Figure 8-2) produces sounds by causing a column of air to vibrate. But instead of a hole to blow *across,* the oboe has a *reed* to blow *into.*

If you were an oboe player (or a bassoonist), you'd spend much of your time *making* reeds. Yes, actual reeds, sliced from the wall of a cane stalk. Talk about low-tech.

Almost all oboists make their own reeds. Reed-performance is considered as much a requirement of the job as the play whereas the mastery of reeds isn't an essential component of performance technique of, say, maracas.

In fact, each oboe player's individual reeds determines the kind of sound that she produces. Oboists keep several reeds available at once, and they save the best on al occasions, such as important concerts and hot dates. Here' ed to know about the oboe — unless you're an oboist, of course

Figure 8-2:
Still life:
Oboe, with
reed.

Making an oboe reed at home

Ingredients:

1 tsp. water

1 short piece of thread

1 small, thin tube

3 to 5 scraping tools

1 med. cane field

1. Select a slice of the wall of a cane stalk from your cane field.*

2. Wet the slice with water and fold it over double.

3. Using thread, bind the ends of it around a thin tube.

4. Cut the now-double reed to the desired length.

5. Taking your special scraping tools, scrape the new ends of the two halves until they're just the right thickness. *Caution:* They shouldn't be too thin or too thick; just right is what you're aiming for here.

6. Repeat several hundred thousand times over a 20-year period until you have the perfect knack.

(*Or just buy the cane from a music supply store.)

Playing the oboe

To become an oboe virtuoso, follow these three easy steps:

1. **Insert a newly whittled reed into the end of an oboe, making sure that the reed is moist.**

   The reed must always — repeat, *always* — be moist.

2. **Place the end of the reed between your lips.**

   Your lips control the vibrations of the reed as you blow.

3. **Blow.**

Now, depending on how many years you've studied the oboe, you may not get any sound out of the thing at all. The oboe is one of the most difficult instruments to play. We'd say that it ranks right up there with the trumpet as the instrument with the most discrepancy between its sound when played badly and its sound when played well. When played by a beginner, an oboe sounds something like a raucous, nasal duck being boiled alive. When played by a virtuoso, the oboe produces one of the most beautiful sounds on earth: clear, vibrant, sweet, plaintive, and full.

Hearing the oboe

The first place to find the sound of an oboe is online at www.dummies.com/go/classicalmusic. Check out the famous oboe cadenza in Beethoven's Symphony no. 5 (Track 4, 4:37).

If you'd like to hear even more of the oboe in all its glory (played by a virtuoso, that is), we heartily recommend the following concertos:

- ✔ **Bach:** Concerto for Violin and Oboe in C minor, BWV 1060 (By the way, BWV stands for three German words that mean, simply, "Bach Work Catalog.")
- ✔ **Mozart:** Oboe Concerto in C major
- ✔ **Ralph Vaughan Williams:** Oboe Concerto
- ✔ **Richard Strauss:** Oboe Concerto in D major

And listen to the following smaller pieces:

- ✔ **Robert Schumann:** Three Romances for oboe and piano, opus 94
- ✔ **Ludwig van Beethoven:** Trio in C major for two oboes and English horn, opus 87

Also see whether you can get your hands on these classical works to hear some truly gorgeous oboe solos:

- **Johannes Brahms:** Violin Concerto (second movement) — really! Right at the beginning of the second movement of this violin concerto is the nicest oboe solo you could ever hope to hear.
- **Brahms:** Symphony no. 1 (second movement)
- **Ravel:** *Le Tombeau de Couperin*
- **Gioachino Rossini:** Overture to *La scala di seta* (*The Silken Ladder*)

The English Horn

English horns are neither English nor horns. Discuss.

Actually, they're a larger cousin of the oboe. Because they're bigger, they play lower notes. The English horn uses a double reed just as an oboe does; in fact, aside from its size, it's identical to the oboe in almost every way. Most oboists can play it because the *fingering* (what fingers to place where to produce a certain note) is the same as on an oboe.

One of the most well-known English horn solos can be found right in an example available at www.dummies.com/go/classicalmusic, near the beginning of Stravinsky's *The Rite of Spring* (Track 9, 0:44).

You can hear an English horn even more prominently in these orchestral works:

- **Hector Berlioz:** *Roman Carnival Overture*
- **Antonin Dvořák:** Symphony no. 9 (*From the New World;* second movement)
- **Jean Sibelius:** *Legends: The Swan of Tuonela*

The Clarinet

The *clarinet* looks somewhat like an oboe, but it makes a very different sound: full, but without the edge of the oboe's sound. One important reason for this difference is that, whereas the oboe has a double reed (a piece of shaved cane doubled over on itself), the clarinet has a *single* reed. Figure 8-3 shows what a clarinet look like.

Figure 8-3:
A clarinet.

Source: Creative Commons

Unlike oboists (and bassoonists), clarinetists don't need to make their own reeds; they can buy reeds ready-made because clarinet reeds are much less temperamental than oboe reeds. Consequently, clarinetists — like their instruments — tend to be quite mellow as a species. The following sections cover the most important clarinet facts to remember.

Transposing instruments

Clarinetists' mellowness is fortunate, because they must contend with one of the strangest musical concepts in this entire book: that the clarinet is a *transposing* instrument (one of several in the orchestra). Which means that when you play one note, you get another.

Don't panic: We explain.

On your average instrument — a flute, for example — what you play is what you get. You see a G on your sheet music, you play a G, and a G comes out. But play a G on a standard clarinet, and the note *F* comes out! In other words, it *transposes* down by one note.

And that's just the *most common* kind of clarinet. Since ancient times — long before the Age of Reason — clarinets have been available in a mind-blowing array of different sizes: big ones to play low notes, small ones to play higher notes. And each size of clarinet transposes by a different amount; that is, on a bigger clarinet, you might play what should be the note G, but an E comes out! As you can imagine, the mathematical complexities of trying to make the correct notes come out of the correct clarinet model drove decades of clarinetists quietly mad.

Thankfully, some hotshot musician of the past had a great idea. How about making the *composer* do all the math? Suppose the composer compensated for the clarinet's tendency to produce notes that were actually *lower* than what the player played — by writing the notes too high *in the first place?* Then all the player would have to do is play what she saw, and the right notes would come out.

So suppose you're playing the most common kind of clarinet, the one that transposes down one note. The composer wants to hear an F. No big deal — he just writes a G in the sheet music. You see the G, you play it — and F comes out. Just what the composer intended in the first place. The composer gets what he wants, nobody has to know about it, no money changes hands, and everybody's happy.

Clarinetists can now play *any* kind of clarinet with no adjustments whatsoever, thanks to composers' extra effort of writing clarinet sheet music in a different *key* than the rest of the orchestra. Composers, conductors, and music lovers have come to accept that this sheet music is printed in the "wrong" key — for the sake of clarinetists all over the world. Most trumpet, saxophone, and French horn music works the same way; all of those are transposing instruments, as well.

Hearing the clarinet

Clarinets are instruments of great grace and agility, with a smooth, lovely sound; they blend beautifully with just about every other instrument in the orchestra. You might say that they're easy to get along with — much like the people who play them.

The musical examples available at www.dummies.com/go/classicalmusic include some wonderful clarinet playing. Check out the finale of Mozart's Piano Concerto no. 22 (Track 3, 0:59). Then listen to a very different sound — a high clarinet bird call in Stravinsky's *The Rite of Spring* (Track 9, 1:14).

If you'd like to hear some great concertos for the clarinet, you should definitely listen to the following compositions:

- **Mozart:** Clarinet Concerto in A major, K. 622
- **Aaron Copland:** Clarinet Concerto
- **Debussy:** *Première rhapsodie* for clarinet and orchestra

Or check out these beautiful pieces:

- **Brahms:** Sonatas for clarinet and piano, opus 120, no. 1 (in F minor) and no. 2 (in E-flat major)
- **Mozart:** Clarinet Quintet in A major
- **Franz Schubert:** *The Shepherd on the Rock,* songs for voice, clarinet, and piano

And, finally, you really should hear these beautiful clarinet parts within the orchestra:

- **Mendelssohn:** Incidental Music to *A Midsummer Night's Dream*
- **Sergei Rachmaninoff:** Symphony no. 2 in E minor (third movement)

The Saxophone

The saxophone, as shown in Figure 8-4, was named after its inventor, Adolphe Sax. (We can be grateful his name wasn't, say, Komarinski or O'Shaughnessy.) The sax enjoyed an enormous surge in U.S. popularity in the 1990s, thanks to a certain president who played it. The saxophone is the newest woodwind instrument and therefore doesn't appear in many old classical works. But the sax is important on the jazz scene, and more and more composers are using the instrument in the classical music of today.

Figure 8-4: The saxophone.

Source: Creative Commons

The saxophone is made of brass, but it's considered a *woodwind* because, playing-wise, it's so similar to the clarinet. Many clarinetists, in fact, play saxophone on the side.

Saxophones come in at least six different sizes. They are transposing instruments, just like clarinets. The most common saxophone is the mid-sized *alto sax;* that's the one Bill Clinton famously played.

If you'd like to hear a really virtuosic saxophone concerto, listen to Alexander Glazunov's Alto Saxophone Concerto, opus 109. Also check out these prominent orchestral appearances:

- **Modest Mussorgsky (orchestrated by Ravel):** *Pictures at an Exhibition*
- **Ravel:** *Boléro*

The Bassoon

Woodwind instruments in general are known for their versatility of sound; none is more versatile than the bassoon (refer to Figure 8-5). This beautiful instrument is capable of sounding completely different in all its registers.

In the highest register, the sound of the bassoon can be strained, throaty, even other-worldly. If you listen to the opening of Igor Stravinsky's greatest masterpiece, *The Rite of Spring,* you hear that unusual sound in all its glory. (If you go to www.dummies.com/go/classicalmusic and check out Track 9, it's right at the beginning.)

In its mid-range, the bassoon has a luscious, full, mellow sound when played by a pro. And in its lowest range, the bassoon can be extremely powerful and heavy (the sound of the grandfather in Sergei Prokofiev's famous children's piece, *Peter and the Wolf*) or lugubrious (as in the passage for two bassoons at the bottom of their range in the last movement of Tchaikovsky's Symphony no. 6 — Track 7 at www.dummies.com/go/classicalmusic).

Concertos for the bassoon are rare; Mozart's Bassoon Concerto in B-flat major is one of the very nicest. While you're at it, take a listen to this lovely bassoon piece: Georg Philipp Telemann's Sonatas for bassoon and harpsichord in E minor, D major, and F minor.

Figure 8-5:
The
bassoon.

Source: Creative Commons

Along with the orchestral appearances we've already listed, you're sure to love these bassoon solos from orchestral literature:

- **Hector Berlioz:** *Symphonie fantastique* (fourth movement)
- **Paul Dukas:** *The Sorcerer's Apprentice*
- **Rimsky-Korsakov:** *Scheherazade* (second movement)

Chapterette: The voice

From the dawn of time, man has sung. And from the dawn of time, his spouse has been unable to do anything about it.

We've nearly accomplished our mission of introducing you to every kind of wind instrument you're likely to encounter in classical music. But failing to mention the voice would be unfair. Nearly every composer who ever lived has been inspired by the human voice.

(continued)

(continued)

In the Middle Ages, the voice was the choice for Gregorian chants, singing praises, and other religious music. These chants were performed by voices alone, in the awesome acoustics of a medieval cathedral or monastery. Even today, to sing *a cappella* — literally, "chapel style" — means to perform without any accompaniment whatsoever.

In the Renaissance era (about 1400 to 1650), most music still gave top billing to singers. But meanwhile, the predecessors of modern strings, woodwinds, and brass were emerging. The human voice began to lose its monopoly on the art form.

One place where the human voice continued to reign was the world of opera. The Renaissance, Baroque, Classical, Romantic, and more modern styles of music all saw the creation of incredible operatic masterpieces.

We can think of far too much juicy stuff to say about opera to fit in this chapter. We've taken the liberty, therefore, of devoting an entire book to it, called *Opera For Dummies* by David Pogue and Scott Speck (John Wiley & Sons, Inc.).

Even today, the human voice is probably the most composed-for instrument in the world. What would rock music or Broadway musicals be without vocals? Muzak, that's what.

For some stunning examples of the human voice in action, listen to these pieces:

- **Johann Sebastian Bach:** *St. Matthew Passion* (voices, choruses, and orchestra)
- **Samuel Barber:** *Knoxville, Summer of 1915* (voice and small orchestra)
- **Gabriel Fauré:** *Requiem* (voices, chorus, and orchestra)
- **Franz Schubert:** *Die Winterreise* (voice and piano)
- **Johannes Brahms:** A German Requiem (voices, chorus, and orchestra)
- **Richard Strauss:** *Four Last Songs* (voice and orchestra)
- **Randall Thompson:** *Alleluia* (voices alone)

Chapter 9

The Top (and Bottom) Brass

"There she blows — she blows — she blows! — right ahead" was now the mast-head cry.

"Aye, aye!" cried Stubb, "I knew it — ye can't escape — blow on and split your spout, O whale! the mad fiend himself is after ye! blow your trump — blister your lungs! Ahab will dam off your blood, as a miller shuts his water-gate upon the stream!"

— Herman Melville, *Moby Dick*

Through the act of blowing, brass players produce some of the strongest sustained sounds of any non-electric instruments in the world.

Not coincidentally, the brass players tend to have the best (some say the raunchiest) sense of humor in any group. They're often bigger in physical stature, stronger in personality, and downright funnier than other players in the orchestra.

We know of four very good reasons for these tendencies among brass players:

✔ **It takes an awful lot of physical strength to play a brass instrument (or, if it's a tuba, just to hold one).** You play by blowing a massive amount of compressed air through the mouthpiece — it's like giving mouth-to-mouth resuscitation to a firehose. A professional trombonist friend of ours used to go kayaking regularly, just to build up the lung capacity to play the trombone well.

- ✔ **It takes an incredible degree of self-confidence, and a true sense of conviction, to play an instrument that can easily be heard above all the others.** This profession is not for the meek or self-conscious.

- ✔ **It takes a good sense of humor to be able to laugh off a bad mistake — or missed note — called a *clam.*** All brass players, even the very best, make occasional clams. And if they do make one, an important realization for them is that, even though the entire world heard it, and even though they may have lost their audition, forfeited an amazing job, and destroyed all chances for a musical future because of it, a clam's not the end of the world. Playing a brass instrument requires a good dose of perspective and humor.

- ✔ **It takes a village to raise a brass player.**

Thus, it's probably fair to say that your typical brass players are, on the whole, more well-adjusted than any other group of people in the world, with the possible exception of surfers, Swedes, and Dalai Lamas.

In this chapter you can read about all things brassy — from the instruments themselves to the brave souls who play them.

Making a Sound on a Brass Instrument

What sets brass instruments apart from woodwinds is *not* the fact that they're made of brass. After all, the saxophone is made of brass, but it's called a woodwind because its reed system and fingering technique are very similar to those of the clarinet. No, what sets brass instruments apart is *the way in which you produce their tone.*

Brass instruments have removable mouthpieces, usually made of metal. Brass players spend a lot of time experimenting with various mouthpieces to find the one that feels best.

As a brass player, you place your lips firmly against the mouthpiece and buzz your lips into it, blowing a very thin but intense stream of air. The vibrations of your lips are transferred to an air column, which stretches all the way through the tubing.

The act of blowing into a mouthpiece, with the intent of producing a beautiful sound, is a real art that takes years to master. Try it sometime. At first, no sound will come out. With plenty of practice, over a number of weeks, you may be able to imitate the sound of a baby elephant dying of starvation. Finally, with enough diligent practice and a good teacher, you'll begin to produce a tone.

About that spit

All the blowing into a brass instrument is bound to have some side effects. One of them is that moisture collects within the tubing of the instrument. If left untreated, this fluid eventually produces an impressive gurgling sound.

Exactly what makes up this moisture is the subject of some dispute. Many players euphemistically claim that it's "condensation." Yeah, right — the kind of condensation that gets lobbed at umpires.

Brass players can pull out various valve slides to empty this moisture from their instruments, which they do regularly — right onto the floor. At the end of a symphony, the brass section of an orchestra can be seen practically floating away on a sea of spit.

We thought you'd want to know.

To play the lowest notes on a brass instrument, you keep your lips relatively relaxed; to play the highest notes, you tighten your lips considerably. Some players are better at the high notes; many more are better at the low notes.

The French Horn

The most noble-sounding of the brass instruments is the French horn. With a full, round, dark tone, the French horn sounds both powerful and elegant. Because the French horn actually *is* a horn (unlike the English horn, which isn't), it's often called *the horn*. (It's *not*, however, actually French.)

You've probably heard the characteristic, majestic hunting call of a French horn. Long ago, these proud instruments were a common fixture in royal hunting parties, until it was discovered, after years of research, that guns worked much better. These sections give you the lowdown on the French horn.

Hunting for notes: The natural horn

In those olden days, the most common kind of horn was the *natural horn*. The natural horn was a coil of brass tubing with a mouthpiece at one end and a bell-shaped opening (called *the bell*) at the other. It had no finger valves or keys at all. To change notes on a natural horn, you had but one recourse: Change the tightness of your lips.

That setup worked fine if you wanted to work with a very limited set of possible notes — along the lines of 16. What if you wanted to play some melody too complex for those 16 notes — for example, *Flight of the Bumblebee?*

You'd need a different horn. No problem. Just switch in the 17 nanoseconds between notes. Either that, or you could insert a tubing extension (called a *crook*). The crook altered the length of the column of air inside the horn, thus giving you a second set of 16 notes to choose from. How convenient!

Adding valves: The modern, treacherous horn

Fortunately, modern technology has solved the nightmare of the French horn player. Today, the horn player doesn't need crooks. Modern horns have rotary valves, as shown in Figure 9-1. These valves are operated by the fingers of the left hand that — in effect — chop off or add on lengths of tubing, thus changing the horn's entire pitch.

Figure 9-1:
The modern
French horn.

Source: Creative Commons

These rotary valves, however, don't take any responsibility away from the lips. On both natural horns and valve horns, the lips must search out just the right tightness from among many, many possibilities. As the notes get higher and higher, the tightness levels get closer and closer together. As a horn player, you must make infinitesimally small distinctions between notes.

Imagine baking a cake, doing your taxes, and reading Braille — all with your lips. Finding notes on a horn is harder.

That's why hitting the wrong note on the horn is so incredibly easy. And that's why you should be in awe of players who consistently hit the right one.

Hearing the French horn

At www.dummies.com/go/classicalmusic you can hear some wonderful horn moments. First, for a blazing fanfare, listen to Track 1 (a movement from Handel's *Water Music*) at 0:23. Then listen to the famous horn call in Beethoven's Fifth Symphony (Track 4 at 0:46). The third movement of Brahms' Symphony no. 4 has a lovely, lyrical, and short melody for horn (Track 5 at 3:03). The last movement of Tchaikovsky's Symphony no. 6 has a horn passage that is extremely low in the range (Track 7, 5:48). Finally, the last movement of Debussy's *La Mer* has a gorgeous, quiet, chorale-like passage for all the horns (Track 0, 3:20).

Following are some wonderful concertos written for the French horn:

- **Wolfgang Amadeus Mozart:** Horn Concerto no. 3 in E-flat, K. 447
- **Richard Strauss:** Horn Concerto no. 2 in E-flat

And these smaller works are not to be missed:

- **Ludwig van Beethoven:** Sonata in F major for horn and piano, opus 17
- **Robert Schumann:** Adagio and allegro in A-flat major for horn and piano, opus 70

The horn has many great moments in orchestral pieces, too. Among them are

- **Johannes Brahms:** Symphony no. 1 (fourth movement)
- **Maurice Ravel:** *Pavane for a Dead Princess*
- **Strauss:** *Till Eulenspiegel's Merry Pranks*
- **Peter Tchaikovsky:** Symphony no. 5 (second movement)

The Trumpet

In sheer sonic force, the trumpet is the strongest of all orchestral instruments (see Figure 9-2). As the highest-pitched brass instrument, the trumpet can be heard over the rest of the orchestra; it's also the instrument from which wrong notes are the most noticeable. The trumpet is the most fleet and agile brass instrument. It can execute impressive runs and leaps at a single bound.

Trumpet players *live* for the great music written in the late 1800s and early 1900s, where the trumpet soars above everyone else. Gustav Mahler's Fifth Symphony, for example, opens with 12 long, glorious bars of trumpet solo before the rest of the orchestra comes crashing in. Moments such as these send trumpet players into fits of twitching ecstasy. But they're not picky; *any* work by Mahler (or Richard Wagner, Strauss, or Anton Bruckner) will do nicely.

Like the French horn, the original trumpet (before the invention of valves) could produce only a few different notes. Have you ever heard a military bugle — an ancient species of "natural" trumpet with no valves — play "Reveille" or "Taps"? Those pieces use only four notes. Over and over and over again.

Modern trumpets are much more versatile. They come in several different sizes, just as clarinets do. On each trumpet, the lips by themselves can produce just a few different notes; valves, just as on modern horns, also enable the fingers to get into the pitch-changing action. But instead of the horn's rotary valves, most trumpets use *piston valves,* which work slightly differently (also shown in Figure 9-2).

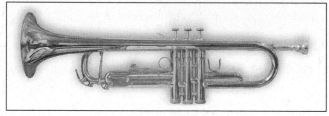

Figure 9-2:
The trumpet.

Source: Creative Commons

In the following sections you can read about some of the techniques that all trumpet players must master.

Tonguing

Although we've been putting it off, we now find ourselves compelled to explore the sensitive and sometimes controversial topic of *tonguing.* All trumpet players (and indeed, all brass and woodwind players) must learn to tongue —*even if they're deeply religious.*

Tonguing is the act of *articulating* (separating) the notes in a piece of music instead of slurring them all together. Any time you hear a burst of staccato trumpetfire, you can be sure that the player is tonguing. "Reveille" (the military "wake up!" piece) is the perfect example of a piece of music where every single note is tongued.

Tonguing essentially involves saying "ta-ta-ta" into your little trumpet mouthpiece, meanwhile pursing your lips into a tight buzzing knot. The result: Each note pops out of the instrument with a clean, sharp attack. With slight variations in technique, you can articulate notes on the French horn, trombone, and tuba this way, as well.

Using mutes

You can change the sound of any brass instrument by sticking a *mute* into its bell. But trumpets get muted more than any other kind of instrument.

Many kinds of mutes exist, and the sounds they produce range from merely muffled to strained and brassy. The most common kind of trumpet mute makes the trumpet sound like it's coming from very far away.

Then there's the "wah wah" mute, used all the time in jazz music. We're betting you can guess what *that* one sounds like.

Hearing the trumpet

For a short and beautiful trumpet fanfare, go to www.dummies.com/go/classicalmusic and listen to Track 1 (a movement from Handel's *Water Music*) at 0:16. And you can hear some thrilling trumpet action going on in Igor Stravinsky's *The Rite of Spring* (Track 9, 6:22).

For sparkling clean brasses . . .

After months of grueling late Romantic works and spit-emptying workouts, a brass instrument can get pretty grungy. Have you ever wondered how these intricate creations get cleaned?

Well, unlike string or woodwind instruments, brass instruments are extremely durable. They are, after all, made of metal. Despite their dozens of finely tuned, interlocking parts, they can safely be wet, swabbed, wiped, brushed, washed, buffed, cleansed, polished, sterilized, or Sanitized For Your Protection.

In fact, you can even take apart a brass instrument and clean it in an electric dishwasher. (Calgon and Joy are fine, but Cascade's sheeting action works best, especially for trumpets in C.)

If you find the sound of the trumpet — muted or not — particularly to your liking, listen to these concertos:

- ✔ **Joseph Haydn:** Trumpet Concerto in E-flat major

- ✔ **Johann Nepomuk Hummel:** Trumpet Concerto in E major (or transposed into E-flat major)

You can also hear some extremely important trumpet licks in these orchestral works:

- ✔ **Beethoven:** Leonore Overture no. 3
- ✔ **Mahler:** Symphony no. 5 (first movement)
- ✔ **Strauss:** *Also Sprach Zarathustra* (*Thus Spoke Zarathustra;* the opening)
- ✔ **Ottorino Respighi:** *Pines of Rome*
- ✔ **Aaron Copland:** *Billy the Kid*

The Trombone

Every red-blooded American of a certain age knows what a trombone is, thanks to a famous song that has 76 of them. The trombone is the quintessential parade instrument (see Figure 9-3); no marching band would be complete without it. It's a powerful *low* brass instrument. But this characteristic is just one of the trombone's many sides. It can also play noble, beautiful tones.

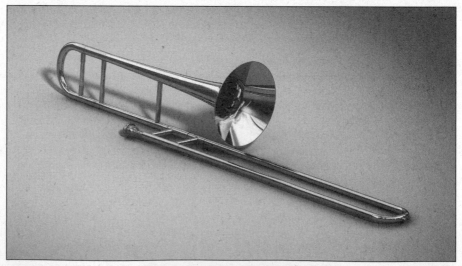

Figure 9-3:
The trombone.

Source: Creative Commons

The trombone's basic design hasn't changed much in more than 500 years! Amazingly, the trombonists of the Renaissance played basically the same instrument that we use today. (But back then, for reasons far too complicated to go into in this book, it was called a *sackbut*. We're not making this up.) Here are some of the things that all budding trombonists must know.

Sliding around

At first glance, you can easily see how the trombone differs from all the other brass instruments: It has a slide. To explain how a trombone works, we'll start with a trombone with its slide pushed all the way in (as shown in Figure 9-3). In this position, the trombone is as short as it can be. We call this *first position*.

In first position, a trombone is capable of producing a handful of notes with the lips alone — just as the natural horn did. Try to play a B-flat with the trombone in this position. Simple enough.

But what if you want to hear the note below this one — the A? That's not one of your available notes. What do you do? You pull the slide out, just a touch, to *second position*.

Now you've effectively made the trombone a bigger instrument, lengthening the tube so it can accommodate a longer column of air. As you may know by now, a longer column of air produces a lower note. Whenever you pull the slide out to the next position, the trombone lowers the sound by a half step.

The trombone has seven slide positions in all; with the slide pulled out as far as it can go, it's in *seventh position*.

Together, the seven slide positions enable you to play any note imaginable. Trombonists become experts at finding the correct slide positions and correct lip positions for each note.

The slide makes the trombone unique among brass instruments — in more ways than one. If you move the slide smoothly between one position and the next, while blowing a constant stream of air into the instrument, you can make your trombone glide *between* the notes.

You've probably heard this comical effect. It's called a *glissando* (which literally means *gliding*.) The biggest glissando that you can make is the one that goes from one end of the slide to the other — that is, from first position to seventh or from seventh to first. A truly impressive effect — used in jazz and cartoon soundtracks even more often than in classical music.

Hearing the trombone

We want to protest the sad fact that trombone concertos are extremely rare. Given the nobility and versatility of the instrument, they should be much more common.

But here are some good ones:

- **Nikolai Rimsky-Korsakov:** Concerto for trombone and band
- **Darius Milhaud:** *Concertino d'Hiver* (*Little Winter Concerto*) for trombone and strings

And don't miss the virtuosic antics of the trombones in these great orchestral works:

- **Ravel:** *Boléro*
- **Rimsky-Korsakov:** *Russian Easter* Overture
- **Gioachino Rossini:** *William Tell* Overture (the storm scene)
- **Wagner:** *Ride of the Valkyries*

The Tuba

If you're a typical product of American pop culture, you may be surprised to find the tuba listed in a discussion of classical music. You're likely to associate the tuba with the fat kid in movie versions of high-school marching bands.

But the tuba (see Figure 9-4) should get more respect. This massive instrument is capable of producing a wall of sound that can blow you away. Keep reading for more about tubas.

A gaggle of tubas

The German composer Richard Wagner first imagined that wall of sound — and he is responsible for today's *bass tuba.* (In fact, he invented a whole flock of tubas in different sizes, but hardly anyone ever uses the smaller ones these days.) He wanted to create a sound that was similar to the French horn but with strong low notes. These so-called "bass" notes can support the entire brass section of an orchestra or band.

Figure 9-4:
The tuba.

Actually, the stereotype of the big tuba player has its basis in reality; we have yet to see a really diminutive tubist, mainly for the same reason that opera singers are sometimes hefty: Playing a tuba takes an incredible amount of breath support. Just think of the size of the thing. It's enormous! And you've got to fill the thing with air continuously.

As for its operation — well, the tuba works much like a French horn. It has a mouthpiece and rotary valves to aid in the pitch-changing. A virtuoso tubist is surprisingly agile and can play amazingly quickly.

Hearing the tuba

Tuba concertos are as rare as trombone concertos.

But here are some very good ones:

- ✔ **Ralph Vaughan Williams:** Tuba Concerto
- ✔ **John Williams:** Tuba Concerto

And you simply must hear these tuba solos from the orchestral literature:

- ✔ **George Gershwin:** *An American in Paris*
- ✔ **Stravinsky:** *Petrushka* (the section called *Peasant with Bear*)
- ✔ **Modest Mussorgsky, arranged by Ravel:** *Pictures at an Exhibition* (the movement called *Bydlo*)

Pet Peeves of the Brassily Inclined

Brass players constantly hear two particular things from orchestra conductors.

- ✔ **Brass players are constantly told that they're playing too loudly.** This sort of thing is perfectly logical, because brass instruments are *made* to play loudly. They're prized for their capability to play *extremely* loudly. By golly, they *should* play loudly! Asking a brass player to play softly is like asking someone to hit a spike gently with a 30-pound sledgehammer.

- ✔ **Brass players in an orchestra are always being told that their sound is** *late,* **that they're playing behind the others.** That's logical, too. Brass instruments are made of yards of tubing, coiled up like a snake. If you unrolled all the tubing in a typical French horn, for example, it would reach to the moon and back four times. (Actually, 12 feet, but we're making a point here.) As you blow into a brass instrument, your air enters the tubing, snakes all the way through its length, deposits some spit on the inside of the instrument, and emerges, refreshed, at the other end. That's bound to take some time. No wonder the sound comes out a wee bit late.

Good brass players often find that they need to compensate for this time lag by anticipating, playing *earlier* than they actually want the sound to be heard. This situation is very uncomfortable; it involves a strange combination of constant mental calculation and imagining that you're in a time warp.

Chapter 10

Percussion's Greatest Hits

Nobody in an orchestra is more dangerous than the percussionists. They come to rehearsal heavily armed and ready to strike.

Percussionists make music by hitting, beating, pounding, whipping, or striking one thing against another. Drums, gongs, cymbals, xylophones, Glockenspiels, triangles, tambourines, castanets, whips, cowbells, and ratchets are percussion instruments. Even the piano is a percussion instrument, because its keys cause hammers to strike the piano strings. Why, this very book, if held at the right height and correctly dropped, could be a splendid percussion instrument.

All percussionists have a personal set of sticks and mallets, perfectly weighted and proportioned, many of which they've made themselves. They're carried in a *stick bag* and go everywhere their owners go; after all, you never know when something's going to need a good whack. Percussionists are proud of their creations and will tell you about them until you ask them to stop.

If you go to an orchestra or band concert where a big piece is being performed, try to get a seat where you can watch the percussion players. The virtuosic antics of these professionals are not to be believed.

Many cash-strapped orchestras scrimp in the percussion department, hiring fewer players than the composer of the music has called for. To cover all the musical parts, therefore, the percussionists are constantly scrambling back and forth across their corner of the stage, practically sprinting from one instrument to the next. Percussion playing is aerobic — and supremely entertaining.

The Timpani

Ah, thou noble Timpanist, how well and proudly dost thou perch above thy orchestra. There you sit enthroned amidst thy noble drums, a hundred feet above the silent decks, striding along the deep, as if the masts were gigantic stilts, while beneath you and between your legs, as it were, swim the hugest monsters of the sea, even as ships once sailed between the boots of the famous Colossus at old Rhodes.

— Herbert Melvole, *Moby Duck*

As you can see in Figure 10-1, *kettledrums* — a more common name for the *timpani* — look exactly like kettles. Upside-down kettles, that is. With no spouts. And no handles. And no openings to pour the water in.

Unlike most other drums, kettledrums are meant to be tuned to specific notes — big, low, booming, walloping, godlike notes. Remember the monumental opening music from the movie *2001: A Space Odyssey?* That music, actually by Richard Strauss, makes dramatic use of the timpani's unique capability to go . . .

Figure 10-1:
A timpani.

© iStock.com

BUM-~bum~-BUM-~bum~-BUM-~bum~ · · ·

What you're hearing is the alternation of two different notes. That's an extremely common effect on the timpani. (Next time the Olympics roll around, listen to the fanfare music they always play on TV — lots of timpani bumming around there, too.)

For an interesting variation of the above, go online to `www.dummies.com/go/classicalmusic` and listen to Track 9. Scan to 6:49, and you'll hear some wild timpani playing.

You tune a kettledrum by tightening or loosening the *head*. (That's the plastic "lid" that's stretched tightly across the opening of the kettle. Now you don't have to ask your doctor why your eardrums are known as the *tympanic membranes* — it's because they're stretched tightly, just like a timpani head.) On old instruments, you adjust the pitch by twisting several screws located around the circumference of the drum — not exactly something you can easily pull off in the three seconds you have between sections of a symphony.

Fortunately, that clumsy process is going the way of eight-track tapes, lava lamps, and fax machines. Nowadays, all timpani come with foot pedals. As you push down the pedal with your toe, you tighten the head; as you push down with your heel (lifting the toe), you loosen the head. In other words, you can tune your kettledrums incredibly quickly.

In fact, you can even change a note *while* you're playing it, making the note slide up or down. You hear this special effect (a *glissando*) in Saturday-morning cartoons, every time the fat guy gets kicked in the rear or shot from a catapult. It's a truly arresting effect. (We got arrested doing it just last week.)

The following sections take a closer look at the timpani.

Drum roll, please!

What timpani are best known for, however, is the *roll*. A timpanist executes a roll with two mallets, striking the drums with each mallet alternately, at blinding speed.

Many timpani rolls are accompanied by a gradual increase in volume. The climax of this increase is generally signaled by a momentous crash from the rest of the orchestra. This effect is so common that it's become a cliché.

The word *timpani* is Italian, and it's plural, because you never see fewer than two in one place (except in Figure 10-1). Composers almost never write for a single kettledrum.

Hearing the timpani

You can hear the timpani strutting their stuff (along with many other percussion instruments) in Béla Bartók's Music for Strings, Percussion, and Celesta — an ingenious, way-out work of music.

For that matter, the timpani make an especially striking appearance in Beethoven's Ninth Symphony (second movement), Strauss's tone poem *Also Sprach Zarathustra* (*Thus Spoke Zarathustra*), and the finale of Dmitri Shostakovich's Symphony no. 5.

The Bass Drum

Whenever the *bass drum* — yes, the same bass drum seen on football fields and in rock groups worldwide — plays at full throttle in a classical orchestra, what the other instruments are doing really doesn't matter; you can't hear them. The intense, rumbling roar that a bass drum produces can make the room shake like an earthquake and drown out all but your most horrified thoughts.

Although a loud note on the bass drum is overwhelming, a quiet one can be even more devastating. Used in the right place in the music, the dull, hollow bass drum note can hit you like a heart-stopping emotional shock.

For a brilliant foray into the world of bass drum possibilities, both loud and soft, listen to Giuseppe Verdi's *Requiem*, Tchaikovsky's Symphony no. 4 (fourth movement), and Igor Stravinsky's *The Rite of Spring*.

The Cymbals

Where the bass drum is, can the *cymbal* be far behind? Ever since the early days of parades, cymbals and bass drums have belonged together.

Smaller cymbals produce a higher-pitched sound, and bigger ones sound lower. Thinner cymbals emit a more vibrant, sizzling sound; thicker ones produce a heavy, weighty, momentous clang. But most of them can produce a stunning metallic crash on demand.

To create this crash — by far the most common cymbal effect — you need *two* cymbals, of course. You hold one cymbal in each hand and brush them together — surprisingly gently, actually; as you pull them apart again, you get plenty of volume.

If the timpani's job is to roll you toward a climax, the cymbal's job is to let you know that you've arrived. Cymbal crashes occur at the most exciting moments of orchestral music. In fact, the timpani roll/cymbal crash is extremely standard punctuation for the climax of any piece.

A cymbal can continue to vibrate and produce sound for an unbelievably long time. If you play a loud crash well and then hold the cymbals above your head, they can keep vibrating for as long as you just took to read all about them.

You can also play a cymbal by suspending it from a stand and rolling on it with some mallets. The result is a wash of sound, similar to the crashing of an ocean wave. In fact, French composer Claude Debussy used it for exactly that purpose in *La Mer* (*The Sea*). Go to www.dummies.com/go/classicalmusic, and you can hear this brilliant effect throughout Track 8.

The Snare Drum

American military bases around the world are equipped with a hefty supply of snare drums. Even if they run out of guns or ammunition, they have snare drums deployed at all times.

The reason for this ample supply is obvious: The snare drum helps brave soldiers march in a synchronized rhythm. And you know how important *that* is.

A typical snare drum is about 14 inches in diameter and 6 inches thick. It has two heads: one on top and one underneath. The heads are usually made of plastic, and the top head is usually hit with two drumsticks. If no drumsticks are available, the white meat or wing may be substituted.

What gives the snare drum its unique sound are the *snares* themselves. These snares are lengths of wire or nylon stretched tightly across the bottom of the drum. As the drum vibrates, the snares buzz against the bottom head, creating the characteristic rasp heard at many a military march.

A lever on the side of the snare drum lets you disengage the snares from the underside of the drum. If you do so, the sound of the drum changes completely, becoming lower and more hollow. This sound is similar to what you may have heard (along with a piccolo) if you'd been with George Washington as he crossed the mighty Delaware.

In orchestras, it's important for percussionists to remember to disengage the snares whenever their snare drums aren't in use. Otherwise, the vibrations made by the rest of the orchestra make the snares rattle abruptly at inopportune moments, such as during the love scene from *Romeo and Juliet*.

Perhaps the most famous example of the snare drum in classical music is in Maurice Ravel's *Boléro*, in which the snare plays nonstop, louder and louder, for 15 minutes. But it also makes illustrious appearances in Sergei Prokofiev's *Lieutenant Kije* Suite, Nikolai Rimsky-Korsakov's *Scheherazade* (fourth movement), and Gioachino Rossini's Overture to *La Gazza Ladra* (*The Thieving Magpie*). And if you'd like to sample the sound of the snare drum without the snares, listen to the second movement of Bartók's Concerto for Orchestra.

The Xylophone

Percussionists, confusingly enough, often use the word *mallets* to refer to certain instruments that *require* mallets. Such instruments, unlike, say, snare drums, can actually play specific notes. In fact, they have the notes arranged in a scale, from bottom to top, almost like a piano keyboard. We're talking your basic xylophone family.

Whether you know it or not, you've heard the xylophone before. For one thing, the instrument figures prominently in that Bugs Bunny "Merrie Melodies" theme song. It's the one making that funny, high-pitched, hollow wooden sound.

In his hugely entertaining work *Danse macabre* (which strangely enough means *macabre dance*), the composer Camille Saint-Saëns uses the xylophone's characteristic sound to imitate the sound of skeletons dancing, their bones clattering against one another.

Percussionists use several different kinds of mallets to hit the bars of a xylophone. The globe-shaped head can be made of yarn (for a softer sound), hard plastic, hard rubber, wood, or ebonite (for a louder sound). As you play, you generally hold one of these mallets in each hand and attack the instrument with both arms flying. Sometimes, however — and this is where percussion playing becomes impossible for novices — you need to play *more* than one note with each hand.

A *chord* is a sound made by three or more notes playing at the same time. If you want to make a three-note chord on the xylophone, you hold one mallet in one hand and *two* in the other. Controlling all three mallets so that they land on the correct xylophone bars, you bring them all down simultaneously.

But composers don't stop there. Xylophonists are often required to play *four*-note chords. You got it: That means *two* mallets in each hand.

Some particularly vicious composers, in fact, even write *six*-note chords for the xylophone, which requires the use of finger and hand muscles that you never even knew you had.

You can hear some truly killer xylophone licks in Aaron Copland's Rodeo (the movement called *Hoe-down*) and Saint-Saëns's *Danse macabre*.

Other Xylo-like Instruments

The xylophone's big half-sister is the *marimba*, whose sound is much deeper, mellower, and fuller. Below each bar on the instrument is a hollow resonator tube that greatly amplifies its sound. The lowest notes, especially, have a flavor reminiscent of African or Caribbean music.

The last mallet instrument that we really want you to know about is the *Glockenspiel* (see Figure 10-2, left side). This instrument is like a xylophone, except that it's much smaller and the bars are made of metal. Correspondingly, the sound that the Glockenspiel produces is silvery and Tinkerbelly. (In fact, the German word *Glockenspiel* means "play of bells.") But don't take the Glockenspiel lightly: It can also make a powerful sound that can be heard above a full orchestra.

You can hear a nice passage for the Glockenspiel in Debussy's *La Mer* (*The Sea*). (Go to www.dummies.com/go/classicalmusic: Track 8, at 5:07.) It also makes a prominent appearance in Gustav Mahler's Symphony no. 4 (first movement).

More Neat Instruments Worth Banging

The variety of other percussion instruments that composers ask for in their music seems to have no end. Here are some of those instruments.

The triangle

If you're talking truth in advertising, the *triangle* has no equal. Unlike the French horn (which is not French), the English horn (which is not English), or even the strings (which are metal wires), the triangle is *exactly* what it claims to be, as shown in Figure 10-2.

You tap the triangle with a thin metal beater, and it produces a delicate, silvery "ding" sound. Thicker beaters (or thicker triangles) produce a heavier "dong."

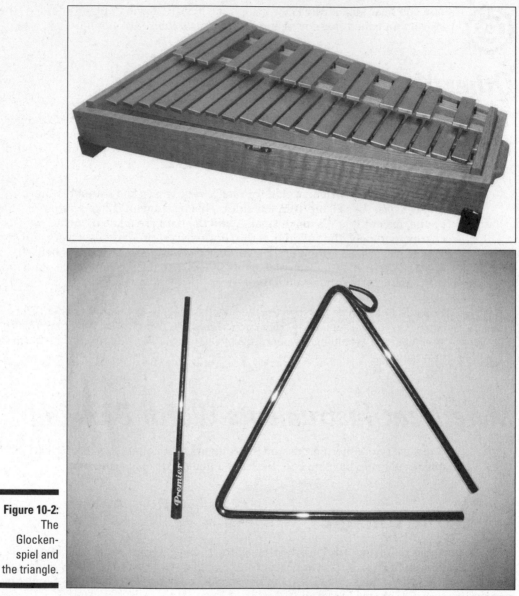

Figure 10-2:
The
Glocken-
spiel and
the triangle.

Besides the ding and the dong, the triangle can make a most satisfying roll, or *trill*, that adds an incredible vibrancy to a loud orchestral sound. You've heard this before, on the opening note of John Williams' music to *Star Wars*, when the whole orchestra enters with a most dramatic crash. If you listen carefully, you'll realize that the triangle trill is what causes the music to sustain its high-intensity, pulse-pounding excitement.

To let a triangle vibrate freely, you attach it from a piece of string and grip it aloft with one hand, using the other hand to strike or roll it with the beater, in the basic wind-chime configuration. Alternatively, you can hang it from your music stand — a very good idea if you happen to be playing six instruments at once.

To get a convincing trill from a triangle, you whack the beater back and forth between two sides of the inside of the triangle. Some people like to roll the beater around *all* inner sides of the triangle, like a dinner bell in the Wild West. On one hand, it's much harder to get an even-sounding, convincing trill this way; on the other hand, it does bring them hungry cowpokes running.

TIP

For another incredible example of the triangle trill, listen to the first two minutes of Strauss's *Also Sprach Zarathustra*.

CHECK IT OUT!

Also, check out the third movement of Johannes Brahms's Symphony no. 4 in E minor (online at www.dummies.com/go/classicalmusic, Track 5). And if you find yourself hooked on the triangle, listen to Franz Liszt's Piano Concerto no. 1 and the Overture of Tchaikovsky's *Nutcracker*.

The tambourine

The *tambourine* is a small, round percussion instrument with a wooden perimeter; a small drumlike head made of plastic (or occasionally goatskin); and small, thin, circular metal disks attached around the edge (see Figure 10-3). Of all the percussion instruments we discuss in this chapter, the tambourine is the one you're most likely to have in your closet. (With the possible exception of the whip. Keep reading.)

Figure 10-3: Hey, Mr. Tambourine Man — here's your instrument!

©iStock.com/ arturoli

This instrument suffers from the misconception of being the easiest percussion instrument to perform on.

In fact, the tambourine is difficult to master. First of all, it's difficult even to *pick up* without making a lot of noise. Those little metal plates, called *jangles*, jangle at the slightest provocation.

Second, many complicated rhythmic licks are written for the tambourine and must be played with virtuosity and finesse, such as the *tambourine roll*. That's the sound of the tambourine continuously vibrating over time. Many percussionists make this sound by holding the instrument overhead and jiggling the wrist back and forth. But others have a trickier method. They wet their thumb and then push it along the perimeter of the tambourine *head* (the flat part). The friction produced makes the thumb skip along the head at a stuttering pace, causing the jangles to vibrate with an even and intense sound.

For some insight into the world of the tambourine, listen to Rimsky-Korsakov's *Scheherazade*, Ravel's *Daphnis and Chloé* Suite no. 2, Georges Bizet's *Carmen* Suite no. 2 (the movement called *Danse bohème*, or *Gypsy Dance*), or anything by the Monkees.

The tam-tam and gong

What you think of as a *gong* isn't one. A true Chinese gong, if you hit it with a gong beater, produces a sound of a certain pitch — a note. Gongs come in many different sizes, and some composers actually write for gongs in C, in A, and so on.

On the other hand, that big, impressive instrument in movies meant to evoke China is not a *gong*. It's actually a *tam-tam*. It's that hanging, gonglike thing that goes *brrrwwwwwwaaaaannnnnggggggg*, without creating any particular hummable note.

The tam-tam makes a powerful appearance in Shostakovich's Symphony no. 5, Stravinsky's *The Rite of Spring,* and Copland's *Fanfare for the Common Man.*

The castanets

If the tam-tam is a cue from moviemakers that something is Asian, the *castanets* cue us that something's Spanish: Flamenco dancers, eyes aglow, costumes aglitter, feet astomping, clasp exotic castanets held high above their heads. Dark and fiery eyes meet from across the room, and Latin passion ignites. The dancers snap the little clamshell-like castanets together repeatedly with the thumb and fingers of each hand. Slowly at first and then with rising speed and volume, the castanets build and build in inflamed Iberian intensity, creating a clattering crescendo of caloric Castilian combustion!

(**Publisher's note:** *We apologize for the preceding excess. The authors have been hosed down.*)

Needless to say, you can find castanets in many pieces about Spain. But orchestral percussionists usually play a *modified* instrument — consisting of two castanets mounted on a flat surface — for convenience. For some evocative examples of castanets in orchestral music, listen to Ravel's *Rhapsodie espagnole* and Manuel de Falla's ballet *The Three-Cornered Hat*.

The whip

Believe it or not, you can find rare occasions in classical music where the sound of a *whip* is just the ticket.

Given the cramped confines of the percussion section onstage, however, and to the great disappointment of certain demographic segments, percussionists never use a real whip in concert. Instead, they use a device that *sounds* like a whip. It consists of two long, thin, rectangular pieces of wood, hinged together at one end.

To create a full, rich whipping sound, all they need to do is hold the pieces of wood open and apart at the hinge — and then slap them together.

Perhaps the most prominent example of whip music in all orchestral music is Ravel's Piano Concerto in G. It's also the only piece we know of that *starts* with a whip solo. (With a whip solo on your résumé, people *have* to take you seriously.)

You can also hear some pretty fierce whipping going on in Mahler's Symphony no. 5, as well as in Benjamin Britten's *The Young Person's Guide to the Orchestra*.

The cowbell

The *cowbell* makes rare and specific appearances in an orchestral setting — whenever a composer wants to create the sound of a cowbell. You can hear some beautiful, nostalgic cowbell playing in Mahler's Symphonies no. 6 and 7.

The ratchet

Our favorite percussion instrument! A ratchet is made of wood and consists of a wooden cog and some slats. If you turn the handle (as you do on a fishing rod), you cause the teeth of the cog to turn against the slats, creating a loud clicking sound.

Not much nuance is available on a ratchet — loud and louder is about it. But you can control how quickly or slowly you turn the handle. Turn it more quickly and the clicks come closer together, producing a more intense sound.

You can listen to the ratchet in *Till Eulenspiegel's Merry Pranks*, by Richard Strauss. It's supposed to sound like the insolent nose-thumbing of our mischievous hero. What instrument could get across this idea better than a ratchet?

Part IV
Peeking into the Composer's Brain

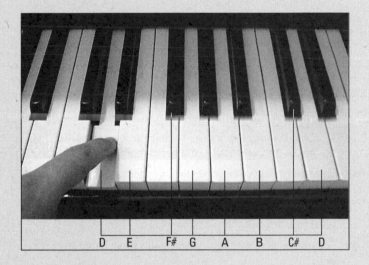

In this part . . .

- ✔ Discover the process of creating and performing music, from the pen of the composer to the ear of the listener.

- ✔ Become familiar with the rhythm, harmony, and dynamics that give music its awesome power.

- ✔ Meet the little marks that make up sheet music and discover what they mean.

- ✔ Try your hand at singing, playing, and even writing your own music.

Chapter 11

The Dreaded Music Theory Chapter

*Y*ou know what the greatest thing about music is? That, when you get right down to it, *nobody knows how the heck it works*. Sure, people study it and take it apart and write, talk, and teach about it — but when you get to explaining how music actually affects our emotions, science pretty much draws a blank. One study proved that fast music can increase your heart rate; another showed that soothing music in the grocery store increases sales by 20 percent; but nobody can figure out *how*.

The best humans can do, therefore, is to *describe* the various components of music and how they work. That's exactly what we intend to do in this chapter. After you understand the components of music, you can enjoy it all the more — and if you really get into it, you can even compose music yourself. Best of all, learning about the pieces that make up music doesn't take any of the magic or mystery out of the listening experience.

Along the way, we're going to dip our literary big toe into a few actual musical terms and theoretical principles — abstruse concepts such as melody and rhythm. If, at any point, the discussion is getting too thick for your taste, you have our permission to close your eyes and breathe deeply until you recover, skip to another chapter, or put on a classical music recording and be amazed that all this tech-talk winds up sounding like that.

Meanwhile, music teachers worldwide are choking back their gag reflex. "These guys think that they're going to teach musical newcomers how to read music in one chapter? Without a teacher? Are they *nuts?!?*"

Yes. But you knew that already.

I've Got Rhythm: The Engine of Music

All music — classical, modern, pop, futuristic, or whatever — has rhythm. Some rhythms are easier to feel than others. But you can boil all rhythms down to their bare essentials — the lengths of the notes themselves. To understand rhythm, you need to be able to *see* it; and to see rhythm, you need to understand a little bit about *sheet music*.

Dividing up time

When you write a piece of music, the first thing you must do is *divide up time*. Just as you can divide up space by using inches, centimeters, rulers, and yardsticks, you can divide up time by using things called measures and beats.

Imagine time as an endless continuum. Composers picture it as shown in Figure 11-1. This series of lines is what we call a *staff*. The staff is made up of five parallel lines, which help us distinguish one note from the next — more on that later. The staff stretches all the way from the beginning of a piece of music to the end.

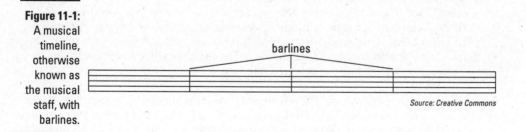

Figure 11-1: A musical timeline, otherwise known as the musical staff, with barlines.

Source: Creative Commons

Like a tape measure without any marks on it, a staff without *vertical* marks is of practically no use to us. To make sense of a staff, we need to mark the divisions in time, just as we do the inches on a tape measure (see Figure 11-1 again).

This staff is divided up by a bunch of vertical lines. The spaces between these lines are called *measures*. A measure is an inch of time; a typical piece of music is dozens or hundreds of measures long.

Feeling the beat

Within each of these measures are a few evenly spaced *beats*. A beat, simply stated, is the length of time it takes to tap your foot once. Music is absolutely teeming with beats. Every note you hear lasts a certain number of beats or a certain fraction of a beat. When you understand that, you understand *rhythm*. (And if you picture beats played really loudly by a drum machine, you also understand *disco*, but that's another book.)

In writing a new piece of music, a composer must first decide how many beats each measure has. This decision is crucial, because it has an important effect on what the music sounds like. Most pieces of music have two, three, or four beats (foot taps) per measure. In a *march* (also known as a *two-step*), every measure gets two beats. All the great marches of John Philip Sousa have two beats in a measure, including "The Stars and Stripes Forever" and the Monty Python theme (which is actually a Sousa march called "The Liberty Bell").

In a waltz, on the other hand, every measure gets *three* beats. (Your fourth-grade music teacher probably represented a waltz by invoking the time-honored phrase, "*OOM*-pah-pah, *OOM*-pah-pah.") And most other works of music, including many pop, Broadway, and jazz tunes, have *four* beats per measure.

In their never-ending quest to improve the state of sheet music, some magnificent monks dreamed up the idea of writing the number of beats per measure at the beginning of the piece of sheet music — something like what you see in Figure 11-2. If you were to write the beats themselves, they'd look like the *notes* in Figure 11-2.

Figure 11-2:
Four beats
to the
measure.

Source: Creative Commons

Probably because most pieces of music have four beats in each measure, each of those notes is called a *quarter note* (because it divides the measure into four pieces). Quarter notes are universally beloved by music fans. When a bandleader starts off his group by shouting, "*And-a-1-2-3-4!*" he's counting off quarter notes. When a rock drummer thuds the bass drum in the dance club, she's thudding quarter notes. Whenever a cheesy mail-order outfit designs a mug that's supposed to appeal to musicians, it paints quarter notes all over it.

Now, back to those ingenious composers of old. They realized that *almost* always, the quarter note is where you want to tap your foot. But even hundreds of years ago, some crackpot composers wrote pieces where *other* kinds of note values got the foot-taps (such as *eighth* notes and *half* notes, which we'll get to in a moment). So everybody mutually agreed to add a second notation at the beginning of every piece of music — a notation that shows which *kind* of note gets the beat. Take a look at the left side of Figure 11-3.

Figure 11-3: Different notation, same meaning.

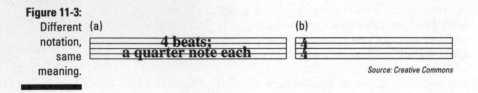

Source: Creative Commons

Over time, musicians learned to abbreviate this notation to look as shown on the *right* side of Figure 11-3. That's what you'd call *standard 4/4 notation,* signifying four beats to a measure with each beat on a quarter note.

Sight-reading for the first time

Check it out: Here you are, only a few paragraphs into the chapter, and we're going to have you reading sheet music already. Ready? Take a look at Figure 11-4.

Figure 11-4: Twinkle, twinkle!

Source: Creative Commons

You recognize the words, right? (We sure hope so. If not, try substituting the famous alternative set of lyrics: "A-B-C-D-E-F-G, H-I-J-K-LMNO-P.") Well, now you can match up the steady parade of quarter notes, four in each measure, with the melody you've always known and loved.

About that squiggly thing at the end of the second and fourth measures: It's called a *rest*. It marks a place where you *don't* sing a note — but you tap your foot anyway, because another beat is going by while you grab a breath. Rests were crucial to the invention of singing, because without them, every singer in history would have died from oxygen deprivation.

Here's another piece of music that uses quarter notes and quarter-note rests (see Figure 11-5). We're not going to tell you what it is until you give the rhythm a try. This one is in 4/4 time, which means four beats to the measure — and again, the quarter note gets the beat. Using your rhythmic skill, tap out the first two measures of this music.

Figure 11-5:
Name that
tune!

Source: Creative Commons

Do you know what it is yet? Think wintertime. Think dashing through the snow. We can't think of any other piece of music, offhand, that begins with the very characteristic rhythm of "Jingle Bells."

Making notes longer

Obviously, a universe of music where the quarter note was the only rhythm available to composers would be a simplistic and boring place. (For proof, ask the nearest kid. Because these all-quarter-note rhythms are so simple and boring and nonthreatening, they're considered ideal for children's songs. Practically every song we learn as youngsters has a rhythm made up mostly of simple quarter notes. "Twinkle, Twinkle" . . . "Frère Jacques" . . . "Old MacDonald" . . . you name it. Just don't sing it. Please.)

For a little variety, therefore, composers began inventing other notes. They came up with the *half note,* which is a note you sing for the duration of *two* beats. Half notes look like albino quarter notes, as shown in Figure 11-6, but they last twice as long. Put another way, in our standard 4/4 world, each half note lasts *half* a measure.

Now that you know about the quarter note and its slow-witted cousin, the half note, you should have no problem understanding the rhythm of the following classic of avant-garde music (refer to Figure 11-6).

Figure 11-6:
The albino
half note.

the half note

I love you, you love me, we're a hap-py fa-mi-ly,

Source: Creative Commons

Without too much mental anguish, now, we think you should be able to grasp the concept of the next rhythmic value, the *whole note*. A whole note (check out Figure 11-7) lasts four times as long as a quarter note; in our 4/4 world, a whole note lasts the *whole* measure.

Figure 11-7:
The whole
note.

the whole note

From sea to shi - ning sea!

Source: Creative Commons

Making notes shorter

On the other hand, some notes are *shorter* than quarter notes — such as the world-renowned *eighth* note. You need two eighth notes to fill your average foot-tap beat. To remind the musician that a pair of eighth notes should be taken together in a single beat, they're often written with a little bracket, or *beam,* joining them, as shown in Figure 11-8.

Figure 11-8:
The joining
of the
eighths.

If I were a rich man, dai-dle, dee-dle, dai-dle, dig-guh,dig guh, dee-dle,dai-dle dum!

Source: Creative Commons

(So what do you do if you want to use one of these short notes by itself? You break the beam in half and draw it as a droopy broken beam, or *flag,* as shown on the last note in Figure 11-8.)

What's more, after witnessing the runaway success of the eighth note, ancient composers wasted no time producing even faster-sounding sequels, such as the sixteenth note, the 32nd note, the 64th note, and, for instrumentalists strung out on caffeine, the rarely seen 128th note.

To notate these ultra-short notes, composers hit upon the idea of adding more and more beams (or flags) to them. Each successive beam or flag shows that the length of the note has been cut in half yet again.

Take a look, for example, at the notes shown in Figure 11-9. You can probably guess what they're called: *sixteenth notes.* They are, as you may expect, exactly half as long as eighth notes. They look like eighth notes, but with an important exception: They each have two flags instead of one. Composers connect the flags of sixteenth notes whenever they appear together. Figure 11-9 shows a lonely sixteenth note by itself (left) and a group of four beamed together.

Figure 11-9:
Sweet
sixteenths.

Source: Creative Commons

You know why that is, right? Because the four sixteenth notes, put together, make up a quarter note — and again, that is *one entire beat.* Connecting the sixteenth notes enables you, the reader, to more easily perceive the whole beat all at once.

Adding a dot

The final concept in your crash sheet-music-reading lesson is that of the *dot.* You put a dot after any kind of note to make it last 50 percent longer. A dotted quarter note (known in the lingo as *a dotted quarter note*), for example, lasts a beat and a half.

The following shows most of the rhythmic symbols you're ever likely to see in a piece of sheet music. We've listed them in groupings that take up the same amount of *time* (or foot taps); that is, one quarter note is the same as two eighth notes, and so on. Notice that each kind of note also has a corresponding *rest* symbol — which, you may recall from earlier in the chapter, means *shut up and breathe* for the specified number of beats.

Almost all the music you hear is made up of combinations of the notes we've explained so far. All rhythm — even the most complicated rhythm — is nothing more than a creative combination of note lengths.

Taking the final exam

Now that you're well versed in wholes, halves, quarters, eighths, sixteenths, and all the dotted versions thereof, it's time for a little freelance rhythmic reading. Remembering that a quarter note is one foot tap, try to figure out which song is represented in each of the written-rhythm examples in Figure 11-10. All you get are the rhythms, not the pitches, so we won't even draw in the five lines of the staff. Answers are at the bottom of the next page.

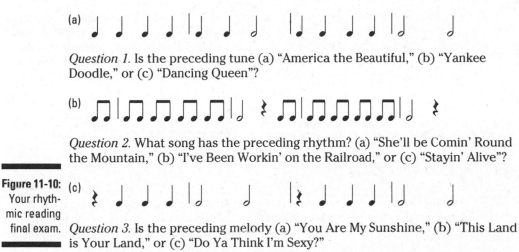

(a)

Question 1. Is the preceding tune (a) "America the Beautiful," (b) "Yankee Doodle," or (c) "Dancing Queen"?

(b)

Question 2. What song has the preceding rhythm? (a) "She'll be Comin' Round the Mountain," (b) "I've Been Workin' on the Railroad," or (c) "Stayin' Alive"?

Figure 11-10:
Your rhyth-
mic reading
final exam.

(c)

Question 3. Is the preceding melody (a) "You Are My Sunshine," (b) "This Land is Your Land," or (c) "Do Ya Think I'm Sexy?"

Source: Creative Commons

I'm a fermata — hold me

One particular musical symbol can bring any rhythm you play or sing to a grinding halt. It's called the *fermata* in Italian. The word fermata means stop, as in "bus stop." A fermata in real life looks like this:

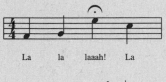

La   la   laaah!   La

And a fermata appearing over any note, anywhere in a piece of music, instructs you to stop and hold that note. For how long? As long as you want. If it feels good, do it. (Unless you're playing in an orchestra, of course — then you hold it as long as the conductor feels like it.)

Below: one of the most famous examples of fermatas ever composed. You definitely know it. Can you identify it by rhythm alone?

It's the opening of Beethoven's Fifth Symphony. (You can hear it online at www.dummies.com/go/classicalmusic, Track 4.) Many people have compared those opening eighth notes to "fate knocking on the door." Others used this rhythm as a symbol for "victory" during World War II. One rock group used it as the basis of a jazzy pop/rock song called "A Fifth of Beethoven" in the '70s. But whatever it means, it's really just three eighth notes plus a half note, with a fermata on the half. We've boiled one of the world's most famous rhythms down to its bare essentials.

Answers: 1. (b) 2. (a) 3. Either (a) or (b) — both songs start out with the same rhythm!

Okay, now you've got rhythm. At this moment, you have the ability to decipher the rhythm of just about any passage you come across in printed music. The rhythmic notation you've just picked up explains how notes are positioned from *left to right* in sheet music. Now comes the fun part — finding out how they're placed from *top to bottom* on the musical staff.

Understanding Pitch: Beethoven at 5,000 rpm

The *pitch* of a note is how high or low it is. The farthest key at the right end of a piano has the highest pitch, and the farthest-left note has the lowest. A soprano after a breath of helium sings with a very high pitch; Darth Vader, in one of his rare concert appearances, would have a very low one.

Performing an experiment for the betterment of mankind

To help explain the concept of pitch, we ask you to participate in a little experiment. You need a car for this exercise. (A stick shift is best, but an automatic with a tachometer — that little "rpm" meter — works nicely, too.)

Put a friend in the passenger seat to read to you from this book. Get in your car and start it. Drive out to the freeway. Now floor it.

As the car accelerates to 5,000 rpm, listen to the engine and observe the tachometer intently. Notice that, as the number of revolutions per minute increases, the sound of the engine gets higher.

Slow down a bit; then floor it again. Notice that the sound your car makes at 5,000 rpm is exactly the same as it was the first time.

Try cruising for a while at a constant speed. Notice that the pitch of the engine stays constant. It's actually playing a note. Can you sing that note?

Slow down just a tad — maybe by ten miles per hour or so. Notice that the pitch goes down? Sing the new note.

Do the same thing one more time, slowing down ten *more* miles per hour; sing the new note. You now have three notes to play with: the beginnings of a musical scale!

With a little experimentation, you can soon play "Mary Had a Little Lamb" on your car. (Be patient. This takes practice.) With continued practice — and perhaps a Ferrari — you can soon master all your favorite classical music solos as you terrorize the residents of your city.

As the car experiment illustrates, musical pitch is a direct function of *frequency*. The faster the engine vibrates, the higher the pitch. As you can read in our chapters on the instruments of the orchestra, all sound is produced by vibrations, or waves, in the air. Sometimes these sound waves are produced by vibrating engine cylinders; sometimes they're made by a vibrating violin string; other times they're made by vibrating air in a horn. In all cases, the faster the vibration, the higher the pitch.

Given that you can rev your car from zero to 5,000 rpm and beyond, a whole universe of pitches is available to you. By making tiny foot muscle adjustments, you can make your car engine play all kinds of notes — an infinite number of different pitches, each barely different from the next. But just as we have names for only a few specific colors out of the trillions in the rainbow, we, in the Western world, make all our music by using only 12 different pitches.

Focusing on 12 pitches

The names these 12 notes have been given are highly unimaginative: They're all called some variation of A, B, C, D, E, F, or G. To see how this principle works, take a look at the portion of a piano keyboard shown in Figure 11-11.

Figure 11-11:
An octave
of notes,
from A to
shining A.

A   B   C   D   E   F   G   A

Source: Creative Commons

The white keys are named for those basic seven notes, A through G. For added variety, most piano makers (all right, *all* of them) include, as a bonus, some black keys. These keys play notes that fall halfway between the white notes.

The black keys are called *sharps* and *flats* (see Chapter 6). In the music biz, *sharp* means slightly higher in pitch, and *flat* means slightly lower. You hear musicians talk about "C-sharp," for example, or "B-flat." And if they're a little tipsy and trying to be funny, you may hear them say, "It's icy out. You'd better C-sharp or you'll B-flat! AHAHAHAHAHA!"

Anyway, a note that's not sharp or flat — in other words, a white key — is formally called *natural,* as in "F-natural."

So how do you know what to call a specific black key on the piano? Consider, for example, the black key between A and B. Do you call it *A-sharp* (because it's slightly *higher* than A)? Or do you call it *B-flat* (because it's slightly *lower* than B)? **Answer:** You're right either way. For our purposes, those two terms are *absolutely synonymous*. Every black key has two different names.

And that's it. You now know the names for the notes. You've got your basic set of seven (A through G), plus the five in-between steps (on a piano, the black keys), for a total of 12 notes. Almost every piece of Western music you ever hear — on your MP3 player, on a CD, on the radio, in the concert hall, or *even in your head* — consists of these 12 pitches alone.

But wait, you're no doubt thinking, with so much emphasis you require italics. *How can there be only 12 notes? Do you mean to tell me that, in the entire Ninth Symphony by Ludwig van Beethoven, which lasts more than an hour, I'm just hearing the same 12 notes over and over again?*

Yep.

Notating pitches

Before we show you how musical notes are written down, a warning: Reading this section may change your life forever in a real and palpable way. From this moment on, whenever you see little notes coming out of Schroeder's toy piano in the *Peanuts* comic strip, you'll theoretically be able to tell exactly what he's playing.

Remember the staff — the timeline graph of music notation (from the beginning of this chapter)? Each line on this staff represents one pitch on the piano keyboard (or on any instrument, for that matter). Because of an obscure union regulation, the second-from-bottom line of this staff is designated as the note G. To help you remember that point of reference, we write an elaborate, stylized letter G (with its tongue wrapped around the G line, as shown in Figure 11-12) called the G *clef.* (*Clef* is French for "key," although we're not sure how that helps you remember anything.)

Figure 11-12:
The glorious
G clef!

G

Source: Creative Commons

To write the note G, you write a little oval exactly on that line, as shown in the figure.

Now that you know where G is, you can figure out where to write the other notes of the alphabet. Each line and each space between the lines corresponds to one of those seven letter names, A through G, as shown in Figure 11-13.

Figure 11-13:
Where
the other
notes of the
alphabet go.

F
D   F
B   C
G   A
E   F

Source: Creative Commons

Learning to read music sure would be easier if the letter names appeared on the staff, just as they do in Figure 11-13. In fact, in the early stages of training, most musicians do rely on a cheat sheet such as this one. This diagram is like a set of training wheels.

But after a while, musicians memorize what the lines and spaces mean. The lines, for example, from bottom to top, are E, G, B, D, and F. You probably can't find a musician in America who hasn't learned *"Every Good Boy Does Fine"* as a memory device. (You'd think, with all the creativity running in their artistic little DNA, musicians could come up with a more clever mnemonic. We hereby propose *"Eggs Generally Bring Down Fever."*)

And the spaces, from bottom to top, spell F-A-C-E. We have no suggestions for improvement on a mnemonic for that one.

Now, clearly, a piano (or any instrument) has more than 12 notes. After you run through the basic 12 notes (A through G and the associated black-key notes), these notes repeat, in sequence. Another A follows G, but at an *octave* higher than the first A. (As we describe in Chapter 6, notes an octave apart sound like the same note — but one's higher. Imagine a child and an adult male singing the same tune. They're hitting the same letter-name notes — A, B, C, and so on — but the child sings "up an octave.")

Okay. So because the musical staff has only enough lines and spaces for about one run through the A-to-G alphabet, how would you, the composer, write notes *higher* than that set of notes? *Answer:* You'd draw in *more* lines. The result would look something like Figure 11-14.

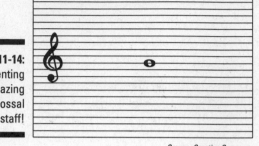

Figure 11-14:
Presenting
the amazing
colossal
infinite staff!

Source: Creative Commons

Clearly, this notational idea has some bugs to work out. Now you have so many lines that identifying the original set of five is impossible! As a compromise, notation scholars hit upon the idea of drawing in extra *mini*-lines, just wide enough to accommodate the note that needs them — as shown in Figure 11-15.

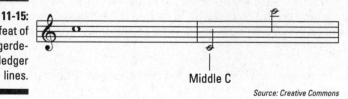

Figure 11-15:
A feat of
legerde-
main: ledger
lines.

Middle C

Source: Creative Commons

These above-the-staff and below-the-staff lines are called *ledger lines.* The first ledger line below the staff is the most important one of all, for it corresponds to the famous *middle C.*

Middle C is so named because it's just about in the middle of the piano keyboard. All the notes on the G clef, falling as they do above middle C, are relatively high notes. Therefore, the G clef is often called the *treble* clef.

Ledger lines are useful only up to a point. Add too many, and musicians would need to stop in mid-concert just to *count how many* are there. *Solution:* Draw in another staff, made specifically for the low notes. This staff, too, has a fancy symbol at the beginning, this time looking like a letter F as drawn by, say, Klingons. Its two dots straddle the line for the note F.

You'd think they'd call this symbol the *F clef*. And professional musicians sometimes do. It's more commonly known, however, simply as the *bass clef,* because it's used for low notes. By the way, as a point of reference, our friend middle C appears at the *top* of this kind of staff, as shown in Figure 11-16.

Figure 11-16:
The bass clef, featuring the Klingon F.

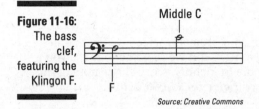

Source: Creative Commons

The bass clef staff works just the same as the G clef (or treble clef) staff in every way. Here, however, notes are assigned based on their distance from the home note F.

A few instruments can play such a large range that they require *both* the bass clef *and* the treble clef to notate all of their notes. The piano is one example. In piano music, a treble clef staff and a bass clef staff are sort of fused together, as shown in Figure 11-17. In this figure, you can see two different ways to write middle C. The second and third notes shown are *both* middle C. In piano notation, the staves are arranged so that they can share middle C, so to speak.

Figure 11-17:
The treble and bass clefs: together at last.

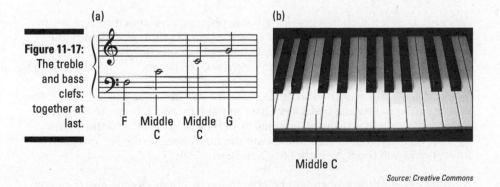

Source: Creative Commons

Reading music

Consider the music in Figure 11-18. Kinda makes you wish you were studying nuclear physics instead, doesn't it?

Source: Creative Commons

If this example of piano music makes your stomach seize up, don't panic. A lot of sheet music looks confusing at first. But we're going to make you a guarantee. If you read on, you'll be able to identify every single note of this music in the next ten minutes — *or you give us $1,000,000!*

To accomplish this feat, we're going to show you how to read and write the notes just by looking at their positions on the staff, with no cheat-sheet of letter names to help you. This is the way that musicians read music.

This task becomes much easier if we identify some *points of reference* — that is, some home notes to hang our hats on. You've already got a few points of reference (if you've been following us so far, that is):

- Middle C
- The F defined by the bass clef
- The G defined by the treble clef

Revisit Figure 11-17 for a refresher on these landmarks.

Anyway, here's the challenge: Using these points as reference, and remembering that you can count lines and spaces up or down, try to identify the notes in Figure 11-18. Heck, we're doing more than teaching you to read music — we're practically teaching you to *play the piano!*

You already know where to write the note for just about any white key on the piano. And notating the black keys isn't much harder. To indicate the black note to the *right* of a plain-letter-name note on a piano, you add the sharp symbol (♯) in front of it. And to indicate the black note to the left (slightly lower), you add the flat symbol (♭). (See Figure 11-19.)

All-righty then. Now you should be able to name, albeit slowly, any note you see on the staff. Try it in the example we showed you back in Figure 11-18 — the same example that seemed so bewildering at the beginning of this section. Our guess is that you can decipher it now!

And just in case you still have trouble, the answer key is in Figure 11-20.

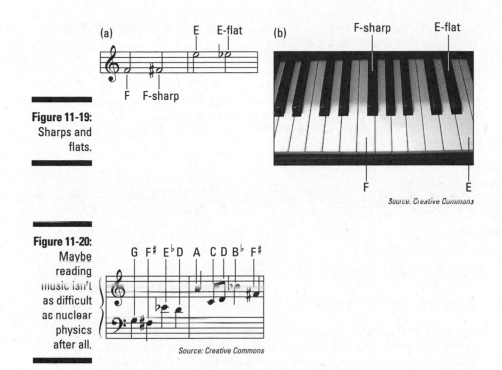

Figure 11-19:
Sharps and flats.

Source: Creative Commons

Figure 11-20:
Maybe reading music isn't as difficult as nuclear physics after all.

Source: Creative Commons

Deciphering key signatures

The world of sharps and flats is fascinating. Composers use them all the time; they've even developed a shorthand for situations where they want to use a particular sharp or flat over and over again.

Figure 11-21 illustrates just such an example. In the piece of music in the figure, the note F-sharp appears four times.

Figure 11-21:
Count the F-sharps.

Source: Creative Commons

Jeez, check out this piece: This composer *never* wants you to play the note F as a white key; he *always* wants it sharped so that you play the black note just to the right of the F key. What tedious and repetitive work, marking all those little sharps! So composers, ingenious folks for the most part, have come up with a solution. At the very leftmost edge of the staff, just after the

G clef symbol itself, they put a sharp on the top line (the line for F). This shorthand has the following meaning:

Henceforth, All Fs Shall Be Sharp.

Not just the F on that particular line of the staff, but the Fs in different octaves, above and below, as well. *All* Fs. Now take a look at the same piece of music, with this little change (see Figure 11-22). Much simpler, no?

Figure 11-22:
A key signature.

Source: Creative Commons

This shorthand is called the *key signature,* and every piece of music has one. The key signature tells you what notes (if any) to play sharp and what notes (if any) to play flat, everywhere in the piece.

Figure 11-23 illustrates some other common key signatures. The first example tells you to play all Bs flat; the second says that you should play all Fs and Cs sharp; and the third, while seemingly key-signature-free, actually *does* have a key signature — it just means that *no* notes in the piece are universally sharp or flat.

Figure 11-23:
Examples of three different key signatures.

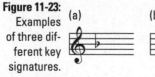 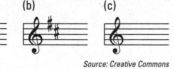

(a)   (b)   (c)

Source: Creative Commons

Figuring out the key

Now we're about to get music-theoretical. Please lower the safety bar and keep hands and feet inside the tram at all times.

The key signature at the beginning of a piece of music is more than just incidental. It specifies the *key* of that piece, a very important characteristic. If you go to a Broadway audition and tell the pianist, "'As Time Goes By' in F major," you're telling him the *key.*

We can explain by way of an example: Go to a convenient piano (or any keyboard) if you can. Touch middle C — or *any* C, for that matter — and then sing that note. You're singing, of course, a C.

Now, starting on that note, sing the first line of that immortal Christmas classic, "Joy to the World." You can play the first line of this song really, really easily: Just walk your fingers down the white keys of the piano, starting on a C and going to the next lower C (refer to Figure 11-24).

Figure 11-24: You can play "Joy to the World" by starting on C and playing each white key in descending order from there.

(a)

Joy to the world, the Lord is come.

(b)

Start here and move down.

Source: Creative Commons

Your first note is a C, and your last note (an octave lower) is also a C. In fact, if you knew how to play this *entire* song, you'd find out that the last note of the whole song is *also* a C. By golly, you'd need to conclude that this song is *in the key of C.*

Any song that you can play completely on the white notes of the piano is very likely in the key of C. Any song that *ends* on a C is usually in the key of C, too.

Okay, now, back to our example. Say that you're a temperamental soprano. Today, you're feeling especially temperamental. Today, you want to sing "Joy to the World" *higher.* Instead of starting on a C, you want to start on a D.

Well, sure, why not? Go back to your piano and locate your beginning note — not C, but the next white key to the right. That's a D. Go ahead and try to play the first line of "Joy to the World" the same way you did before, just by walking down the white keys of the piano.

GAAK! What happened?!? Some of the notes definitely sounded wrong.

Right, because when you started the song on D, you moved the whole melody to a new place on the keyboard. And that opened up a whole can of worms.

Now, feel free to skip over the following explanation if you want. Your life will go on just as well without it.

A *melody* is recognizable because of the relationships between its notes — just like a person, actually. Your brother's eyes are a certain distance apart. If that distance were to change, he'd cease to look like your brother. You probably wouldn't recognize him.

Similarly, if you want a melody to always stay the same, so that you can recognize it no matter what key it's in, you need to keep all the relationships between the notes the same. But — alert! — you've picked up the melody and placed it down on a different part of the keyboard from where it was. And the keyboard has an *irregular pattern* of white and black keys.

So to make the melody sound right, you must *sharp* some of the notes — that is, play black notes instead of white ones. In this case, the key of D, you must sharp two of them: F and C. So F becomes F-sharp, and C becomes C-sharp.

Temperamental soprano that you are, you insisted on singing "Joy to the World" in the key of D. And *every piece in the world* that's in the key of D requires the F and the C to be sharp. The key signature that tells you so looks like the one shown in Figure 11-25. It indicates that you should raise the two circled notes to black keys.

Figure 11-25:
"Joy to the World" again — but this time in the key of D.

Joy   to   the world,   the   Lord is come.

Source: Creative Commons

Go ahead and try this experiment again. Play "Joy to the World" on the piano, starting on D. But this time, as you go down the keyboard, substitute black notes for white ones on your second and sixth notes. That is, play notes in the following order: D, C♯, B, A, G, F♯, E, D.

This business of sharps and flats can get complicated. Some keys have up to *seven* sharps or flats in their key signature. (Want to make a beginning piano player turn green? Put a piece of seven-sharp sheet music on the music stand.) Fortunately, you don't need to know that to appreciate what a key is.

Dave 'n' Scott's 99.9999% Key-Determining Method

A tiny, tiny percentage of musicians are blessed with a bizarre and practically ESP-like talent known as *perfect pitch*. These lucky, lucky fools can tell you what key a piece is in just by *listening* to it. Many musicians would give just about anything to have this talent.

If you're not among the gifted 1/10 of 1 percent, we have a clever cheat for you. This method is foolproof 99.9999 percent of the time. What you do is this: Wait until the music you're listening to (the song or symphony or whatever) *ends*. Listen carefully to the *final note*. Rush over to a piano and hunt around until you match the note that the music ended on. Almost invariably, that final note matches the key of the piece. "That piece was in F!" you can triumphantly proclaim to your party guests as the music ends.

If you're looking at the sheet music of a piece, determining its key is even easier. Trained musicians, of course, can look at a wad of sharps and flats at the beginning of the staff and immediately declare, "Key of G-flat." Once again, however, we have a shortcut for you. Using your new-found mastery of music notation, just sneak a glance at the final note of the melody. Once again, that note is almost always the same as the key.

Try determining the key of the pieces shown in Figure 11-26. If you're having trouble remembering the letter names of the different lines and spaces, cheat by checking back to Figure 11-13.

Figure 11-26: Can you determine the keys of these pieces from their last notes? (No peeking at the answers, which appear at the bottom of the page.)

Source: Creative Commons

Answers: (1) Key of B. (2) Key of F. (3) Key of D.

Understanding why we have keys

When we, your present authors, first learned to play the piano, it became rapidly apparent that music with a lot of sharps and flats — black notes — was harder to play than all-white-meat music. We were absolutely mystified as to why any composer would knowingly write music in any key *other* than C, where every note is a white one. Wouldn't life be so much simpler (we asked, and you're probably asking) if everything was written in the key of C? Why not start a movement (our little nine-year-old thoughts went) to phase out key signatures and black keys on the piano?

Actually, we can name some pretty good reasons for the existence of different keys:

- **Sometimes, there's going to be a singer.** Shifting all the music into a non-C key is often necessary to fit the kind of voice (soprano, tenor, or whatever) singing the song.

- **On other instruments, the key of C *isn't* the easiest one.** Sure, no-black-notes music is easy to play on a *piano*. But each orchestra instrument has its own quirks — and its own "easy keys" to play in. For a considerable population of the standard orchestra — the players of most clarinets, many trumpets, and a few others — *B-flat* is the easiest key.

- **Some people say that the key makes a difference.** We bet that you couldn't tell the difference between the same music played in two different keys if you heard them an hour apart. But some musicians *swear* that certain keys have an intangible something, a certain quality, a sonic *je ne sais quoi.* "F-sharp major is such a *bright,* glimmering key," you hear a musician say. Well, okay. Just so we don't have to play it on the piano.

- **If the piano had no black keys, you'd never know where middle C was.** If you didn't have little clusters of three black keys and two black keys to break up the sea of white piano keys, you'd *never* know where you were on the keyboard!

But as you'll soon discover, the keys aren't all that different from one another after all. As we explain in the "Joy to the World" example in the "Figuring out the key" section earlier in this chapter, the relationships between the various notes of a melody remain constant no matter what key you're in. And this fact brings us to the important concept of *intervals* — the building blocks of every melody and harmony in the world.

Making the Leap into Intervals

An *interval* is the distance between two notes, measured (for our purposes) in piano keys. Determining the interval between two notes is easy: You name Piano Key #1 as one and count how many notes are in between it, spatially speaking, and the next note of the melody. If you count five keys in all, you declare that the two notes are "a fifth apart." If you count seven, you say that they're "a seventh apart." Not exactly organic chemistry, is it?

After you come to recognize intervals by *listening* to them, however, music gets to be fantastically fun. You begin to recognize the characteristic intervals used by your favorite composers — classical, rock, Broadway, or whatever. You really begin to understand what makes music sound the way it does. "Another Andrew Lloyd Webber hit," you can say. "The guy hardly ever uses intervals larger than a second, does he?" Or "John Williams wrote the music for this movie. What do you wanna bet he uses an interval of a fifth as the opening notes?"

We're going to use famous melodies to help you identify some of history's most famous intervals. You, like millions of music students before you, are never again going to be able to hear "Here Comes the Bride" without thinking, "Here comes the *fourth.*"

This section is either going to be great fun or horribly embarrassing for you to read, depending on whether (a) you're surrounded by other people, or (b) you're self-conscious about singing to yourself while you read.

The major second

The interval of the second is extremely common — it simply means that two notes are next to each other, on the keyboard or otherwise. Can you sing only the first *two notes* of "Rudolph, the Red-Nosed Reindeer" — and *stop?* ("Ru-dolph" — right, that's it.) If so, you've just sung an interval of a second. If that particular melody escapes you right now, you may also want to try singing the first two notes of "Silent Night" — just "Si-i." That much. That's a second, too: two notes next to each other. (Check out Figure 11-27.)

Both of those Christmassy examples feature *ascending seconds* — the line goes *up.* Plenty of famous tunes use seconds going *down,* too, however; try singing to yourself, in your best Barbra Streisand impersonation, "Mem'ries light the corners of my mind." You got it — the notes of the word *mem'ries* form a *descending* second.

Figure 11-27:
The major
second
interval in
one of your
favorite
Christmas
songs.

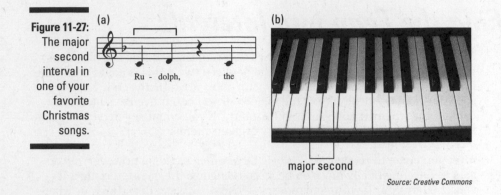

Ru - dolph,   the

major second

Source: Creative Commons

The major third

A *third,* obviously, is where you go *three* notes from one note of the melody to the next (counting both piano keys, of course). Perhaps the most famous third in classical music is the opening of Beethoven's Fifth Symphony. You know, the one that goes "Da-da-da-DAAAAAAAAAAAAAAAAAH!" (To refresh your memory, go online to www.dummies.com/go/classicalmusic and listen to Track 4.) But you can find plenty of other familiar examples containing both descending and ascending thirds. Hum to yourself, for example, the first two notes of "Swing Low, Sweet Chariot."

That's a descending third. For ascending thirds, look no further than the first two notes of "I Could Have Danced All Night." (Refer to Figure 11-28.) In fact, give yourself a moment of drill right now: Walk around your home or workplace singing just those first two notes, over and over: "I could —! I could —! I could —!"

If anyone looks at you funny, assume a highbrow expression and explain that you're working on your ascending major-third intervals.

Figure 11-28:
Dance all
night to
THIS inter-
val, baby!

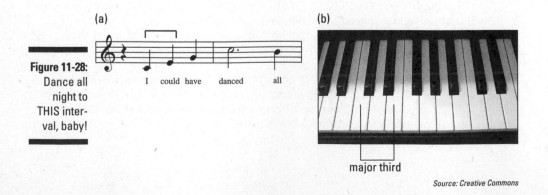

I   could   have   danced   all

major third

Source: Creative Commons

The fourth

This interval is easy to love. It's one of the catchiest, most easy-to-sing, beloved musical leaps of all time. Especially at Christmastime — holiday carols are positively riddled with melodies that begin with leaps of a fourth. You've got yer "Oh, Come, All Ye Faithful." (Listen to the ascending fourth between "all" and "ye.") And you've got yer "Hark the Herald Angels Sing!" (Here the first two words are an interval of a fourth, this time going up.) And you've even got yer "O, Christmas Tree!" But forget about Christmas; fourths abound in every kind of music. The "Mexican Hat Dance" music begins with an ascending fourth repeated three times. The original *Star Trek* TV show began with two consecutive ascending fourths, one built upon the other (Listen to the horn solo as they're saying, "Space . . . the final frontier.") Come to think of it, the theme for *Star Trek: The Next Generation* begins with a fourth, too. And don't forget the classic song "Here Comes the Bride," in which the first two notes form an interval of a fourth (see Figure 11-29).

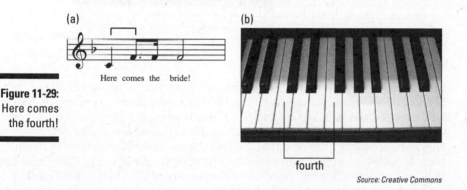

(a)

Here comes the bride!

(b)

fourth

Source: Creative Commons

Figure 11-29: Here comes the fourth!

If you're singing these quietly to yourself as you read, you can't help hearing the similarity of all these pairs of notes.

Most of all, for some mysterious reason, the opening theme music of every TV news broadcast in the country contains as many consecutive ascending fourths as possible. Someone probably did some market research and found out that, the more ascending fourths the theme music uses, the more trustworthy the news station seems. And indeed, this belief must contain some truth. After all, would you prefer to get your news from a station that used "Hound Dog" as its theme music?

Then again, if our theory is correct, the "Mexican Hat Dance" music would make a splendid opening theme for CNN.

The fifth

Yes, the fourth is everywhere. But leaps that are *five* notes apart are neck-and-neck in popularity. Think "*Flint*stones! Meet the *Flint*stones!" Each time the family name is invoked, you're singing a descending fifth. Fifths that leap *up* abound, too. Take, for example (as in Figure 11-30), the "Rest Ye" notes in "God Rest Ye, Merry Gentlemen."

Figure 11-30:
Pick up a fifth of musical pleasure with this interval.

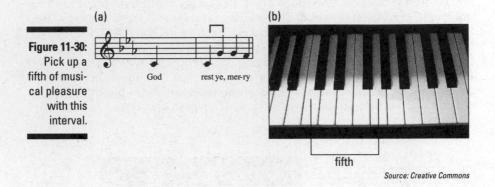

(a)

God   rest ye, mer-ry

(b)

fifth

Source: Creative Commons

TIP

But if you *really* want to meet a composer who's fond of fifths, check out the brilliant movie-music composer John Williams. Just about every movie theme he's ever written is based on a fifth. Take *Star Wars,* for example: Those first two triumphant notes form an ascending fifth. Or how about *Superman* — another ascending fifth. And that soaring theme from *E.T.* (as they're flying their bicycles) — yep, it's an ascending fifth, no doubt about it. How 'bout the famous five-note alien call from *Close Encounters of the Third Kind?* The final two notes of that form an ascending fifth.

But don't think that John Williams writes nothing but ascending fifths. Heavens, no. He also writes movie themes based on *descending* fifths, such as the mournful violin-solo theme from *Schindler's List.*

The major sixth

Can you take still more? As intervals go, the *sixth* is a superstar in pop-culture music. To get it into your head quickly, hum the old three-note NBC tune: "N . . . B . . . C." As you've probably guessed, the "N . . . B" is an ascending sixth. (See Figure 11-31.) So is the first couple of notes of "My Bonnie Lies over the Ocean" and "Hey, Look Me Over."

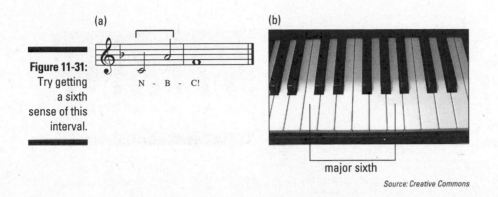

(a)

N - B - C!

(b)

major sixth

Source: Creative Commons

Figure 11-31: Try getting a sixth sense of this interval.

Sadness, anyone? You can find a descending sixth in the opening two notes of "Nobody Knows the Trouble I've Seen."

The major seventh

If fourths, fifths, and sixths are the Rolling Stones, the major seventh is Slim Whitman. That is to say, it's somewhat less likely to be the basis of your favorite tunes. Frankly, it doesn't sound all that great. And we can't think of a single famous melody that's based on it. If you can grab a piano, you may as well listen to just how *off* it sounds by playing a middle C together with the B above it — the *seventh* note above it if you count middle C as one.

The octave

In Chapter 6 we introduce you to the interval called the *octave* — so named because it contains eight notes within it. The two notes of an octave interval are really the *same* note played in two different ranges.

Try singing "Somewhere over the Rainbow" — but stop on the second syllable. Bravo! Why, Judy Garland herself couldn't sing a more perfect ascending octave than you just sang. (But then, you have the unfair advantage of being alive.) Figure 11-32 shows the octave in action.

If you've understood this discussion, and (especially) if you've enjoyed it, congratulations are definitely due you. This stuff is college-level music theory. The good news: Now you know all the major intervals.

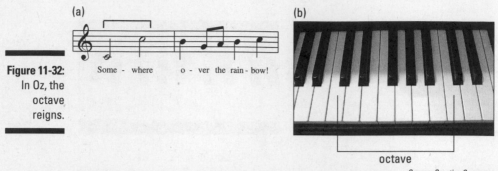

Figure 11-32: In Oz, the octave reigns.

Some - where   o - ver the rain - bow!

octave

Source: Creative Commons

Telling the difference: major and minor intervals

The bad news: Whenever we say *major* intervals, we *don't* mean "important." We mean that music has two different classes of intervals: *major* and *minor*. We can explain the distinction in this way: A major interval is slightly bigger than a minor interval. Makes sense, right?

Of course, the *best* way to understand the difference between major leaps and minor ones is to listen a lot, play them on an instrument a lot, and hum them a lot. But in our usual fashion, we'll attempt to help you experience the difference for yourself right now.

The minor second

A *minor second* is the smallest possible interval in the music of the Western Hemisphere. Remember the *Jaws* theme (another John Williams movie-music classic)? The main theme, the sharky music, is simply two notes repeated again and again; two notes, need we point out, that form an interval of a minor second (see Figure 11-33). Something about this interval, played down low, just makes you think of a shark.

A minor second goes an ultra-short distance — usually from a white key to the nearest black key or vice versa. Because it stretches only halfway between two white keys, it has the nickname *half step*.

Now a *major second,* also known as a *whole step,* by contrast, is the second-smallest interval in Western music. But compared to a *minor* second, it feels absolutely spacious. Compare the major second that begins "Happy Birthday" with the white key/black key interval of the *Jaws* theme. Hear the difference?

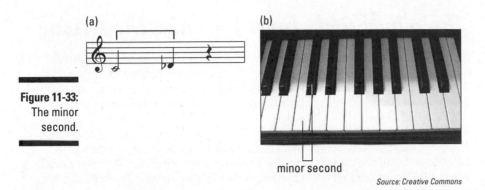

Figure 11-33:
The minor
second.

The minor third

You may remember the *major* third as the happy first two notes of "I Could Have Danced All Night." Compare that leap with the first two notes of "Greensleeves" (also known as "What Child Is This?"), as shown in Figure 11-34.

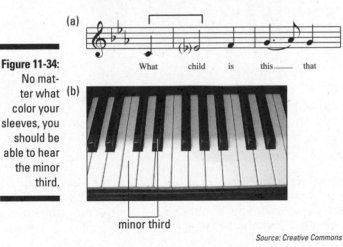

Figure 11-34:
No mat-
ter what
color your
sleeves, you
should be
able to hear
the minor
third.

What   child   is   this___   that

minor third

Wanna try going down? Then listen to the minor third that begins the "Star-Spangled Banner" (on the word "Oh-oh"); the words "get no" in the Rolling Stones' "I Can't Get No Satisfaction"; and the Stevie Wonder hit, "You Can Feel It All Over," which begins with one minor third after another.

The minor fifth (not!) — aka the tritone

So far, we've taken each happy little major interval and made it slightly smaller to provide the minor version. But if you shrink the *fifth* by a half-step in that way, you have what musicians call a *diminished fifth,* otherwise known as a *tritone.* But in medieval times, pious people called this interval the *DEVIL'S INTERVAL!*

This one particular interval was considered so awful and dissonant and scary-sounding that it was actually banned by the church. (We're *not* making this up!) Composers were forbidden to use this interval on pain of *death.*

Because the death penalty for using a tritone has been repealed in most states, these days you can hear this jarring sound in the privacy of your own living room. You can get it by making a fifth just a half step narrower — or by making a fourth just a half step wider — as in Figure 11-35.

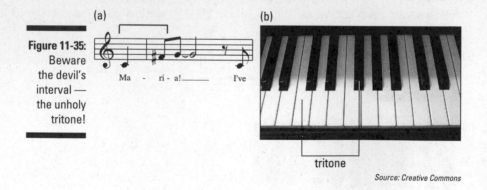

Figure 11-35: Beware the devil's interval — the unholy tritone!

Source: Creative Commons

In our time, this interval was made famous by one particular song: "Maria." This song comes from that great Bernstein/Sondheim musical, *West Side Story,* which absolutely teems with devil's intervals — for example, the first two notes of the song "Cool" (where they sing "Bo-y!").

We'll admit that the tritone does sound somewhat cool. But we don't find it evil at all. Not in the least.

The minor sixth

The first two notes of the old NBC musical logo form a happy little *major* sixth (from middle C to the A above it, if you're checking this tune out on a piano). If you go from C up to A-*flat* or from A-flat down to C, you get a *minor* sixth — a much sadder interval. You can prove this point to yourself if you've ever heard that tear-jerking melody from *Love Story.* The words are "Where do I begin . . . to tell the story of how great a love can be?" And the minor sixth is the leap forming the first two notes (and practically all the leaps thereafter), as shown in Figure 11-36.

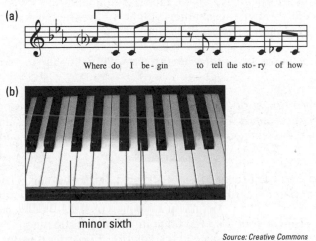

Source: Creative Commons

Figure 11-36: Love that minor sixth interval!

The minor seventh

We mention earlier in this section the surprising lack of popular melodies based on the *major* seventh. Interestingly, the *minor seventh* (C to B-flat, if you're at a piano) is much more common. It's the first two notes in "Somewhere" from *West Side Story,* for example (the first two notes of "There's a place for us . . ."). The main spaceship-flying-by-during-opening-credits theme of the original *Star Trek* series, too, is brought to you by the minor seventh. (See Figure 11-37.)

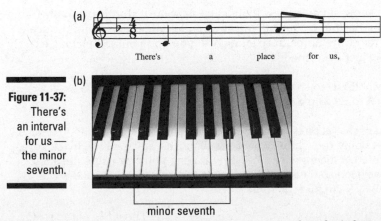

Figure 11-37: There's an interval for us — the minor seventh.

Source: Creative Commons

Getting on the Scale

Throughout this book, we make occasional casual use of the term *scale,* but we've saved the thorough explanation for this moment. And for good reason! If you've made it through this chapter, you now have the musical training necessary to grasp the *technical* definition.

Technically speaking, a *musical scale* is a way of dividing up an octave into various intervals.

Now, in the Western world, all the intervals within a scale are seconds — major and minor seconds, that is. The characteristic sound, feel, and identity of any scale are determined by the arrangement of those major and minor seconds.

Someday you may want to learn about all the different breeds of scales, each with its own personality traits. But for now, we're going to tell you about the most common of all scales, known as the *major scale.* You've got a very handy major scale at your disposal on your versatile little piano keyboard. All the white keys form a major scale in the key of C. Earlier in this chapter, we directed you to play "Joy to the World" — if you did so, you've even *played* a scale.

Locating the major and minor seconds of the C major scale on the piano keyboard is very easy. Any two neighboring white keys with a black key between them are a *whole step* (a major second) apart. If no black key divides the two white keys, they're just a *half step* (a minor second) apart. Simple enough?

So if you play a C major scale, what you're really doing is playing whole steps and half steps in a particular pattern. And that pattern is as follows:

   Whole, whole, half, whole, whole, whole, half

We know, we know; if you're new to music, this theory stuff is probably frying your brain. But try it at a piano. If you start on middle C and go up the scale, playing only the white notes, sure enough — you find yourself playing exactly the pattern we just described:

   C to D (whole), D to E (whole), E to F (half), F to G (whole), G to A (whole), A to B (whole), B to C (half)

This particular scale is so easy to figure out — and so often cited — precisely because it uses only the white keys of the piano, skipping all the black keys. But we can create a major scale from *any* starting point by using the same scheme. All we need to do is make sure that the interval sequence is the same, and skip keys in just the right places.

Here's an example. Start on the note D. If you skip keys in exactly the pre-scribed pattern (whole-whole-half, whole-whole-whole-half), you find yourself landing on black keys here and there, as shown in Figure 11-38. That's totally okay.

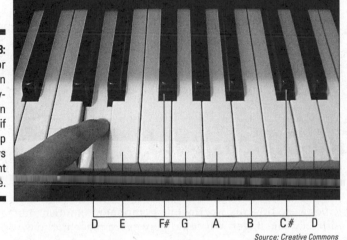

Figure 11-38:
A major scale can start any-where, even on a D, if you skip over keys in the right sequence.

D E   F# G   A   B   C# D

Source: Creative Commons

Fantastic, isn't it? No matter what note you start on — white or black — you can play a major scale if you step through the whole steps and half steps in the prescribed order. You may even accidentally write a top-ten hit in the process.

Constructing a Melody

There's no such thing as a melody that *isn't* made up of a combination of scales and intervals — the exact scales and intervals that we talk about in the previous sections. If you name a hit song, we can show you that one note connects to the preceding one by using only off-the-shelf, over-the-counter scales and intervals.

Classical pieces are no different. Figure 11-39, for example, shows the melody from the third movement of Brahms' Symphony no. 4, which you can hear online at www.dummies.com/go/classicalmusic, Track 5.

If you hear this piece performed at a concert, you're likely to read in the pro-gram an analysis that goes something like this:

> At the opening of the third movement, Brahms employs a descending C major scale fragment.

Source: Creative Commons

Figure 11-39:
It's Brahms!

Now you can smile smugly, knowing exactly what that fancy lingo means. If you played the melody on a piano, you'd find that it begins with a C major scale, *going down* — C, B, A, G, F. Because it's not an entire scale, but just five notes of it, it's called a scale *fragment*. Don't you wish that the IRS's tax forms were this easy to translate?

Getting Two-Dimensional: Piece and Harmony

Now, if *melody* were the only worthwhile component of music, humans would be born with only one finger. We could play every piece in the world on the piano, one note at a time.

But music, even on the page, has more than one dimension. At any moment, you hear more than the melody note; underneath, you hear a specific group of additional notes that form the *harmony* — the chord. (See Figure 11-40.)

Figure 11-40:
The two-dimensional shape of music: melody and harmony.

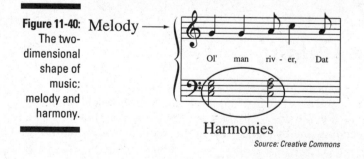

Source: Creative Commons

To identify a harmony for sure, you need at least three notes played simultaneously. Fancy jazz chords may have four, six, or even more — but three notes is the minimum.

Studying harmony is like studying math: The intricacies and interrelationships of the various chords can be enlightening and addictive, but understanding them doesn't come in a day. Still, you can get a lot more out of the music you hear even if you understand the basic idea — which is exactly what we intend to explain to you.

Major, minor, and insignificant chords

You can create hundreds of different chord types; just drop your hand on a random glob of piano keys, and your local jazz-bar pianist can happily tell you its name. It may take him 35 minutes to get *through* saying its name — "That's an E-flat minor seven with a diminished fifth over D" — but he'll do it.

Fortunately for the classical-music lover, however, the great majority of chords used in classical music fit into two types: *major* and *minor*.

To build a chord, you first choose the bottom note — the *root*. For this example — especially if you have a piano nearby — choose middle C. Already, you know the first part of this chord's name; it's going to be a "C-something."

To choose the other two notes of this chord, you can call upon your existing knowledge of intervals. You make a *major* chord by adding two notes: a major third above the root note and a fifth above the same root note. On the piano, this chord looks like the diagram shown on the left in Figure 11-41.

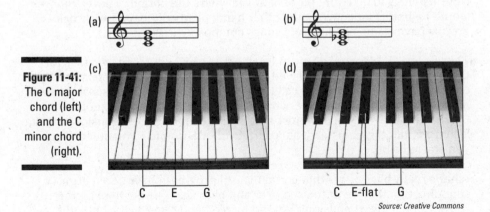

Figure 11-41:
The C major chord (left) and the C minor chord (right).

Source: Creative Commons

The chord you just played (or imagined playing) is called the *C major* chord. Any piano player on the planet will smile at you in instant recognition if you say "C major" at a post-concert get-together. Said pianist may be even more impressed if you call it a C major *triad,* because it does, after all, contain three notes. (If you just say "C chord," by the way, people assume that you mean "C *major* chord.")

Now then, if you lower the middle note so that it's a *minor* third above C instead of a major third, you get the configuration shown on the *right* in Figure 11-41. This chord is called, of course, a *C minor* chord.

Notice that, whereas a major chord sounds bright and happy, a minor chord sounds sadder, haunting, or even, sometimes, evil (if played forcefully). Trust us on this one: The happy/sad nature of major and minor chords has never been lost on the composers for the TV shows and movies you watch. It's a rare stalker flick with background music that wasn't deliberately filled with *minor* chords — or a rare sports movie that doesn't end with triumphant *major* chords as the motley crew of underdogs wins the final game and the crowd goes wild.

In your musical life, you'll eventually hear about other kinds of chords: diminished, half-diminished, augmented, dominant seventh, and so on. Each has a characteristic sound, each contains notes at specified intervals above the root note, and none is used nearly as frequently as the major and minor types you just created.

Friends and relations: harmonic progressions

Now, listening to an entire piece of music where the harmony never *changes* would be boring indeed. (On the other hand, plenty of heavy metal rock groups have made millions from songs composed just that way.)

Therefore — in classical music at least — the usual course of events is for the harmony (chord) being played underneath the melody to *change* every couple of seconds. Musicians call this string of changing chords a *harmonic progression* (or a chord progression). If you want your piece to sound "normal," however, you can't just switch chords *randomly,* a C major here, an F-sharp minor there. Instead, only certain chords sound right after the chord you started with.

What's really hilarious is that certain chord progressions are so natural-sounding that they've been used over and over again throughout history. "Blue Moon," "Heart and Soul," "Stand by Me," and "Stay Just a Little Bit Longer," for example, as well as hundreds of other songs, all have this chord sequence: C major, A minor, F major, and G major — and back to C. In fact, if you play us almost any pop song from the 1950s, for example, you can pause it at any point — and we can *predict* the next chord, even if we've never heard the song before.

Friends, Romans, chord progressions

Okay, we lied. It turns out that "Blue Moon," "Heart and Soul," and "Stay Just a Little Bit Longer" have that C major–A minor–F major–G major chord sequence *only* if you play them all in the key of C. And if you dig out your old recordings, you'll discover that they *weren't* all played in the key of C; some were played higher or lower to suit the voices of the teen idols who sang them.

This little detail leaves music-theory experts like us in a bit of a dilemma. How can we make our point that all these songs use the same underlying harmony *patterns,* using the same chords *relative to the starting note,* even though each actually has a different starting note? *Answer:* Refer to them by *number,* using "one" to refer to the starting note. And use Roman numerals to make the system seem more scholarly.

If C is your starting note, for example, you can assign Roman numerals as shown in Figure 11-42.

Figure 11-42:
Starting at C, you can denote the different keys by using Roman numerals.

Source: Creative Commons

Using this system, our favorite '50s pop-song chord sequence, formerly known as C/A minor/F/G/C, is now more simply notated as I, vi, IV, V, I. You pronounce that "one, six, four, five, one." (In classical music studies, lower-case letters indicate *minor* chords, and capitals represent major chords.)

Now, using these same Roman numerals, you can shift the music into other keys. Whether you sing one of those 1950s hits in the key of C, B-flat, F-double-sharp, or whatever, the Roman numerals of those chords are always the same: I, vi, IV, V, I. That particular pattern brings a smile of warm familiarity to camp-fire folk guitar players the world over.

Listening to the oldies

So what does all this have to do with classical music? Well, you can apply these handy Roman numeral harmony labels to any piece ever played. Although the chord sequences aren't quite as predictable as they were in the '50s, certain familiar patterns do emerge.

A huge majority of classical music pieces, for example, *end* with the same two chords: V-I. (That's "five-one," if you're reading aloud.) In the key of C major, V-I means the G major chord followed by the C major chord. If you can fake these two chords (or even those two *notes,* G and C) at a piano, they should sound familiar — especially if you go back and forth between them a million times really fast (a cliché of many a classical symphony's final moments).

While we're on the topic of final chord progressions, also check out IV-I ("four-one") at a piano. (In the key of C, this is an F chord followed by a C chord.) That's the "A-men" chord sequence that ends virtually every church hymn, ever.

On two occasions in your upcoming life, understanding these chord relationships can be useful. First, if you start to recognize familiar and recurring patterns of chords, you're in a better position to appreciate how classical composers made them *sound* fresh and interesting — by writing above those stock harmonies clever and surprising melodies, rhythms, and orchestration, for example. Second, you may well find references to these famous chord progressions (especially V-I) in the program notes of concerts or recordings you listen to. If you read that "Beethoven, in his early years, frequently relied on the I-V," you'll know that doesn't mean an intravenous drip.

Put in Blender, Mix Well

In this challenging chapter, you've heard about the *horizontal* component of music (the melody) and about the *vertical* component (the harmony). Before we release your brain to a well-deserved hour or two of intellectually devoid TV-watching or bathtub-soaking, we're obligated to point out that these two dimensions are *related.* You, like the long-dead classical composers, can't come up with a masterful melody and stick just any old chord sequence under it, even if it *is* the "Blue Moon" sequence. The two are conceived and written simultaneously, and one affects the other.

You can prove this point to yourself by examining almost any great melody — classical, rock, or any other popular style. You'll discover that many a melody has been created by *spelling out* the notes of the chord (harmony) being played underneath it! Remember when you played (or imagined playing) a C-major chord on the piano? The three notes you played were C, E, and G. Lo and behold, these are the three notes that constitute the melody notes of many a song that begins with a C chord, as in Figure 11-43.

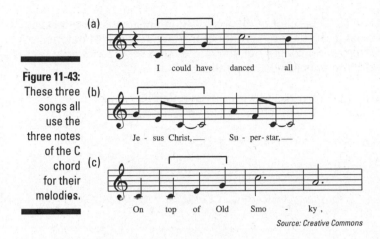

Figure 11-43: These three songs all use the three notes of the C chord for their melodies.

Source: Creative Commons

Real creative, huh? To write the melody, those composers simply played the three notes of the chord one at a time!

In other cases, the composer has *based* the melody on the chord notes, but fleshed it out with in-between notes (known in music-theory circles as *passing tones*). In the example in Figure 11-44, however, you can still find the familiar C, E, and G notes forming the foundation of the melody.

Figure 11-44: Passing tones aplenty.

Source: Creative Commons

Getting the hang of this? The point is that *you* can compose melodies of your own, and this trick — using the three notes that make up the chord as the basis — is a great way to get started. Beethoven, Mozart, and Elton John all have done it; you'd be in good company.

Getting Your Music Theory Degree

If you're still with us, you're amazing. You now have an understanding of how rhythm, pitch, intervals, and scales form the basis of melody, and how major, minor, and other chords make up harmony — which makes you more knowledgeable than 99.99 percent of the world's non-musicians. Not only can you understand what people are talking about in conversations about music (and in concert program booklets), but you may even be able to identify scales, chords, and intervals as you hear them.

And when *that* happens, it's a great feeling: Even unfamiliar music has familiar elements, making you much more at home, no matter where your ears take you.

Chapter 12

Once More, with Feeling: Tempo, Dynamics, and Orchestration

*I*f you've read Chapter 11 (and you're still alert and haven't wandered off to your neighborhood bar), you're painfully aware of how much trouble composers go to in writing down their masterpieces. They immerse themselves in the finer points of notes, rhythms, pitches, measures, key signatures, and the rest. Despite all these details, however, whenever a composer's work is performed, the music may come out sounding quite a bit different than the composer intended! The conductor and the musicians who perform the work may make the piece sound much worse than the composer imagined — or much better.

Music is a collaborative art. The composer is only one participant in a long line of creative types who stand between the original sheet music and your ears. Movies and plays are also like that, by the way; a great screenplay may make a lousy movie because of bad acting and bad direction. The difference is, of course, that the screenwriter gets $500,000 anyway, whereas even the greatest composers in history generally struggled just to make their minimum credit-card payments — a proud tradition that continues to this day.

This chapter explains why the same composition can sound completely different, depending on who's performing it. Here you can read about the various mushy, intangible, touchy-feely qualities of music that can't be specified precisely — only interpreted and perceived.

Meet the Dynamics Duo: Soft and Loud

Dynamics are volume levels: quiet, loud, and everything in between. Most composers specify exactly how loudly each section of music should be played. They do so by marking special symbols — called, sure enough, *dynamic markings* — underneath the music they're supposed to affect.

Fortunately, understanding the various dynamic markings isn't tough. The Big Two Letters you need to know are *p* and *f,* which essentially stand for "soft" and "loud" in Italian. Either one of these letters can be modified by an *m,* which means "medium." Composers use these letters in combinations such as those in Table 12-1.

Table 12-1	Dynamic Markings Demystified	
Marking	*Means*	*Stands for*
ppp	Unbelievably quiet	*pianississimo*
pp	Pretty darn quiet	*pianissimo*
p	Quiet	*piano*
mp	Sorta quiet	*mezzo-piano*
mf	Medium (normal)	*mezzo-forte*
f	Loud	*forte*
ff	Really loud	*fortissimo*
fff	Incredibly loud	*fortississimo*
fffff	Deafening	*Ow! Jeez!*

Like so many music students before you, you may well ask, "What's the deal with these pretentious Italian words? Why don't we just make the markings *s, m,* and *l,* pronounced 'soft,' 'medium,' and 'loud'? Then all you'd need to do for '*really* soft' or '*really* loud' is add a letter R in front . . . or something."

Well, you've got a point. The funny thing is, that's exactly what the Italians *thought* they were doing when they dreamed up these symbols to begin with! To them, *piano* (pronounced "PYAHHH-noe") *is* the word for "soft," and *forte* (pronounced "FOR-tay") is the word for "strong" or "loud." It isn't their fault that the rest of the world picked up on their system and has used it ever since.

Honey, I shrunk the LoudSoft™

Speaking of unpretentious Italians, based on your newfound knowledge of the term *piano,* you may find somewhat peculiar the fact that, whenever you say the name of the most popular keyboard instrument of all time, the piano, you're actually saying "the soft" in Italian. What a stupid name for an instrument, right?

Well, not if you consider the background. Before the invention of the piano, what high-society types had sitting in their living rooms were *harpsichords.* As we discuss in Chapter 6, the harpsichord, for all its classiness, has a disappointing drawback: No matter how hard or softly you strike a key, a harpsichord gives you exactly the same volume. Until you break it.

Therefore, when the first piano came along around 1709, the big attraction was that you could *change* the volume of the notes while you played. Hit a key harder and it played more loudly. Hit it lightly and it played more softly. Seeking to capitalize on the new invention's most attractive feature, and seeking to entice thousands of harpsichord owners to upgrade, the inventors named the new instrument the LoudSoft™ — or rather, because they were Italian, the *Fortepiano.* Eventually, through a series of miscommunications, this name was turned around: *Pianoforte.* As things turned out, all those syllables proved to be a tad time-consuming for the busy Type-A types of the 18th century. So, over time, people started using the shorthand word *piano* to refer to the new instrument.

As for the third Italian musical marking — the prefix *mezzo* (pronounced "MET-soe") — it means, obviously, "medium" or "middle." As in *mezzanine* (between two floors). Or *mezzo-soprano* (medium-high female singer). Or *intermezzo* (music played between two other pieces). Et cetera. Ad lib. That's amore.

Wearing Italian hairpins

The beauty of live musical performance, of course, is that the music doesn't always snap sharply from one dynamic level to another. More often, it smoothly ebbs and flows, as emotion and energy carry the players along.

A composer can't really specify emotion and energy, but she *can* inform the players that she'd like a gradual change from soft to loud. To do so, she just writes in a long, sideways V shape between the two markings involved, like this:

p ⊂———————— *f*

That symbol, which means to get smoothly louder as you play, is called a *crescendo* ("creh-SHEN-doe"). This musical term, like others you've met in this book, has been co-opted by jealous wannabes from other art forms. In a sports article, for example, you may read "a crescendo of energy"; in cooking magazines, you encounter "a crescendo of flavor"; we'd even wager that at least one hotel-industry newsletter out there has used the phrase "a crescendo of toiletries."

You can hear some mighty powerful crescendo effects if you go to www.dummies.com/go/classicalmusic. The last movement of Tchaikovsky's Symphony no. 6 (Track 7) is just teeming with them. Listen to 0:37, and pay special attention to the long crescendo starting at 6:57!

The opposite symbol, meaning "get gradually softer," is called a *decrescendo* ("day-creh-SHEN-doe") or a *diminuendo* ("dee-mee-noo-END-oe"). (We bet you can figure out where those words came from without our help.) That symbol looks like this:

f ═══════════════════ p

Interestingly, the word *hairpin* has a real, specific meaning in music circles. It means a crescendo *followed by* a diminuendo, like this:

On the other hand, a diminuendo followed by a crescendo (a somewhat rarer dynamic bird) has no name at all. We'd like to suggest *toothbrush*.

Getting into matters of sonic taste

So if a composer writes these elaborate "get loud!" and "get soft!" commands in the sheet music, why doesn't the music sound the same regardless of who performs it?

Answer: Who's to say what loud *is?* Head-banging rock concert attendees certainly have a different "too loud" threshold than harp aficionados. And even among classical music buffs, the *degree* of loud, soft, or motion from one dynamic to another can vary, even from one night to the next.

And one more thing just between us — this is not to leave this room: When you get right down to it, certain conductors and other interpreters we know sometimes *deliberately ignore* certain dynamic markings and substitute their own fluctuations in volume. If they think that the music would be more exciting, more passionate, or otherwise more effective with a different interpretation of the dynamics, they often change it. Classical music composers rarely complain when their dynamics are overridden. Then again, they're generally dead.

Throwing Tempo Tantrums

Composers write on the sheet music not only how loudly the music should be played, but also how quickly. The speed of a piece can be indicated in dozens of ways. Table 12-2 lists a few greatest hits of the tempo markings.

Table 12-2	Tempo Markings Made Comprehensible	
Marking	*Pronounced*	*Means*
Adagio	"ah-DAH-joe"	Restful
Lento	Just what you'd think	Slowly
Largo	You guessed it!	Broadly, unrushed
Larghetto	"lar-GET-toe"	A little bit broadly
Moderato	"moder-AH-toe"	Medium speed
Andante	"ahn-DAHNN-tay"	Walking speed
Andantino	"ahn-dahn-TEE-noe"	A bit faster than walking speed
Allegretto	"ah-leg-RET-toe"	A little bit lively and fast
Allegro	"ah-LEG-grow"	Lively and fast
Presto	C'mon, you know	Really fast
Prestissimo	"press-TEE-see-moe"	The cops are after you

Incidentally, the tempo indication sometimes includes words to describe the *character* of the music in addition to its tempo. It may say "With vigor," for example, or "Violently" or "Smugly" or "*Con brio*" (which we always thought meant "with cheese," but in fact means "with spirit").

And as a bonus, the composer can also add a *metronome marking* to the tempo indication — specifying an exact speed at which the music should go. For more about metronome markings and how they get ignored, see Chapter 4.

Telling 'Bones from Heckelphones: Orchestration Made Easy

In addition to volume and speed, another important factor in determining how music sounds is who's playing it. By that we don't mean which *people;* we mean which *instruments.*

Playing with sound colors

Orchestration is the art of assigning all the notes in a particular piece of music to the different players of the orchestra. Depending on how the composer makes these assignments, she can completely change the effect that the music has on the audience. The same notes that sound nasal and sharp when played on an oboe may sound smooth and sweet when played on a flute. Multiply those variations by the 30-odd different kinds of instruments in a standard orchestra, and you get a hint of the incredible possibilities available to the composer.

Notating orchestrations

When you orchestrate, you write down each player's part on a gigantic sheet of staff-lined music paper that looks like Figure 12-1.

The flute player's music is written on the top line; what the oboists play simultaneously is written just below that; the clarinetists' music is just below that; and so on down the page. Orchestration is a difficult act, because you can't just run over to the piano to discover how something you've just written sounds. You must "hear" your work in progress in your head — at least until the first day of rehearsal with the actual players.

Who's the orchestrator?

These days, in the Broadway theater world, the composer is never the orchestrator; the composer writes the melody and maybe a piano part, and another person is hired to arrange that music for full orchestra.

But in the days of yore (yore great-grandparents, that is), composers almost always orchestrated their own music. Composers often served as their own *copyists,* too — charged with recopying every note off that full-page score into individual instrument parts, writing all the flute players' notes on one set

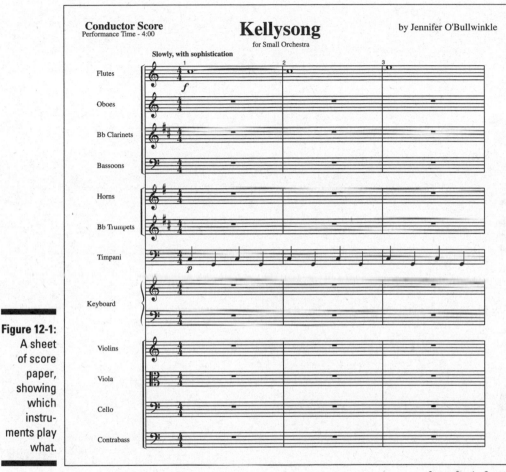

Figure 12-1:
A sheet of score paper, showing which instruments play what.

Source: Creative Commons

of pages, the clarinet's notes on another set, and so on. (Believe it or not, this process — so time-consuming and tedious in Beethoven's time — remained exactly as time-consuming and tedious right up until about 1985, when personal computers finally made a dent in the copying job.)

For more on the individual instruments that make up the orchestrator's palette, see Part III. For now, just remember that, whenever you listen to a piece of classical music, you're hearing the representation of a huge amount of composer labor. You're not hearing just melodies and harmonies; you're hearing them played by a carefully chosen group of instruments.

And in case you were wondering about the title of this section: a *heckelphone* is a type of bass oboe, and *'bones* is short for trombones. May you win your next game of trivia.

Part V
The Part of Tens

Head to www.dummies.com/extras/classicalmusic for an extra Part of Tens article on ten great chamber music pieces.

In this part . . .

- Find out why most people's conceptions of classical music are completely wrong and how you can correct them.

- Arm yourself for stress-free cocktail party conversations about music.

- Uncover how to make the glorious art of classical music a permanent part of your life.

- Discover the best jokes that even classical musicians like to tell about one another.

Chapter 13

The Ten Most Common Misconceptions about Classical Music

In This Chapter

▶ Debunking the myths

▶ Enjoying the cheap seats

▶ Uncovering the truth about clapping

As in any field of endeavor that's been talked about nonstop for 1,000 years, a few old wives' tales and rumors have cropped up regarding classical music. Allow us to debunk them.

Classical Music Is Boring

Classical music can be the most exciting thing on earth! If you have even a hint of the Number One Misconception, we have just the ticket for you: Listen to the last movement of Tchaikovsky's Fourth Symphony. This music is passionate; it's romantic; and it bubbles over with an effervescent love of life. We bet that it has an actual, measurable effect on your heart rate — really.

But we could name dozens of decidedly unboring pieces such as this symphony — and we *have*. Listen to the pieces we mention in Appendix A, and *then* tell us what you think!

Classical Music Is for Snobs

Classical music is for everybody, snobs included. But we don't particularly like snobs. We'd rather hang out with normal people — the people for whom all the composers were writing.

In any art, some people think that they're somehow superior just because they *know* more. They develop their own terminology and use it like a password to an exclusive club. They meet over cocktails and revel in their learnedness. They even dress alike.

The world of music is no exception. We only hope that, in their vast superiority, these people remember to listen and feel and enjoy once in a while. Otherwise, they won't get half as much out of the music as you do!

All Modern Concert Music Is Hard to Listen to

You've probably heard snippets of 20th-century or 21st-century classical music — that is, "avant garde" music that sounds alien, dissonant, random, and unapproachable. Many audience members are afraid to listen to any classical music written after 1900.

We sympathize. True, a lot of fiercely dissonant works were composed in the 20th century — the musical equivalent of expressionist, surrealist, and modernist "modern art." *Some* of the music that resulted from these experiments is indeed hard to listen to.

But a huge number of modern pieces are *very easy* to listen to. They're incredibly beautiful: lush, romantic, and thrilling. We'd hate for you to miss out on them. Bottom line: It all depends on what you listen to.

Many famous composers who wrote in the emotional, highly charged style — what we call Romantic music (including Sergei Rachmaninoff, Antonín Dvořák, Richard Strauss, Nikolai Rimsky-Korsakov, Camille Saint-Saëns, Jean Sibelius, Edvard Grieg, and Gustav Mahler) — actually wrote music well *into* the 20th century. And so did American composers Samuel Barber, Aaron Copland, and George Gershwin!

So give 20th-century classical music a chance — especially now that we're well into the 21st.

They Don't Write Classical Music Anymore

The world of classical music composition is alive and well. Conservatories offer courses in composition as well as performance, and, recently, exciting new composers have appeared on the scene.

Many of these new composers have made a conscious effort to create works that are melodic and fun. This trend may be a backlash against the bad rap that 20th-century classical music has acquired. It may also be a response to the incredibly lucrative careers that a few star composers — John Williams, for example — have made for themselves in the entertainment business.

Don't forget that Beethoven lived at a time when hundreds of other composers (some of whom were much more famous at the time) were writing really mediocre music. We've forgotten all about them. But aren't we glad that Beethoven existed? Somewhere out there in the world today, a future Beethoven just might be gearing up.

You Have to Dress Up to Go to the Symphony

This misconception prevents some would-be classical music lovers from even setting foot in the concert hall. If you want to dress up, fine. But don't feel that it's an obligation — and please don't let a simple thing like this prevent you from going to a concert. (See Chapter 4 for much more on this topic.)

If You Haven't Heard of the Guest Artist, She Can't Be Any Good

The concert world is *teeming* with amazing musicians, and only a few can be famous at a time. The musicians whose names you've heard — especially the violinists and pianists among them — regularly reap between $50,000 and $100,000 for a single performance.

Rare are the musical organizations that can afford to hire a soloist of that caliber for every concert. So many orchestras turn to lesser-known musicians, often right out of conservatory.

Some of these musicians play *much better* than some of the famous names. First, they're young and full of talent and energy. And second, they *need* to play well to make a name for themselves. By contrast, some of the more established talents gave up practicing years ago.

If an orchestra in your area is featuring a soloist you haven't heard of, the chances are good that she's fantastic. Otherwise, she wouldn't have been chosen from the thousands of others available.

Professional Musicians Have It Easy

Recently, while attending a party, a pianist friend of ours was asked if she'd sit down at the piano and knock off a tune. She sat down to play, but grudgingly. Her lack of enthusiasm surprised people: Why would a musician hesitate to play? After all, musicians get to do what they love all day long!

Actually, *all day long* is about the size of it. To make ends meet, most professional musicians must take on a number of jobs: a full-time position in a good orchestra, part-time "ringer" duty in a not-so-good one, solo performances, quartet gigs, and hours and hours and hours of practicing and teaching.

Professional musicians begin their training early in childhood — sometimes as early as the age of three! But although the average professional classical musician spends more years in intensive training than any doctor or lawyer, society doesn't put the same value on this training. Only in the most prestigious symphony or opera orchestras can a performing musician make a full-time living in one job.

So please understand if the off-duty pianist is uneager to sit down and play at the party where she's a guest. She's a professional; she plays all day long. Asking her to "play us some tunes" is just like asking a dentist to "pull us some teeth"!

The Best Seats Are Down Front

In 99 percent of the world's auditoriums, the *worst* seats are front row center! The best seats are in the back, way at the top of the highest balcony. If you sit near the front, your ears are at or below the level of the stage itself. The musicians, who sit on top of that stage, send their beautiful music right over your head, up to the cheap seats. At the back of the concert hall, the sound has had a chance to blend, and you can hear it in all its glory. See Chapter 4 for more on this phenomenon.

Clapping between Movements Is Illegal, Immoral, and Fattening

An unspoken rule at many classical music concerts concerns clapping. When a piece of music consists of more than one movement (or section), recent tradition holds that you should not clap between the movements, but instead wait until the whole thing is over. Some classical music snobs are so insistent on this rule that they will shame you (with a glare) for daring to disobey it.

As Chapter 4 mentions, we think this is a silly tradition. But surprisingly, the "No-Clap Policy" isn't just silly — it's also a relatively recent invention. When most of the great old masterpieces were first performed, not only did the audience commonly clap (or boo, or cheer, or gossip) between movements, but they often expressed themselves right in the *middle* of a movement, as well. Sometimes a single movement was so popular, the audience demanded that it be repeated on the spot! In fact, the word *encore* literally meant "Play it again!"

In fact, pieces that are now always performed together — such as the four movements of a symphony — were often broken up in the old days. A famous concert in Beethoven's time consisted of the first two movements of his latest symphony, followed by a piano concerto, some concert arias for singer and orchestra, and then the *last* two movements of the symphony. So much for the idea that separating the parts from one another is blasphemy. If clapping between movements was good enough for Beethoven, it's good enough for us.

Classical Music Can't Change Your Life

This final misconception is the biggest one of all. If people knew the truth the way we do, everyone would be a classical music lover.

The reason that classical music becomes an obsession for so many people, including us, is that it has incredible power. This power can be compared to the power of nature, the power of religion, or even the power of an incredibly forceful and magnetic personality. If you're attuned to it and are within its sphere of influence, you simply can't remain unchanged.

We hope that this book helps you tune in to the life-affirming force of classical music. We hope that you want to experience more. And we hope that this incredible art continues to move you and change you as long as you live.

Chapter 14

The Ten Best Musical Terms for Cocktail Parties

At a cocktail party, you overhear this typical (and extremely realistic) conversation. How much can you understand?

André: Did you hear the concert last night?

Zubin: Did I? *Did* I? It was the highlight of my life!

André: Oh, I agree. Incredible. From the first moment of Berg's *Three Pieces,* I noticed how attentive the audience was — even in *atonal* music like that!

Zubin: And I felt that Kurt conducted in a way that brought out the melodies with an incredible clarity, even amid such thick *orchestration.*

André: What did you think of the violin *concerto* afterward?

Zubin: Masterful. The way Isaac played — just like the old days. His *intonation* was in top form.

André: Yes — and in the Brahms *concerto,* of all things. One of the hardest pieces in the *repertoire.* He must have practiced 'til his fingers bled.

Zubin: Exactly. You know, during the *exposition,* I sat there thinking, "This piece I know extremely well, and yet I feel that I'm hearing it for the first time." His use of *rubato* was just stunning.

André: The *tempo* was a little slow.

Zubin: But I love it that way. You hear all that *counterpoint.*

André: What did you think of his *cadenza?*

Zubin: Incredible. I've never heard anyone play it so beautifully, with such a dramatic *crescendo* toward the end. It took my breath away.

This conversation uses all 11 of the following Ten Best Musical Terms for Cocktail Parties, which you can master in this chapter.

Atonal

Most music is based on harmonies and scales. We say that it's in a key (for example, the key of C), and it's *tonal.* Even without a knowledge of music theory, you can tell that the notes sound "right." But some modern music is extremely dissonant. You can't say that it's in the key of C; you can't say that it's in *any* particular key. In other words, it's not tonal — it's *atonal* (pronounced "A. Tonal").

Cadenza

Near the end of nearly every movement of a concerto comes a moment when everything seems to stop — except the soloist. The soloist takes off on a flight of fancy, all by himself, in an elaborate solo lasting anywhere from ten seconds to five minutes. This solo is called the *cadenza* ("ca-DENN-zah"): a moment devised by the composer for the soloist to show off.

Concerto

A *concerto* ("con-CHAIR-toe") is a piece of music for a soloist with orchestra. Typically, the soloist sits or stands at the front of the stage and plays the melody, while the orchestra accompanies her. In the best concertos, the soloist and orchestra actually appear to have a musical conversation. The concerto is by far the flashiest part of any concert program, and many people go to a symphony orchestra concert just to experience an exciting soloist.

You can hear a movement from a concerto by going to www.dummies. com/go/classicalmusic and listening to Track 3: the final movement of Mozart's Piano Concerto no. 22.

Counterpoint

Counterpoint is a combination of two or more different melodies that sound good together. The music of Johann Sebastian Bach, for example, is full of masterful counterpoint. One instrument or voice plays one melody while another instrument or voice plays a second melody; at every moment, the simultaneous notes work well together.

Go to www.dummies.com/go/classicalmusic and listen to Track 2 for a glorious example of Bach's counterpoint. Listen to the way the voices enter one at a time and imitate one another, starting at 2:22.

Crescendo

Italian for "growing." In music, a composer writes crescendo ("creh-SHEN-doe") whenever he wants the players to get gradually louder. Crescendo doesn't mean "climax," although some people wrongly use it that way, as in, "The music rose to a crescendo." The right way to use this term would be, "The music made a crescendo to the climax!"

Exposition

It's the beginning part of a piece, where the main themes are heard for the first time. Most symphonies have an exposition in the first movement. For more on exposition, see Chapter 3.

Intonation

Intonation is tuning. If a player performs with good intonation, she's playing in tune; if her intonation is bad, she's out of tune.

Orchestration

If a composer writes a new piece for orchestra, he doesn't usually write down all the instrumental lines right away. He usually jots down a simple version first — perhaps just for the piano. His next job is to figure out what each instrument is going to play. The art of assigning different melodies to different instruments is called *orchestration*. (For details, see Chapter 12.) The word *orchestration* can also refer to the number of musicians who are playing at a given moment, as in "thick orchestration" or "thin orchestration."

Repertoire

This term means "a list of musical pieces available for playing." *The piano repertoire* ("REPP-per-twar") refers to all the commonly played works for piano. *My repertoire* refers to all the pieces I can play. *Tonight's repertoire* refers to the pieces that are being performed tonight.

Rubato

A player uses *rubato* ("roo-BAH-toe") by making slight variations in tempo for the sake of expression in music. This word originally meant "robbed," as in taking a little extra time to play a phrase and then "giving it back" by speeding up later (or vice versa).

Tempo

Tempo means "speed." The Germans use the word *tempo* to refer to driving speed: a tempo of 150 kilometers per hour, for example. In music, we refer to a certain number of beats per unit of time: 150 beats per minute, for example.

Using Your New-Found Mastery

Now that you understand the Ten Best Musical Terms for Cocktail Parties, see if you can understand the following conversation, overheard in a pianist's dressing room backstage, just before a concert:

> **Vladimir:** What's wrong, Rudolf? Why are you crying?
>
> **Rudolf:** It's this Rachmaninoff *concerto*. I just can't master the *cadenza*.
>
> **Vladimir:** Well, when must you perform it?
>
> **Rudolf:** In 20 minutes. It's part of tonight's *repertoire*.

Vladimir: Well, we need to work fast then. Play it for me.

Rudolf: All right. *(Plays.)*

Vladimir: Well, there's your first problem, Rudolf. The *tempo* is much too fast.

Rudolf: Ah, but that's the tempo from the *exposition.* I wanted to be consistent.

Vladimir: Nonsense. Play it slower. Now here, emphasize this *counterpoint* between the left and right hands.

Rudolf: All right. *(Plays again.)* What do you think of this *rubato?*

Vladimir: Splendid. Now make a *crescendo* here to anticipate the full *orchestration* when everyone starts to play again.

Rudolf: Like this?

Vladimir: Oh, my goodness, what are you doing? You make it sound *atonal!*

Rudolf: No, no, that's just the *intonation* on this piano. It's horribly out of tune.

Vladimir: Oh, I see. No matter. But the piano onstage, *that one* has been tuned, yes?

Rudolf: Yes, of course! *(They both laugh heartily.)*

Chapter 15

Ten Great Classical Music Jokes

Classical musicians work harder than most people we know. At the end of the day, they *really* unwind. This chapter introduces you to some of the jokes that musicians love to tell.

Master of Them All

Three famous conductors — George Szell, Leonard Bernstein, and Herbert von Karajan — were discussing which of them is the greatest.

"I believe that I am the greatest," said Szell, "because I took a relatively unknown orchestra and turned it into one of the greatest in the world."

"Well, I believe that *I* am the greatest," Bernstein replied, "because I am a composer as well as a conductor. When I conduct music, I can feel the soul of the composer. And when I conducted my own Mass, God himself inspired me."

To which Karajan responded, "No, I didn't!"

The Heavenly Philharmonic

A great violinist died and went to heaven. But when she joined the Celestial Philharmonic, she found, to her amazement, that she was sitting at the very back of the violin section.

As she looked around, she found out why. In front of her were all the greatest violinists in history: Paganini, Heifetz, Joachim . . . all of them were there. Similarly, all the other positions in the orchestra were filled by the greatest virtuosos of all time.

Then the maestro entered, raised his baton, and started to beat time — but not all that well, to tell the truth. His beat was unclear and sloppy, and his musical ideas weren't well thought out.

Our friend the violinist turned to her stand partner and asked, "Who's that, anyway?"

"Oh," replied the stand partner, "that's God. He thinks he's a conductor."

Brass Dates

A woman went out on a date with a trumpet player. When she came back, her roommate asked, "Well, how was it? Did his trumpet skills make him a great kisser?"

"Nah," she replied. "That dry, tight, tiny little pucker — it was no fun at all."

The next night, she went out with a tuba player. When she came back, her roommate asked, "Well, how was his kissing?"

"Ugh!" she exclaimed. "Those huge, rubbery, blubbery, slobbering slabs of meat — oh, it was just gross!"

The following night, she went out with a French horn player. Once again, her roommate asked afterward, "Well, how was *his* kissing?"

"Well," she replied, "his kissing was just so-so, but I loved the way he held me!"

The Late Maestro

The famous conductor finally passed away, but his agency kept getting calls from people asking to speak with him. "I'm sorry; he's dead," was the standard reply.

Finally, the receptionist began to notice that the same person seemed to be making all these calls. She finally asked the caller what the story was.

The reply: "I was in his orchestra, and I just like to hear you say it."

Basses Take a Breather

In the Ninth Symphony, the bass players didn't have a thing to do. Not a single note for 20 minutes.

Therefore, at one particular concert, the bass players decided that, after playing their parts in the opening of the symphony, they'd quietly lay down their instruments, leave the stage, and visit the bar next door to the concert hall for a while. They planned to return just in time to play their final notes.

That's just how it went. But after ten minutes at the bar, two of the bassists passed out, and the rest of the players in the section were rather drunk. Finally, one of them looked at his watch and exclaimed, "Look at the time! We'll be late!"

On their way back into the concert hall, the bassist who had suggested this excursion in the first place said, "I think we'll still have enough time — I anticipated that something like this could happen, so I tied a string around the last pages of the conductor's sheet music. When he gets to that spot in the score, he'll have to slow the tempo way down while he waves the baton with one hand and fumbles with the string with the other!"

Sure enough, when they got back to the stage, they discovered that they hadn't missed their entrance. But one look at their conductor's face told them that they were still in serious trouble.

After all, it was the bottom of the Ninth, the basses were loaded, and the score was tied, with two men out.

Houseless Violist

A viola player came home to find his house burned to the ground. "We're so sorry," the police told him. "Apparently, the conductor of your orchestra came to the house, abducted your wife, stole everything worth stealing, and then set fire to the place."

The viola player's eyes lit up with excitement. "Really? The maestro was *here?!?*"

Ludwig's Grave

A guy goes to Vienna to pay his respects to the great composers. But when he gets to the graveyard, he hears a strange scratching sound coming from Beethoven's tomb.

Unable to restrain himself, he pries the lid off the tomb, and there sits the long-dead master, furiously crossing out musical notation from a piece of old music paper.

"What are you doing?" asks the guy in astonishment.

"What do you think I'm doing?" Beethoven retorts. "I'm decomposing!"

The Weeping Violist

The concert was about to begin, and the principal viola player was nowhere to be seen. The conductor rushed backstage and found the violist in the dressing room, weeping.

"What's the matter?" the conductor asked.

"Oh, it's that darn principal bass player," the violist cried. "He put one of my strings out of tune — and he won't tell me which one!"

Musicians' Revenge

Q. What's the ideal weight for a conductor?

A. About 2½ pounds, including the urn.

One Last Viola Joke

An American orchestra had just arrived in Europe for a two-week tour. One hour before the first concert, the conductor became very ill and was unable to conduct, and the orchestra suddenly had to find a substitute. The orchestra manager asked whether anyone in the orchestra could step in and conduct. The only person to volunteer was the last-chair viola player.

The manager was nervous. "You have no time to rehearse," she said. "You'll have to conduct the concert cold."

"I know. It'll be all right," said the violist.

The violist conducted the concert, and it was a smashing success. Because the conductor remained ill, the violist conducted all the concerts, getting rave reviews and standing ovations every time.

Two weeks later, the conductor had recovered, and the violist returned to the back of the viola section. As he sat down, his stand partner asked, "So where've *you* been for the past two weeks?"

Chapter 16

Ten Ways to Get More Music in Your Life

There's more to enjoying classical music than going to a concert once a year or putting on some music while you wash the car. We live in an age in which alternative forms of musical contact are plentiful, easy, and fun. Don't just listen to it — *live* it! This chapter gives you ten easy ideas.

Get Involved with Your Orchestra

If you live near a city with an orchestra, you don't have to be a mere audience member; you can get far more involved. For example, as we mention in Chapter 4, more and more orchestras offer pre-concert talks to their audience: usually free, often short (30 to 45 minutes), and incredibly interesting.

Most orchestras also offer subscription plans, which give you the chance to enjoy live classical music for much less money than you'd pay to hear all the concerts individually. Depending on the size of the orchestra or concert series, a subscription can contain anywhere from 3 to 25 concerts, spread out between September and June. Often you can choose how many concerts — and which ones — you want to hear.

Subscription series have another advantage, too: They're often conceived as a whole, meaning that the orchestra has determined that these concerts go together well. Some series have a theme: Music from Faraway Lands, for example, or Music about Food, or Music to Nuzzle By.

Orchestras and other concert series usually plan their seasons so that subscribers constantly get introduced to a variety of interesting music. These organizations know that, by subscribing to a series, you're placing your trust in their ability to help you discover music afresh, year after year.

Join a Classical Music Tour

"Join a classical music tour?" we can hear you asking. "Like a rock group tour? Do we go around the country wearing tie-dyed tuxedos? Do we help haul harp equipment? Do we drop rosin? Wowww, dude — that's so *andante!*"

No, no, we're talking about touring with *other music fans,* not musicians. Every once in a while, groups take tours to some cool place to check out the classical music there. Some trips are elaborate and expensive — to Europe, for example. But others are much more modest and affordable. You may find a group that's taking a day trip to the next city or somewhere only a couple of hours away.

The advantages of this type of tour are twofold. First, you find out all about the music you're going to hear from people who love to talk about it. And second, you're guaranteed to make friends.

Meet the Artists — Be a Groupie

It's a well-kept secret: Most classical guest soloists are just as friendly as you and I. (Well, just as friendly as *I* am, anyway.) They *love* to meet their fans. Just think: They're in a strange town, just for a day or two, and they don't know anybody there. They're lonely, bored, and depressed. In fact, a friendly visit from you may be just the ticket to prevent a horrible drinking binge in a hotel room.

Just go backstage at the end of the concert (or during intermission if the soloist plays only in the first half of the concert) and say hi. Shoot the breeze a bit. Invite him out for drinks or dessert. Don't worry that you don't know enough about music. He doesn't know much about what *you* do, either.

Now then: If the idea of waylaying the superstar is too self-assertive for your comfort zone, consider joining the orchestra groupies: people who love an orchestra so much that they go to every rehearsal and concert that they can attend legally.

If you become a groupie, the people who make up the orchestra eventually begin to look more and more familiar to you. You start to see the same faces.

After a while, the members of the orchestra notice *your* familiar face, too. Go right up and talk to them. For the most part, they're friendly and even grateful that someone would take the time to listen to them again and again. When you become an orchestra groupie, each concert is more of a pleasure than you could have imagined.

Load Up on Free or Cheapo Recordings

These days, you can find no end of bargains on classical recordings. The iTunes store, Amazon, and ArkivMusic.com are full of them. Many go for $4 or less, and a surprising number of them are *good!*

Cheap recordings fall into two categories:

- **Recordings that used to be expensive:** These recordings contain excellent older performances that have been cheaply repackaged. The CBS Great Performances series is one example — all the recordings in this series are excellent.

- **Recordings that were always cheap:** Certain recording companies — such as Laserlight, Excelsior, Point Classics, and Vienna Masters — make a living by recording performances of obscure Eastern European orchestras and conductors and selling them cheap. The quality on these recordings is mixed; sometimes it's good, sometimes not. But these recordings often go for less than $2, so they're a decent option of last resort. We know people who regularly buy cartloads of these things.

If you find yourself falling in love with a particular piece of music, you may actually want to own *more than one* recording of it. It's fascinating to hear the effect that a different set of performers can have on a piece of music. And in this case, you may want to spring for a more mainstream, more expensive label (such as EMI, Decca, RCA, Philips, or especially Deutsche Grammophon) to have a better chance of getting a terrific performance.

And speaking of cheap — how does *free* strike you? YouTube has multiple recordings of nearly every classical music piece you can imagine. And if you haven't noticed, public libraries aren't just about books anymore. They've got videos, Internet access, sheet music, computer programs — and hundreds of *classical music CDs!* Arm yourself with the list we provide in Appendix A and *get over there.* This is your chance to immerse yourself in classical music under the best of all possible circumstances: in your own room, with expensive recordings, all for free.

Make Music Friends on the Internet

If you've got a computer and signal, you can find about 1,000 years' worth of information, lists, discussions, and news about classical music all over the Internet.

Here are a couple of Web addresses great for classical music exploration:

- ✔ Talk Classical (www.talkclassical.com) has news, entertaining discussions, Top Ten lists, and lots more. Pack a suitcase.

- ✔ Classical Music Mayhem!! (http://classicalmusicmayhem. freeforums.org/portal.php) offers no end of discussions on nearly every aspect of classical music.

- ✔ Good Music Guide (www.good-music-guide.com) is a comprehensive guide to all types of classical music, and it throws in links to composers, performers, and music reviews.

Finally, for pure discussion (and nothing else), the Internet offers several extremely lively and interesting bulletin boards catering to music lovers. Try searching for rec.music.classical, rec.music.classical.recordings, and even rec.music.opera. The topics, as you can see, are pretty much revealed in the titles.

Join an Unlimited Music Service

The competition among music providers has become fierce, and some services are offering *unlimited* music streaming and/or downloading for a monthly or yearly fee. The two most prominent such services are Spotify and Amazon Prime.

Spotify (www.spotify.com/us) is now free. Spotify offers literally millions of music tracks to choose from. But there's a catch: You have to listen to ads. Or, if you prefer your listening experience ad-free, you can upgrade to Premium for about $10 per month.

Prime Music (www.amazon.com/primemusic) is a service of Amazon Prime. If you've already paid for Amazon Prime, you can listen to more than a million music tracks, without ads, at no additional cost. If you don't already have Amazon Prime, you can sign up for about $100 per year — which is cheaper than Spotify Premium in the long run. Prime Music's selection isn't as good as Spotify's, but the Amazon membership does include other benefits, such as free shipping of any CDs (or anything else) you may want to buy.

Listen to Your Local Classical Station

More than likely, your city or town has a classical music radio station. It's almost always a public radio station, often affiliated with a college, and you can usually find it between 87 and 92 on the FM dial.

The advantages of public classical stations are enormous:

- They own a huge variety of classical music that you've never heard, and they play it day and night.
- They tell you a little bit about each piece of music before they play it.
- They take requests.
- No ads!

In fact, we can think of only two *disadvantages:*

- Depending on the station, the announcer may be a self-important twit who overenunciates all his syllables as if you're the biggest idiot on Earth. Luckily, such announcers are becoming rarer as normal, enraged humans pick them off.
- About every six months, these radio stations have a weeklong fund drive, during which the various announcers enumerate the many advantages of having a classical music station and make you feel like an ax murderer for not having pledged money. Lost in the illusion that their entire listenership is hanging on every word, they go on and on like that for days — improvising in long sentences, the ends of which bear no relationship to their beginnings, to the effect that volunteers are standing by, and that, if you'd just stop being such a nasty tightwad, they could reach their goal of $5,000 this half-hour, and that the lonely phone you hear ringing in the background is actually someone just like yourself calling to pledge his life savings and his wife's precious heirlooms, and that the other phones really are lighting up even though they don't have ringers.

Those are the weeks when we listen to a lot of rock music.

One more idea: Digital radio services, such as SiriusXM, are taking over the airwaves. The advantage of digital radio is that the sound is much better than the average radio signal. These digital stations have a published schedule, and you can record anything you want directly from the cable, getting a perfect, crystal-clear recording.

Oh, and one other thing: no announcers.

Watch Classical Music Movies

Composers tend to be expressive and passionate souls, and as such they're the perfect subject for movies — especially the composers from the Romantic era (basically the 19th century). Of course, these movies are dramatizations; they range from farfetched to pure fiction. But they do tend to capture the spirit and personality of the composer — and they're *filled* with awesome music.

Here are some of the most interesting:

- ✔ *Amadeus:* Based on the play by Peter Shaffer, this movie tells the apocryphal story of Wolfgang Amadeus Mozart's demise at the hands of his vengeance-seeking rival, Antonio Salieri. Probably the best movie ever made about a composer.

- ✔ *Immortal Beloved:* In this film, Ludwig van Beethoven's friend (and executor of his estate) tries to find the "Immortal Beloved" to whom Beethoven referred in his will. A very powerful movie. (Especially after you find out who the "Immortal Beloved" was. Can we talk?)

- ✔ *Impromptu:* Starring Judy Davis, Hugh Grant, and Emma Thompson, this movie's about Frédéric Chopin's impetuous romance with the female author who wrote under the name George Sand.

- ✔ *Mahler:* A dark — and mostly true — Ken Russell movie about Gustav Mahler, one of classical music's most tormented composers.

- ✔ *The Music Lovers:* A detailed account of Tchaikovsky's notoriously stormy marriage to Glenda Jackson. No, wait . . . Glenda Jackson is the actress who *plays* Tchaikovsky's wife, and the actor playing Tchaikovsky is Richard Chamberlain.

- ✔ *Shine:* This Oscar-winning film dramatizes the real-life story of pianist David Helfgott, giving a vivid chronicle of his nervous breakdown, rehabilitation, and triumph with Rachmaninoff's Piano Concerto no. 3.

- ✔ *Song of Love:* This 1947 flick portrays the relationship of Clara Schumann to her husband, Robert, and to her closest, um, *friend,* Johannes Brahms. Katherine Hepburn plays Clara.

- ✔ *Song without End:* Starring Dirk Bogarde and Genevieve Page, this film tells the story of Franz Liszt's scandalous affair with a countess and dramatizes his attempts to give up performing in favor of composition.

- ✔ *Wagner, the Complete Epic:* If you ask us, *this* is the one that should have been called *Song without End.* It lasts nine hours and stars Richard Burton as the composer, with Vanessa Redgrave and Sir Laurence Olivier.

Study Up on the Classics

It's amazing how much you can discover by looking up a piece of music online or opening up the liner notes (the little booklets) that come with a CD. You can find out when each piece was written, the circumstances surrounding its composition, and something about the life of the composer.

You can also find great *books* on almost all aspects of classical music. Hit the library, as well as the very bookstore where you found *this* monumental work.

Then, if this classical music thing *really* starts to interest you, you may be a prime candidate for a music course offered at a local college or university.

You can find a class in general music appreciation. Or, if you want a more hard-core education, you can study music history (either all or in part), music theory (which includes harmony and counterpoint), composition, orchestration (the composer's art of assigning musical lines to instruments in the orchestra) — or even conducting. You can also find courses in *ear training* (the skill of hearing and distinguishing musical lines, intervals, and harmonies) and *sight singing*.

If you're really serious about pursuing music this way, call the music department at your local college and ask for a course catalog. Even if you don't enroll in a course, you may be able to *audit* it (attend the classes without having to take the tests) — sometimes for free.

Make Your Own Music

We've saved the best for last. The greatest way to make classical music part of your life is to make it *yourself*. Of course, practicing an instrument daily — or at least several times per week — takes quite a commitment. To see results, you've got to set aside a regular period of time and then stick with it.

When choosing an instrument, consider the sound. What do you enjoy listening to? You're going to hear that instrument an awful lot while you practice it. This book and the accompanying online examples (at www.dummies.com/go/classicalmusic) can help. Read Part III to discover how each instrument makes its sound. Then listen to the recordings to hear what each instrument sounds like. By that point, you should have a pretty good idea of what you like and what you don't.

Then you can go out and get yourself an instrument. If you're a beginner, check a local music shop for good deals. Don't buy anything expensive right away — you may even want to *rent* your first instrument. You're going to have plenty of time to upgrade after you reach the next level.

The music shop should also have some good leads on teachers. But beware: Prices vary widely. Depending on experience and reputation, a professional music teacher can charge anywhere from $20 to $100 for an hour-long lesson. Go with the more reasonable fees at the beginning. As long as you're making good progress, there's no need to pay more.

Another place to find a teacher is a local university. Sometimes music students make excellent teachers, and they charge only about $15 to $20 per lesson — much less than, say, the principal oboist of the Boston Symphony.

After you take lessons for a few months and practice diligently, you're ready for the real fun. Get together with a group of fellow beginners and make some music together. It's probably going to sound excruciating at first, but you'll get better and better as time goes on. Plus, it's a blast!

If all this stuff is making you break out in a cold sweat, calm down. Nobody said you *have* to take up a musical instrument to be active musically. Instead, you can join a local chorus. Singing in a group — especially a top-notch one — is another of life's all-time best joys.

We know from our own lives that nothing is so liberating and uplifting as participating in the creation of music. And we hope that some of our suggestions strike a chord with you, inspiring you to create some of your own.

We wish you a lifetime of true discovery and enrichment through classical music.

Part VI
The Appendixes

Click on www.dummies.com/extras/classicalmusic for a bonus article on classical music of the 21st century.

In this part . . .

- ✔ Discover how to create a killer classical music collection, choose the best of the best, and enjoy it to the fullest.

- ✔ View the whole history of classical music at a glance so you can better understand how music changed with the times.

- ✔ Get to know some of the most commonly used terms in classical music, and then carry on a conversation like a virtuoso.

Appendix A

Starting a Classical Music Collection

• •

You're lucky enough to live in a time and place where you can hear all the classical music you want for free. You can hear it on YouTube, on a podcast, or on the radio, or you can check it out of the library.

Nevertheless, a time may come when you want to own your own recordings. For that moment, we've compiled five lists of musical masterpieces, beginning with the most accessible "easy listening" and working up to great pieces that have challenged many a listener. We offer our promise that every piece on every list is worth hearing.

List 1: Old Favorites

This list consists of incredibly beautiful pieces that you'll probably recognize when you hear them:

- **Bach:** Brandenburg Concerto no. 5
- **Beethoven:** Piano Concerto no. 5 (*Emperor*); Symphonies no. 5 and 9
- **Bizet:** *Carmen* Suites 1 and 2
- **Dvořák:** Symphony no. 9 in E minor (*From the New World*)
- **Gershwin:** Rhapsody in Blue
- **Grieg:** Piano Concerto in A minor; *Peer Gynt* Suite no. 1
- **Handel:** *Messiah*
- **Haydn:** Symphony no. 94 in G major (*Surprise*)
- **Mendelssohn:** Symphony no. 4 in A major (*Italian*)
- **Mozart:** Piano Concerto no. 21 in C major

- **Rachmaninoff:** Piano Concerto no. 2 in C minor
- **Ravel:** Boléro
- **Rimsky-Korsakov:** *Scheherazade*
- **Rodrigo:** *Concierto de Aranjuez*
- **Rossini:** *William Tell* Overture
- **Schubert:** Symphony no. 8 (*Unfinished*)
- **J. Strauss:** *Blue Danube* Waltz
- **Tchaikovsky:** *Nutcracker* Suite; *Romeo and Juliet* Fantasy-Overture; Violin Concerto in D major; Piano Concerto no. 1 in B-flat major
- **Vivaldi:** *Four Seasons;* Guitar Concerto in D major

List 2: MILD on the Taste Meter

You may not recognize these great pieces, but they are quite accessible:

- **Bach:** Orchestral Suite no. 3
- **Barber:** Overture to *The School for Scandal*
- **Bartók:** Romanian Dances
- **Beethoven:** Symphonies no. 3 (*Eroica*) and no. 7; Violin Concerto in D major
- **Berlioz:** Roman Carnival Overture
- **Brahms:** Symphonies no. 1 and 2
- **Britten:** *Young Person's Guide to the Orchestra*
- **Dvořák:** Cello Concerto in B minor; Serenade for Strings in E major; Serenade in E-flat major
- **Gershwin:** Piano Concerto in F; *An American in Paris*
- **Handel:** *Water Music;* any Concerto Grosso
- **Haydn:** Symphony no. 104 in D major
- **Liszt:** Hungarian Rhapsody no. 2
- **Mendelssohn:** Symphony no. 3 in A minor (*Scottish*)
- **Mozart:** Violin Concerto no. 5 in A major; Piano Concerto in C minor, K. 491; and Symphony no. 40 in G minor — or just about anything else he wrote

- **Prokofiev:** Symphony no. 1 (*Classical*)
- **Rimsky-Korsakov:** Capriccio Espagnol
- **Rossini:** All his overtures
- **Saint-Saëns:** *Carnival of the Animals*
- **Schubert:** Symphony no. 5 in B-flat major
- **Schumann:** Symphony no. 2 in C major
- **Sibelius:** *Finlandia*
- **Smetana:** *The Moldau* (the second tone poem from *Má Vlast*)
- **Stravinsky:** Pulcinella Suite
- **Tchaikovsky:** Symphonies no. 4 and 5
- **Vivaldi:** Any concerto (especially Concerto for Four Violins)
- **Wagner:** *Rienzi* Overture
- **Weber:** *Der Freischütz* Overture

List 3: MEDIUM on the Taste Meter

The following are moderately challenging pieces for hungry ears (and they can change your life):

- **Adams:** The Chairman Dances
- **Bach:** B-minor Mass
- **Barber:** Adagio for Strings; *Knoxville, Summer of 1915*
- **Berlioz:** Symphonie fantastique
- **Bernstein:** Symphonic Dances from *West Side Story*
- **Brahms:** Symphonies no. 3 and 4
- **Bruckner:** Symphony no. 4
- **Debussy:** Prelude to *The Afternoon of a Faun*
- **Elgar:** Enigma Variations
- **Falla:** *Three Cornered Hat:* Three Dances
- **Franck:** Symphony in D minor
- **Holst:** *The Planets*
- **Kodaly:** Dances of Galanta; Peacock Variations

- **Mahler:** Symphonies no. 1 and 4

- **Mussorgsky-Ravel:** *Pictures at an Exhibition*

- **Orff:** *Carmina Burana*

- **Rachmaninoff:** Rhapsody on a Theme of Paganini; Piano Concerto no. 3

- **Ravel:** *Daphnis and Chloé*

- **Sibelius:** Violin Concerto; Symphonies no. 1 and 2

- **R. Strauss:** *Till Eulenspiegel's Merry Pranks; Don Juan*

- **Stravinsky:** Firebird Suite

- **Tchaikovsky:** Symphony no. 6

- **Verdi:** Requiem

- **Wagner:** *Flying Dutchman* Overture; *Tannhäuser* Overture

List 4: MEDIUM HOT on the Taste Meter

The following are spicier pieces for somewhat adventurous ears:

- **Adams:** *Short Ride in a Fast Machine*

- **Barber:** First and Second Essays; Symphony no. 1

- **Bartók:** Divertimento for Strings; Concerto for Orchestra

- **Bloch:** Concerto Grosso no. 1

- **Bruckner:** Symphony no. 5

- **Debussy:** *La Mer*

- **Gorecki:** Symphony no. 3

- **Higdon:** *Blue Cathedral*

- **Ives:** *The Unanswered Question*

- **Mahler:** Symphonies no. 2 and 5; *Rückertlieder*

- **Nielsen:** Symphony no. 3 (*Sinfonia espansiva*); Symphony no. 4 (*The Inextinguishable*)

- **Prokofiev:** Symphony no. 5; *Romeo and Juliet*

- **Rachmaninoff:** Symphonic Dances

- **Ravel:** Rhapsodie espagnole

- **Schoenberg:** *Verklärte Nacht*

- **Shostakovich:** Symphony no. 5
- **R. Strauss:** *Don Quixote; Ein Heldenleben*
- **Stravinsky:** *Petrushka*
- **Torke:** Color Music
- **Wagner:** *Tristan and Isolde:* Prelude and Liebestod

List 5: HOT on the Taste Meter

These challenging pieces for more adventurous ears are incredible master-pieces of human expression:

- **Adams:** Harmonielehre
- **Adès:** Violin Concerto ("Concentric Paths")
- **Barber:** *Medea's Meditation* and *Dance of Vengeance*
- **Bartók:** Music for Strings, Percussion, and Celesta; *Miraculous Mandarin Suite*
- **Berg:** Violin Concerto
- **Corigliano:** Symphony no. 1
- **Hindemith:** *Mathis der Maler* Symphony
- **Ives:** Symphony no. 2
- **Janácek:** *Taras Bulba*
- **Mahler:** Symphony no. 9
- **Prokofiev:** Scythian Suite
- **Ravel:** *La Valse*
- **Schoenberg:** Gurrelieder
- **Shostakovich:** Symphony no. 1
- **R. Strauss:** *Also sprach Zarathustra (Thus Spoke Zarathustra)*
- **Stravinsky:** *The Rite of Spring*
- **Webern:** Passacaglia, opus 1

Appendix B

Classical Music Timeline

• •

Gregorian chant, Mozart, Beethoven . . . after several hundred pages, you'd be forgiven for getting confused about which musical events happened when. Here, for your reference pleasure, is a timeline of the major composers, pieces, and events that made classical music what it is today.

Sorry about not having an actual, graphical time*line*, by the way; the publisher told us that the book would need to be 18 feet wide to accommodate it.

Dawn of Man: Humans begin to make musical sounds with their voices and with other primitive instruments, such as pipes, whistles, drums, and rocks. Many a millennium of music-making madness passes.

about A.D. 600: Pope Gregory I ("The Great") comes up with a system to organize musical scales. *Gregorian chant* is named for him.

1025: Guido of Arezzo begins writing about music. He eventually devises such breakthroughs as music notation (*writing down notes* — what a concept!), as well as the *solfège* syllables ("do, re, mi, fa . . .").

1066: The Normans conquer England.

1098: Hildegard von Bingen, one of the first notable female composers, is born.

1215: King John I (the only) of England signs the Magna Carta. Somebody probably plays some music for the occasion.

about 1400: The Italian Renaissance starts gearing up.

1492: Columbus sails the ocean blue.

1517: Martin Luther nails his 95 theses to the door of a church in Wittenberg.

1533: Italian madrigals appear: multiple melodies sung simultaneously by different voices within a choir.

1587: Claudio Monteverdi (1567–1643) publishes his first book of madrigals.

1601: Shakespeare writes *Hamlet*.

1607: The Jamestown colony is founded in America. Monteverdi writes *Orfeo*, his first opera, in Italy.

1620: The Pilgrims arrive at Cape Cod and sign the Mayflower Compact.

1643: Louis XIV becomes the Sun King of France at the age of five.

about 1650: The Baroque era gets going.

1678: Antonio "Four Seasons" Vivaldi is born in Italy.

1685: Johann Sebastian Bach is born in Eisenach, Germany. George Frideric Handel is born in Halle, Germany.

1709: Bartolomeo Cristofori invents the first piano (*gravicembalo col piano e forte*).

1717: Handel writes his *Water Music* and performs it on a barge floating down the Thames behind King George.

1722: Bach writes his *Well-Tempered Clavier*.

1732: Franz Joseph Haydn is born in Austria, near Slovakia and Croatia.

1742: Handel's *Messiah* premieres in Dublin, Ireland.

1750: Bach dies. The Classical period begins at about this time.

1756: Wolfgang Amadeus Mozart is born in Salzburg, Austria.

1770: Ludwig van Beethoven is born in Bonn, Germany.

1776: The American Declaration of Independence is signed.

1785: Mozart writes his Piano Concerto no. 22 in E-flat major.

1787: The American Constitutional Convention begins. Mozart writes *Don Giovanni*.

1789: The French Revolution begins. George Washington becomes the first president of the United States.

1791: Mozart dies at age 35 in Vienna after beginning his *Requiem.* Haydn writes his Symphony no. 94 (*Surprise*).

1798: Franz Schubert, leader of the *Lieder,* is born.

1804: Napoleon crowns himself emperor of France. Beethoven, realizing that Napoleon is a self-important boob, tears up the title page of his Third Symphony (*Eroica*) originally dedicated to Napoleon. The Romantic Era is born.

1805: Fanny Mendelssohn, a gifted pianist and composer, is born, destined to be overshadowed by her younger brother Felix.

1806: Beethoven writes his Fourth Symphony.

1807: Beethoven writes his Fifth and Sixth symphonies.

1809: Haydn dies in Vienna at age 77. Felix Mendelssohn is born in Hamburg, Germany.

1810: Robert Schumann is born in Zwickau, Saxony.

1812: The United States goes to war with Great Britain. Napoleon is defeated in Russia. Beethoven writes his Seventh and Eighth symphonies.

1815: The metronome is invented. Napoleon is defeated again at the Battle of Waterloo.

1819: Clara Wieck, the future wife of Robert Schumann and a great composer in her own right, is born.

1823: Beethoven finishes his Ninth Symphony, using solo voices and a choir for the first time in that form. Franz Schubert writes his song cycle *Die schöne Müllerin* (*The Miller's Beautiful Daughter*).

1826: Felix Mendelssohn, age 17, writes his Overture to *A Midsummer Night's Dream.* Carl Maria von Weber dies.

1827: Beethoven dies.

1828: Schubert dies. Funeral homes prosper.

1829: Hector Berlioz's (1803–1869) *Symphonie fantastique* premieres in Paris. Mendelssohn rediscovers Bach's *St. Matthew Passion* and conducts its first performance in 100 years.

1833: Johannes Brahms is born in Hamburg, Germany.

1838: Music is taught in an American public school for the first time, in Boston. Robert Schumann writes his piano pieces *Kinderszenen* (*Children's Scenes*) and *Kreisleriana*.

1840: Peter Tchaikovsky is born in Votkinsk, Russia.

1842: The New York Philharmonic and Vienna Philharmonic orchestras are founded. Richard Wagner (1813–1883) writes his first successful opera, *Rienzi*. Mikhail Glinka (1804–1857) writes his opera *Ruslan and Ludmila*.

1847: Felix Mendelssohn dies in Leipzig.

1848: The Potato Famine hits Ireland. Gold is discovered in California. Karl Marx and Friedrich Engels write *The Communist Manifesto*.

1851: Hermann Melville writes *Moby Dick*. Robert Schumann writes a whale of a Third Symphony.

1856: Robert Schumann dies in an asylum at age 46.

1861: The American Civil War begins. The serfs are emancipated in Russia. Wagner's opera *Tannhäuser* premieres in Paris.

1867: Amy Beach, the first successful American female composer, is born.

1868: Johannes Brahms writes his *German Requiem*.

1874: Modest Mussorgsky (1839–1881) writes the opera *Boris Godunov,* as well as *Pictures at an Exhibition*.

1875: Bedrich Smetana (1824–1884) writes his cycle of tone poems *Má Vlast* (*My Fatherland*). Edvard Grieg (1843–1907) composes incidental music to Henrik Ibsen's play *Peer Gynt*. Antonín Dvořák (1841–1904) writes his *Serenade for Strings*.

1877: Johannes Brahms finishes his First Symphony at the age of 43 and then writes his Second Symphony in a matter of months. Thomas Edison invents the phonograph.

1882: Igor Stravinsky is born in Russia.

1885: Brahms completes his Fourth Symphony.

1887: Nadia Boulanger is born in France — destined to be the teacher and inspiration for myriad composers and conductors, including Aaron Copland, Elliott Carter, and Philip Glass.

1888: Nikolai Rimsky-Korsakov (1844–1908) writes *Scheherazade*. Vincent van Gogh paints *Sunflowers*.

1889: Richard Strauss (1864–1949) writes the tone poem *Don Juan*. Gustav Mahler (1860–1911) writes his First Symphony.

1892: Dvořák arrives in New York.

1893: Tchaikovsky writes his Sixth Symphony (*Pathétique*) and dies a week after conducting its premiere.

1894: Nicolas II, the last tsar of Russia, is crowned in Moscow. Dvořák writes his Ninth Symphony (*From the New World*). Claude Debussy (1862–1918) writes *Prelude to the Afternoon of a Faun*.

1897: Brahms dies in Vienna at age 64.

1899: Jean Sibelius (1865–1957) writes his nationalistic tone poem *Finlandia*. Scott Joplin (1868–1917) writes *The Maple Leaf Rag*.

1900: Copland is born.

1901: Sergei Rachmaninoff (1873–1943) writes his Second Piano Concerto after undergoing hypnosis to get over composer's block. Mahler writes his Fourth Symphony.

1905: Debussy completes *La Mer,* his three-movement portrait of the sea.

1907: Music is broadcast over the radio for the first time. Mahler becomes conductor of the Metropolitan Opera in New York.

1909: Continuing his grand slam of conducting success, Mahler becomes conductor of the New York Philharmonic.

1910: Maurice Ravel (1875–1937) writes the ballet *Daphnis and Chloé,* as well as the *Mother Goose Suite*. Igor Stravinsky writes his ballet *The Firebird* for the Ballets Russes. Mahler's Eighth Symphony (*Symphony of a Thousand*) is first performed. Samuel Barber is born.

1913: Stravinsky's *The Rite of Spring* premieres in Paris, causing a riot — and World War I begins a year later.

1917: The Bolsheviks take over Russia. The United States enters World War I.

1918: Sergei Prokofiev (1891–1953) writes his First Symphony (*Classical*). World War I ends. Leonard Bernstein is born in Massachusetts.

1922: Arnold Schoenberg (1874–1951) develops his 12-tone technique. Carl Nielsen (1865–1931) writes his Fifth Symphony. James Joyce finishes *Ulysses*. Benito Mussolini becomes dictator in Italy after the fascist revolution.

1924: Joseph Stalin becomes dictator in Russia upon the death of Vladimir Lenin. George Gershwin (1898–1937) writes *Rhapsody in Blue*.

1926: Dmitri Shostakovich (1906–1975) writes his First Symphony as his final exam for the Leningrad (now St. Petersburg) Conservatory.

1929: The stock market crashes, plunging the United States into the Great Depression. William Faulkner writes *The Sound and the Fury*.

1935: Alban Berg (born in 1885) writes his Violin Concerto and dies (in that order). Gershwin writes his jazzy opera *Porgy and Bess*. Barber writes his Adagio for Strings, destined one day to make everyone sob as the soundtrack to sad movies.

1937: Shostakovich writes his Fifth Symphony as "A Soviet Artist's Reply to Just Criticism."

1939: World War II begins. Prokofiev writes music for the movie *Alexander Nevsky*.

1944: Aaron Copland writes his ballet *Appalachian Spring*.

1945: World War II ends.

1948: John Cage (born in 1912) writes his Sonatas and Interludes for Prepared Piano.

1953: James Watson and Francis Crick develop the first model of a DNA molecule. Prokofiev dies in Moscow on March 5, the same day as Stalin.

1957: The Soviet Union launches its first Sputnik. Bernstein launches *West Side Story*.

1969: American astronauts walk on the moon for the first time.

1971: Stravinsky dies.

1981: Barber dies.

1982: Philip Glass (born in 1937) writes the score to the movie *Koyaanisqatsi.*

1987: John Adams (born in 1947) writes his opera *Nixon in China.*

1990: Bernstein and Copland die.

1997: The first edition of *Classical Music For Dummies* is published.

2012: John Williams receives his 48th Oscar nomination for his music to the film *Lincoln,* based largely on the American style of Copland.

2015: The second edition of *Classical Music For Dummies* is published.

Appendix C

Glossary

accelerando (Italian): A sheet-music marking that means "gradually speed up." Abbreviated accel.

accessible: Refers to music that's easy to listen to and understand.

adagio (Italian): Restful, at ease.

allegretto (Italian): A little bit lively and fast.

allegro (Italian): Lively and fast.

andante (Italian): Walking speed.

andantino (Italian): A little faster than walking speed.

atonal: Refers to music that's not in any specific key. Sounds alien and dissonant to many people.

Baroque (French): The period of music history from the mid-1600s to the mid-1700s; characterized by emotional, flowery music written within very strict forms.

beat: The length of time it takes to tap your foot once.

brio (Italian): Briskness, spirit.

cadence: A simple progression of harmonies, one chord to another, ending with a natural resting-place chord.

cadenza (Italian): A moment near the end of a concerto movement for the soloist alone, usually a stretch of fast and difficult notes, originally designed for showing off.

cantata (Italian): A piece of music for chorus and orchestra, usually on a religious subject.

chops (slang): Technical skill in musical performance.

chord: A sound made by three or more notes playing at the same time.

chord progression: A string of changing chords, one after the other. The same as *harmonic progression*.

Classical: The period of music history from the mid-1700s to the early 1800s; music of this time is sparer and more emotionally reserved than music of the Baroque and Romantic periods.

concerto (Italian): A piece of music where one player (the "soloist") sits or stands at the front of the stage, playing the melody, while the rest of the orchestra accompanies her.

counterpoint: Two, three, four, or more melodic lines played at the same time.

crescendo (Italian): Literally means "growing"; getting progressively louder.

deceptive cadence: A chord progression that seems just about to settle happily on the ending chord — and then doesn't.

decrescendo (Italian): Getting progressively softer. Means the same as *diminuendo*.

development: The middle section of a movement in sonata form, in which the composer develops the musical themes, varying them and making interesting musical associations.

diminuendo (Italian): Getting progressively softer. Means the same as *decrescendo*.

dissonant (Italian): Harsh, discordant. Sounds as though the notes are wrong.

divertimento (Italian): A suite of dance pieces usually written as background music for a social function.

dynamics: The loudness or softness of a musical composition, or the markings in the sheet music that indicate volume.

exposition: The first section of a movement in sonata form; its purpose is to introduce, or expose, the two main melodies, or themes.

fantasy: A piece in which the composer is liberated from most of the normal constraints and conventions of musical form.

forte (Italian): Loud — or, literally, "strong."

fortissimo (Italian): Very loud — or, literally, "very strong."

fugue (Italian): A composition written for three or more musical lines, or voices. Each voice has similar music, but they enter at different times, creating counterpoint with one another.

glissando: Italian for "gliding." A musical technique in which an instrument slides up or down between notes rather than stopping on each individual note.

Gregorian chant: A simple, meandering melody, usually with Latin words, originally sung in unison by monks with no accompanying instruments.

harmonic progression: See *chord progression.*

harmony: The particular chord that plays in the background while a melody is playing. Also, the study of chord progressions.

Impressionist: A style in visual art and in music, in which the artist attempts to portray the impressions created by sights, sounds, fragrances, and tastes.

interpretation: A combination of personal ideas about tempo, instrumental balance, volume levels, note lengths, phrasing, and dramatic pacing in performance.

interval: The distance between musical notes.

intonation: Tuning; being in tune or out of tune.

larghetto (Italian): A little bit broadly.

largo (Italian): Broadly.

ledger line: A line written above or below the musical staff.

Leitmotif (German; pronounced "LIGHT-mo-teef"): A musical theme assigned to a main character or idea of an opera; invented by Richard Wagner in his *Ring Cycle* and used with great success by John Williams in the *Star Wars* movies.

lento (Italian): Slowly.

Lied (German; pronounced "LEED"): A song. Plural: *Lieder.*

madrigal (Italian): A piece of music from the Renaissance period, written for at least three voices, with overlapping melodies, usually without accompaniment.

maestoso (Italian): Majestically.

march (or **two-step**): A piece of music for marching, in which every measure gets two beats.

measure: A basic unit of musical time, usually containing two, three, or four beats.

mezzo forte (Italian; abbreviated *mf*): Literally, "half strong." Medium-loud (normal).

mezzo piano (Italian; abbreviated *mp*): Literally, "half soft." Somewhat quiet.

minimalism: A style of music involving very repetitive snippets, with subtly shifting rhythms and harmonies.

minuet: An old, courtly dance in which every measure has three beats. A precursor to the waltz.

moderato (Italian): Moderately; at medium speed.

motive or **motif:** A small musical idea, often made up of only two or three notes.

movement: One of the contrasting sections of a symphony, concerto, sonata, or chamber piece. Movements are usually separated by a pause.

Neoclassical: Literally, "new-classical." A musical style used by some 20th-century composers, such as Sergei Prokofiev. A return to the restraint and balance of the Classical style, but with a lot of "wrong notes" added.

opera: A music-drama, as in "He's been up in his room all day, reading that new book he's so crazy about, *Opera For Dummies*."

oratorio (Italian): A musical piece for solo singers, chorus, and orchestra, with words usually taken from the Bible.

orchestration: The art of arranging a piece of music for an orchestra; also, the study of instruments and their sounds.

pianissimo (Italian; abbreviated *pp*): Pretty darned quiet.

pianississimo (Italian; abbreviated *ppp*): Unbelievably quiet.

piano (Italian; abbreviated *p*): Quiet.

pitch: A particular note. The exact frequency of a sound, as defined by the number of vibrations per second.

programmatic music: Music that's *about* something or that tells a story. Programmatic music often takes the form of a tone poem.

prestissimo (Italian): Really, *really* fast.

presto (Italian): Really fast.

recapitulation: The third section of a movement in sonata form, in which the composer restates his themes.

Renaissance: French for "rebirth." The period of history dating from about 1400 to the mid-1600s.

rest: A place marker in sheet music, at moments when no notes are to be played.

rhapsody: A musical composition with a very free form.

roll: A technique executed on a percussion instrument, in which the player strikes the instrument with two mallets alternately, at blinding speed.

Romantic: A period of music, art, and literature (mostly the 1800s and beginning of the 1900s) that's often characterized by the unabashed expression of emotion.

rondo (Italian): A musical form in which a recurring melody alternates with contrasting themes.

rubato ("roo-BAH-toe"): Italian for "robbed." An expressive technique making use of slight variations in tempo, creating a musical ebb and flow. A very important characteristic of Romantic music.

scale: A standardized series of ascending or descending notes (such as the white keys on a piano), played in sequence.

scherzo: Italian for "joke." A quick, boisterous movement, usually the third, in a symphony or sonata.

serenade (Italian): A suite usually written as background music for a social function.

solfège (French): A system of singing standardized syllables on certain notes of the scale ("do, re, mi, fa . . .").

sonata: Italian for "sounded." A composition meant to demonstrate the sound and technique of a particular instrument, sometimes with piano accompaniment.

sonatina (Italian): A short sonata, usually without a development.

song cycle: A series of songs, usually grouped together thematically.

Sprechstimme: German for "speak-voice." A technique in which a singer doesn't dwell on notes as in traditional music, but just touches on them, sliding up and down between them.

staff: The five parallel lines (and the spaces between them) on which composers write their notes.

string quartet: (1) A group consisting of two violins, a viola, and a cello. (2) Music written for this group.

suite: A series of movements, usually of dance music.

symphony: (1) A piece of music for a large body of instruments, usually consisting of four different movements in a prescribed form. (2) An orchestra that plays symphonies.

tempo (Italian): Speed.

tonal: Refers to music that is in an identifiable key.

tone poem: A freeform orchestral work meant to depict something or tell a story.

trill: The quick alternation of two adjacent notes.

trio (Italian): A group of three instruments, a work written for that group, or the contrasting middle section of a minuet or scherzo.

twelve-tone music: Music composed by self-imposed rules of math, in which each note is used the same number of times.

vibrato: A vibration that produces barely noticeable variations in pitch of a note, adding an amazing warmth to the tone of an instrument.

vivace (Italian): Vivacious.

waltz: A lively ballroom dance in which every measure has three beats.

Index

• *I* •

• *J* •

About the Authors

David Pogue has a degree in music from Yale and a doctorate in music from Shenandoah Conservatory. He spent ten years working on Broadway shows as a conductor, orchestrator, or synthesizer programmer.

More recently, he founded Yahoo Tech (*yahootech.com*), a job for which he was groomed by 13 years of writing the weekly tech column for *The New York Times*.

He's also a columnist for *Scientific American*, a two-time Emmy-winning correspondent for "CBS News Sunday Morning," and the host of several NOVA miniseries on PBS. He's written or co-written 75 books, including 30 in his own "Missing Manual" series, six in the "For Dummies" line (including Macs, Magic, Opera, and Classical Music), two novels (one for middle-schoolers), and *Pogue's Basics,* a *New York Times* bestseller.

He lives in Connecticut with his wife, Nicki, and three awesome children. Links to his columns and videos await at www.davidpogue.com. He welcomes feedback about his books by email at david@pogueman.com.

Scott Speck has conducted the world's great musical masterpieces, including symphonies, concertos, operas, oratorios, and ballets, in hundreds of performances around the world. He has conducted at London's Royal Opera House at Covent Garden, the Paris Opera, Moscow's Tchaikovsky Hall, Washington's Kennedy Center, San Francisco's War Memorial Opera House, and the Los Angeles Music Center. In recent seasons, he has led symphony orchestras of Chicago, Baltimore, Houston, Paris, Moscow, Beijing, Oregon, Buffalo, Honolulu, and many others.

Speck has been a regular commentator on National Public Radio, the BBC, the Australian Broadcasting Corporation, and Voice of Russia, broadcast throughout the world. He has been featured in TED talks and at the Aspen Ideas Festival. His writing has been featured in numerous magazines and journals.

Born in Boston, Speck graduated *summa cum laude* from Yale University. There he founded and directed the Berkeley Chamber Orchestra, which continues to perform to this day. He was awarded a Fulbright Scholarship to Berlin, where he founded an orchestra called Concerto Grosso Berlin. He received his master's degree with highest honors from the University of Southern California. He was a conducting fellow at the Aspen School of Music and studied at the Tanglewood Music Center.

Speck is fluent in German and French, has a diploma in Italian, speaks Spanish, and has a reading knowledge of Russian.

Scott Speck can be reached at www.scottspeck.org, on Facebook at www.facebook.com/ConductorScottSpeck, and on Twitter @ScottSpeck1.

Dedication

This book is dedicated to our families. You know who you are!

Authors' Acknowledgments

This edition was made possible by the efforts of our serene and supremely talented manager, Linda Brandon; development editor, Chad Sievers; and our hard-working copy editor, Ashley Petry. Thanks are also due to Brian Noble for his technical review.

Michael Wartofsky masterfully created the Finale-generated sheet-music examples in record time; Michael A. Lewanski, Jr. provided tireless research, as well as the first drafts of our history timeline and glossary; and Gene Jarvis, Mark Barville, and Caroline Camp offered advice and information. Moral support was graciously provided at no charge by our families and friends.

Publisher's Acknowledgments

Acquisitions Editor: Tracy Boggier

Project Manager: Linda Brandon

Development Editor: Chad R. Sievers

Copy Editor: Ashley Petry

Technical Editor: Brian Noble

Art Coordinator: Alicia B. South

Production Editor: Selvakumaran Rajendiran

Cover Photos: ©iStock.com/Svemir

pple & Mac

ad For Dummies,
h Edition
'8-1-118-72306-7

hone For Dummies,
h Edition
'8-1-118-69083-3

acs All-in-One
r Dummies, 4th Edition
'8-1-118-82210-4

S X Mavericks
r Dummies
'8-1-118-69188-5

logging & Social Media

acebook For Dummies,
h Edition
'8-1-118-63312-0

ocial Media Engagement
r Dummies
'8-1-118-53019-1

ordPress For Dummies,
h Edition
'8-1-118-79161-5

usiness

ock Investing
r Dummies, 4th Edition
'8-1-118-37678-2

vesting For Dummies,
h Edition
'8-0-470-90545-6

Personal Finance
For Dummies, 7th Edition
978-1-118-11785-9

QuickBooks 2014
For Dummies
978-1-118-72005-9

Small Business Marketing
Kit For Dummies,
3rd Edition
978-1-118-31183-7

Careers

Job Interviews
For Dummies, 4th Edition
978-1-118-11290-8

Job Searching with Social
Media For Dummies,
2nd Edition
978-1-118-67856-5

Personal Branding
For Dummies
978-1-118-11792-7

Resumes For Dummies,
6th Edition
978-0-470-87361-8

Starting an Etsy Business
For Dummies, 2nd Edition
978-1-118-59024-9

Diet & Nutrition

Belly Fat Diet For Dummies
978-1-118-34585-6

Mediterranean Diet
For Dummies
978-1-118-71525-3

Nutrition For Dummies,
5th Edition
978-0-470-93231-5

Digital Photography

Digital SLR Photography
All-in-One For Dummies,
2nd Edition
978-1-118-59082-9

Digital SLR Video &
Filmmaking For Dummies
978-1-118-36598-4

Photoshop Elements 12
For Dummies
978-1-118-72714-0

Gardening

Herb Gardening
For Dummies, 2nd Edition
978-0-470-61778-6

Gardening with Free-Range
Chickens For Dummies
978-1-118-54754-0

Health

Boosting Your Immunity
For Dummies
978-1-118-40200-9

Diabetes For Dummies,
4th Edition
978-1-118-29447-5

Living Paleo For Dummies
978-1-118-29405-5

Big Data

Big Data For Dummies
978-1-118-50422-2

Data Visualization
For Dummies
978-1-118-50289-1

Hadoop For Dummies
978-1-118-60755-8

Language &
Foreign Language

500 Spanish Verbs
For Dummies
978-1-118-02382-2

English Grammar
For Dummies, 2nd Edition
978-0-470-54664-2

French All-in-One
For Dummies
978-1-118-22815-9

German Essentials
For Dummies
978-1-118-18422-6

Italian For Dummies,
2nd Edition
978-1-118-00465-4

e **Available in print and e-book formats.**

Available wherever books are sold. **For more information or to order direct visit www.dummies.com**

Math & Science

Algebra I For Dummies,
2nd Edition
978-0-470-55964-2

Anatomy and Physiology
For Dummies, 2nd Edition
978-0-470-92326-9

Astronomy For Dummies,
3rd Edition
978-1-118-37697-3

Biology For Dummies,
2nd Edition
978-0-470-59875-7

Chemistry For Dummies,
2nd Edition
978-1-118-00730-3

1001 Algebra II Practice
Problems For Dummies
978-1-118-44662-1

Microsoft Office

Excel 2013 For Dummies
978-1-118-51012-4

Office 2013 All-in-One
For Dummies
978-1-118-51636-2

PowerPoint 2013
For Dummies
978-1-118-50253-2

Word 2013 For Dummies
978-1-118-49123-2

Music

Blues Harmonica
For Dummies
978-1-118-25269-7

Guitar For Dummies,
3rd Edition
978-1-118-11554-1

iPod & iTunes
For Dummies, 10th Edition
978-1-118-50864-0

Programming

Beginning Programming
with C For Dummies
978-1-118-73763-7

Excel VBA Programming
For Dummies, 3rd Edition
978-1-118-49037-2

Java For Dummies,
6th Edition
978-1-118-40780-6

Religion & Inspiration

The Bible For Dummies
978-0-7645-5296-0

Buddhism For Dummies,
2nd Edition
978-1-118-02379-2

Catholicism For Dummies,
2nd Edition
978-1-118-07778-8

Self-Help & Relationships

Beating Sugar Addiction
For Dummies
978-1-118-54645-1

Meditation For Dummies,
3rd Edition
978-1-118-29144-3

Seniors

Laptops For Seniors
For Dummies, 3rd Edition
978-1-118-71105-7

Computers For Seniors
For Dummies, 3rd Edition
978-1-118-11553-4

iPad For Seniors
For Dummies, 6th Edition
978-1-118-72826-0

Social Security
For Dummies
978-1-118-20573-0

Smartphones & Tablets

Android Phones
For Dummies, 2nd Edition
978-1-118-72030-1

Nexus Tablets
For Dummies
978-1-118-77243-0

Samsung Galaxy S 4
For Dummies
978-1-118-64222-1

Samsung Galaxy Tabs
For Dummies
978-1-118-77294-2

Test Prep

ACT For Dummies,
5th Edition
978-1-118-01259-8

ASVAB For Dummies,
3rd Edition
978-0-470-63760-9

GRE For Dummies,
7th Edition
978-0-470-88921-3

Officer Candidate Tests
For Dummies
978-0-470-59876-4

Physician's Assistant Exam
For Dummies
978-1-118-11556-5

Series 7 Exam For Dummies
978-0-470-09932-2

Windows 8

Windows 8.1 All-in-One
For Dummies
978-1-118-82087-2

Windows 8.1 For Dummies
978-1-118-82121-3

Windows 8.1 For Dummies
Book + DVD Bundle
978-1-118-82107-7

e **Available in print and e-book formats.**

Available wherever books are sold. **For more information or to order direct visit www.dummies.com**

Take Dummies with you everywhere you go!

Whether you are excited about e-books, want more from the web, must have your mobile apps, or are swept up in social media, Dummies makes everything easier.

Leverage the Power

For Dummies is the global leader in the reference category and one of the most trusted and highly regarded brands in the world. No longer just focused on books, customers now have access to the For Dummies content they need in the format they want. Let us help you develop a solution that will fit your brand and help you connect with your customers.

Advertising & Sponsorships

Connect with an engaged audience on a powerful multimedia site, and position your message alongside expert how-to content.

Targeted ads · Video · Email marketing · Microsites · Sweepstakes sponsorship

21 Million Monthly Page Views & 13 Million Unique Visitors